The Warehouse Prison

Disposal of the New Dangerous Class

John Irwin
San Francisco State University

Afterword by
Barbara Owen
California State University, Fresno

Roxbury Publishing Company
Los Angeles, California

Library of Congress Cataloging-in-Publication Data

Irwin, John, 1929–
The warehouse prison: disposal of the new dangerous class / by John Irwin
    p. cm.
Includes bibliographical references and index.
ISBN 1-931719-35-7
1. Prisons—United States 2. Prisoners—United States 3. Imprisonment—
    United States. 4. Corrections—United States I. Title.

HV9471.I786 2005
365'.973—dc21   2004007917

Publisher: Claude Teweles
Managing Editor: Dawn VanDercreek
Production Editor: Monica Gomez
Production Assistant: Susan O'Brien
Typography: Robert Leuze, RLeuze@rcn.com
Cover Design: Marnie Kenney
Cover Photo: California Department of Corrections,
Communications Office

Printed on acid-free paper in the United States of America. This
book meets the standards for recycling of the Environmental Protection Agency.

ISBN 1-931719-35-7

ROXBURY PUBLISHING COMPANY
P.O. Box 491044
Los Angeles, California 90049-9044
Voice: (310) 473-3312 • Fax: (310) 473-4490
E-mail: roxbury@roxbury.net
Website: www.roxbury.net

Contents

Foreword

After I had stood by for 20 years in horror while prison popula-tions exploded, I was compelled to revisit the prison environ-ment to conduct this study. First, I knew as well as I knew anything that there was no rational justification for this escalation. I knew from a careful examination of crime rates that crime in the United States had remained virtually level from 1973 through the 1980s and then had declined after 1993. Second, James Austin and I had studied intake populations in the mid-1990s and discovered that most of the persons being sent to prison were guilty of unserious felonies, crimes for which they would have received probation or short jail sentences in the decades before the punitive swing in pe-nal practices in the United States. Moreover, we were able to dem-onstrate that the dramatic increase in the use of incarceration was having no impact on crime rates.

Furthermore, I was disturbed by the images of prisoners that were disseminated by the mass media—the scans of prison yards filled with muscled, tattooed, swaggering convicts; the barrage of stories of prisoner rapes; and the silly, distorted characterizations of the prison world in shows such as HBO's *Oz*. I had not been in prisons to conduct research for 20 years, and I could not stop won-dering what was really going on in them. In my last close contact conducting the studies that led to my book *Prisons in Turmoil* (1980), I had witnessed the escalation of prisoner riots, assaults, homicides, and other disturbances and the breakdown of the infor-mal prisoner social order that obtained in earlier eras. But I had no idea what was going on in the hundreds of new prisons that had been thrown up in the imprisonment binge of the 1980s and 1990s. There were no new ethnographies of male prisons, even though the women's prisons were being studied by sociologists such as

Angela Devlin, Karlene Faith, Meda Chesney-Lind, Joy Pollock, and Barbara Owen. So I was drawn back to the prison one more time.

Actually, it has been difficult for me to stay away from the prison since being released from one in 1957. I intended to stay away, but when I was attending UCLA, planning to finish a degree in physical science and go on to study oceanography, which fit with my new passion, surfing, I became more interested in social science than math and physics. So I went to the chair of the combined Sociology and Anthropology Department, Donald Cressey, to seek his advice on career possibilities in sociology. He encouraged me to pursue a degree in sociology and to take his criminology course. I took his class, and when he started lecturing on the "prisoner social organization," I realized that there was something wrong with the current theories. Thus began a series of discussions with him that resulted in our writing a *Social Problems* article, "Thieves, Convicts, and the Inmate Culture," which established me as a bona fide "criminologist."

I went on to the University of California, Berkeley, to obtain a Ph.D. I plunged into sociology with an emphasis in "deviance," under the guidance of Herbert Blumer, Erving Goffman, and David Matza. When I completed all the requirements for the Ph.D. except a dissertation, Sheldon Messinger, a student of the prison and the assistant director of the Law and Society Center at Berkeley, asked me to join a study of parole that was being administered at the Center. The Center's director, Philip Selznik, after some difficulty, was able to obtain permission for me to conduct a study in the California prison system. I was suddenly back in the prison. Looking back on this trajectory, prison-school-prison, I saw that it was inevitable that I end up a criminologist studying prisons. A great deal of my attention has been on prisons, prisoners, and ex-prisoners ever since.

My prison experiences—five years at Soledad, a medium-security California prison, after several years of living the life of a thief and drug addict—as well as my postprison years not only determined my academic career path but also shaped my sociological perspective in definite and profound ways. I had lived on both sides of the fence—first on the deviant, illegal, and unconventional side and then on the conventional side (with a great deal of initial difficulty). While becoming formally educated and mastering all

ix

the habits, mannerisms, and viewpoints of "squares," I made an essential discovery. They, conventional people and even the academics who studied criminals and other deviants, did not fully appreciate that the people on the other side—the deviants, "offenders," and convicts—were mostly ordinary human beings. This insight guided my interest and influenced all of my academic and political activities.

In my first study, which led to *The Felon*, (1970) an underlying theme was the unfair and counterproductive practices that resulted from the prison overseers' misunderstanding of the intentions and meanings of prisoners. Likewise, prisoners usually misunderstood the intentions and meanings of the overseers. My subsequent studies and books, as well as the reform activities I have pursued, have all been informed by this insight. I knew that prisoners were human beings. I also knew that with few exceptions, the people overseeing them, studying them, and making decisions affecting them did not view these men and women as full or worthy human beings.

When I obtained permission from the California Department of Corrections to conduct the study that resulted in this book, I began my research at Solano, a new, middle-range California prison. After receiving permission from the warden, Anthony Newland, I was escorted around the prison by the associate warden, Tim Rougeau. I admit that I was anxious. I had not been on a prison yard in 20 years. I had nothing but the distorted images that are flashed throughout the mass media, movies, and TV shows to inform me about what contemporary prisoners were like. When the associate warden and I approached a group of prisoners with whom he was acquainted, we stopped to talk with them. I pulled a couple of them aside and talked to them privately. (I have no trouble establishing rapport with prisoners.) Then I walked around and talked more freely to other prisoners we met. I was greatly relieved. Prisoners were still the same bunch of ordinary human beings they had always been. Oh, I was not naive or romantic. I knew there were a lot of very tough and dangerous guys among them. But there were a lot of very tough and dangerous guys outside, too. And not just in the ghettos or lower classes. There were dangerous and tough guys in police departments, in the Army, in the National Football League, in our work sites, and in our high schools. I was fully aware that prisoners are a skewed sample of the population—but not so much because of villainy and dangerousness as because of race, class, and disreputability. Once you could get beyond these latter characteristics of prisoners, however, there were human beings with about the same weaknesses, strengths, desires, and needs as most other people everywhere.

That first day at Solano, I began gathering prisoners who were willing to participate in my study, and I began a series of meetings that lasted for two years, which formed the basis for my analysis of what was going on in the new type of prison—the warehouse prison. My underlying purpose was the same as it had been in my earlier studies: (1) to demonstrate that prisoners are human beings who are not being treated as human beings and (2) to show that the outcome of this mistreatment is unnecessary, unfair, and counterproductive.

I discovered at Solano that prison planners and administrators have succeeded in devising and administering a prison that keeps up to 6,000 prisoners—crowded together in limited space and with limited access to rehabilitative or recreational programs—almost completely controlled. This control is accomplished through the physical design of the prison, the rigid enforcement of extensive rules, and the possibility of transferring troublesome prisoners to highly punitive supermax prisons. I also discovered that prisoners, most of whom are serving relatively long sentences (more than five years), although not brutalized, are profoundly harmed by this new form of imprisonment and have tremendous difficulties in adjusting to the outside society after their release. I was convinced by my colleague, Barbara Owen, that it is even worse for women prisoners in the new prisons (see her Afterword in this book, which presents the differences in women prisoners' treatment).

The discovery of the insidious nature of the new prisons led me to carefully examine the forces that helped create our present penal situation: We are the most punitive nation in the world, perhaps in history. My subsequent analysis forms the second theme of the book, which is conveyed in the subtitle, *Disposal of the New Dangerous Class.* ◆

Acknowledgments

Many people helped me in my research and in writing this book. John Berecochea, the Chief of the Office of Research of the California Department of Corrections, was instrumental in my acquiring approval for the study. Warden Anthony Newland granted me permission to conduct my study at Solano State Prison. My wife, Marsha Rosenbaum, advised me and edited drafts. Barbara Owen, once my student and now my colleague, helped at every stage of my research and critiqued and edited drafts of the book. She also enriched the book by writing the Afterword, which covers unique issues of women prisoners. Maria Belknap edited the book and smoothed out many of my sentences. Above all, I must acknowledge the contribution of the convicts with whom I met over a two-and-a-half-year period and shared ideas, descriptions, and analyses of prisoner behavior and relationships. These "experts" read and critiqued drafts of most of the book's chapters. They—Eric Borchert, Anthony Crane, Bret Goodhart, Richard Karr, Robert Laucella, Alfredo Monteon, William Mothershed, Ignacio Pena, Kevin Wharton Price, and Kevin Williams—have served a total of 207 years in prison. ✦

Chapter 1

The Imprisonment Binge

America has undergone a massive imprisonment "binge." Between 1980 and 2000, the country's prison populations increased fivefold. The rate of incarceration zoomed from 100 to over 500 per 100,000. As a result of this expansion and the punitive ideology that underpinned it, hundreds of new prisons were built at a cost in the billions of dollars, and completely new prison regimens were introduced. In this book, I examine the causes of this binge, the new forms of imprisonment it produced, and the particular and broader effects it caused.

In 1992, as this binge was well under way, James Austin and I conducted a study of prison expansion to learn what was driving it and to see who was being sent to prison in this punitive convulsion.[1] We found that a conservative rhetoric on crime in America, based on several fallacious concepts, had prevailed and dictated penal policies. We identified the following misconceptions:

1. The war on poverty—which tried in the 1960's and 1970's to fight crime through education, job training, and rehabilitation—was a total failure.

2. Dangerous criminals repeatedly go free because of liberal judges or decisions made by the liberal Supreme Court that help the criminal, but not the victim.

3. Swift and certain punishment in the form of more and longer prison terms will reduce crime by incapacitating hardened criminals and making potential lawbreakers think twice before they commit crimes.

4. ~~Most inmates are dangerous and cannot be safely placed in the community.~~
5. ~~It will be far cheaper to society in the long run to increase the use of imprisonment.~~
6. ~~Greater use of imprisonment since the 1980s has reduced crime.~~[2]

The first two of these ideas were patently false. The war on poverty was never waged. The courts were not relatively lenient, and the number of "defendants" who escaped prosecution because of the "exclusionary rules" established by Supreme Court decisions was insignificant. We were able to demonstrate that escalation of punishment and the incapacitation of more and more "criminals" had little or no impact on crime rates. We also discovered that the majority of persons sent to prison in this punitive binge were charged with unserious felonies, crimes that would have received short county jail sentences or probation before the punitive era, and that the binge disproportionately incarcerated African Americans, other nonwhites, and women. Since then, it has become increasingly apparent that the financial cost of the binge damaged other government undertakings, particularly education and social welfare.

Since our study (published in 1994), the punitive binge has continued, hundreds more prisons have been built, prison populations have further escalated and changed composition, and prison management regimens have dramatically altered. Though James Austin and I did not conduct a close study of prisoner social organization, I suspected that prisoner routines were radically different than in earlier eras of imprisonment. It had been years since I had the opportunity to conduct the type of study—close, participant observation—that would inform me of what was happening in that world. In my last close examination of the prison world, during the 1970s, prisoner society had been shattered by conflict and violence.[3] Since then, like the general population, I have been bombarded by the mass-media camera scans of throngs of muscled, long-haired, tattooed, menacing convicts milling about prison yards and conservative criminologists threatening us with the proliferation of new "career criminals" and "criminal predators."[4] I know these images both provide a distorted perspective on the prisoners and continue to justify punitive policies.

I was sent to prison as a young adult and after that spent most of my academic career studying prisons. I remain emotionally attached to the prisoner world, so during the imprisonment binge my curiosity and concern about prisoner issues mounted. In 1999, I received permission from the California Department of Corrections to study prisoners and parolees. I started my study at California State Prison at Solano, one of 22 large prisons built in California during the 1980s and 1990s. After two years, I shifted to the San Pedro Parole unit and studied parolees.

This book is about the contemporary "warehouse" and "supermax" prisons, how prisoners cope in these new prisons, and how they fare after release.[5] I also attempt to explain why the United States has the world's largest prison system. To this end, I examined the role of punishment in society, the development of the prison as society's primary penal device, and the history of American prisons. A grasp of this history is necessary to understand prisoners' contemporary modes of adjustment to prison life.[6]

The Punitive Swing

It is popularly believed that public reaction to rising crime rates since the mid-1940s is responsible for the excessively punitive penal policies and the escalation in prison populations. Many prominent academics share this belief. David Garland, a leading scholar of the history of punishment, examined the punitive swing in England and America. He concluded that this swing is mainly due to rising crime rates and the threat of crime to the middle classes:

> [I]ncreasing levels of concern about crime were certainly triggered by the steep increases in reported crime (especially violent offending) that occurred in the decades after 1960. As more and more of the population were themselves burgled or robbed or assaulted, or else had a close friend or relative who had been; as theft of and from cars became a normal concomitant of car ownership in many cities; as the visible evidence of vandalism and drug abuse began to manifest itself on city streets and schools; and as U.S. statistics showed an increasing percentage of homicides committed by unknown assailants, rising crime rates ceased to be a statistical abstraction and took on a vivid personal meaning in popular consciousness and individual psychology. The anxieties about

crime, on top of the more inchoate insecurities prompted by rapid social change and economic recession, paved the way for a politics of reaction in the late 1970s.[7]

The actual patterns of crime rate increases cannot explain the growing fear of crime experienced by Americans. The best evidence suggests that crime rates in America remained relatively steady from 1950 to 1966, rose significantly between 1967 and 1973, leveled off again, took a slight upward swing around 1981, leveled off until 1995, and then began a steady decline.[8] In reality, the public concern for crime followed more closely politicians' and the media's attention to crime than the fluctuations in crime rates. Garland admits: "This politics, in its turn, helped shape these diffuse middle-class anxieties into a more focused set of attitudes and understandings, identify the culprits, naming the problem, setting up scapegoats."[9]

I contend that in the 1970s, '80s, and '90s, politicians aroused public fear of crime and mounted the punitive penal response— mainly imprisonment of hundreds of thousands of "offenders" in the new warehouse or supermax prisons—for the following reasons: (1) to divert the public's attention away from other serious social and political problems; (2) to exploit an expedient issue to win elections; and (3) to mount a penal response to control, manage, and dispose of the new dangerous class. This class is largely composed of nonwhite, inner-city youths whose life opportunities had been severely restricted by the economic changes that occurred from the 1970s into the 1990s, and who, it was believed, posed a threat to the lives and property of middle-class Americans. This development is treated thoroughly in Chapter 8.

Punishment in Society

Society's response to crime is a complex issue. To unravel it, we must examine the social forces that define crime and design punishment. Emile Durkheim, the eminent grand theorist of sociology, suggested that the punitive response is a function of the moral outrage that members of a society experience toward those who violate shared social standards or mores. As he put it, the passion experienced by members of society toward violations of the "collective conscience," that is, the shared moral precepts, was the "soul of punishment."[10] It is starkly apparent, particularly today after a sustained 25-year expression of public concern regarding crime and the leniency of the criminal justice system, that moral outrage toward many forms of crime plays an important role in public policy toward crime and therefore influences imprisonment. However, there are forces other than public outrage toward violations of public morality that influence lawmakers and the various criminal justice functionaries—policemen, prosecutors, and judges.

My analysis rests on the assumption that society's response to crime is not merely the translation of public morality into law and into a system of official actions to enforce this morality. To understand the prison today, and particularly the experience of prisoners in it, we must examine the various purposes and processes that create and influence law and its enforcement.

Making Law

Laws are rules enforced within a sovereign society that has the capacity to enforce its rules through an organized response that includes punishment. This process requires "rulers" to make the rules and direct the enforcers and punishers. Customs, standards, and folkways—extralegal rules that guide social behavior—accrue over long stretches of time and may not come into being through conscious decisions made by specially empowered leaders. Laws, however, are consciously made and enforced. Consequently, to understand the nature of law and law enforcement, we must start with the "purposes" of the particular decision makers who make and enforce the law.[11] I have divided these purposes into four sets: (1) formalizing traditions, (2) advancing self-interest, (3) pursuing rational/utilitarian goals, and (4) pursuing humanitarian arrangements. Formalizing traditions has occurred in rapid and dramatic fashion in some of the historic codifications, such as the making of Hammurabi's "code." In these codifications, rulers attempted to establish order among heterogeneous groups that possessed conflicting mores. The "legislation of morality," as it has been referred to, is also a factor in the ongoing making and enforcing of the law whenever rulers believe there is widespread nonconformity to central, sacred, or crucial standards or mores. This frequently occurs when rulers believe that minority or "inferior" groups, such as the Irish immigrants in America at the end of the nineteenth century, are not following the morality of the superior group.[12]

Self-interest motivates lawmakers and enforcers. There are abundant examples of despotic rulers who arbitrarily established self-serving laws and backed these up with brutal force. More relevant for my analysis are the persistent and largely successful activities of judges, legislators, executives, lobbyists, Political Action Committees (PACs), and influential power brokers who decide or influence the law to effect outcomes beneficial to some group, particularly the elites of a society. In fact, ever since societies have had sufficient central organization and power to make and enforce law, the advancement of the self-interest of the rulers, the ruling class, or the elites has been the dominant force in making and enforcing law.

Some lawmakers and law enforcers do work to make the society function more efficiently and effectively. As in the case of the famous codifiers of disparate traditional systems, there are historical examples of notable lawmakers, such as Solon in fourth century B.C. Athens, Napoleon in France at the beginning of the nineteenth century, and the framers of the American Constitution, who, to a great extent, were trying in a rational fashion to set down laws and legal procedures to make things work for the "good of the society." Also, in the ongoing lawmaking processes, a few (some would argue many) lawmakers—legislators, executives, judges, and administrators of criminal justice organizations—make efforts to work toward the public good. Of course, all leaders and law enforcers frame their activities in a rhetoric of the "public good," but their actual purposes are usually very different. However, they sometimes do work to fulfill socially pragmatic goals.

Finally, from the beginning of the development of law, some individuals and groups have worked persistently to make the law fair, humane, and just. Invariably, these "humanitarians," "political activists," "reformers," and "do-gooders" are reacting to the conditions that exist because of the efforts of lawmakers who have pursued other purposes, particularly self-serving ones.

Many "natural law" theorists have suggested that the legal enterprise contains within itself impetus for reform and seeking justice.[13] Their argument suggests that when people are forced to live according to rules, they naturally recognize unfair practices, such as punishment without due process, inconsistent application of rules, ex post facto enforcement, and cruel and unusual punishment. For the most part, these theorists have focused on procedural matters and have not addressed the absence of "social justice." However, some have.[14] When we examine the history of humans living in societies governed by law, it is clear that unfair, unjust, cruel living conditions precipitate steady efforts on the part of individuals and groups to correct these conditions and to make things more humane and just. In fact, it is from the reformers' efforts that legal systems have become as fair, just, and humane as they are. Legal systems left to evolve from the acts of unrestrained rulers will remain despotic, tyrannical, and unjust.

Since law is the outcome of these different purposes, particularly those of self-interest, it is important to recognize that not all laws are related to deeply held morals or mores. Many are. All modern legal systems outlaw murder, assault, many forms of theft, and other "crimes," which are clearly violations of widespread moral values. However, modern systems also outlaw loitering, tax evasion, stalking, prostitution, the use and possession of some drugs, and many other acts toward which there is a lack of unanimous or intense public moral repugnance. Also, there is more vigorous law enforcement toward relatively less serious crimes committed by lower-class people, such as petty street crime, than toward serious white-collar crimes, such as the embezzlement of large amounts of money and political corruption. A young Rio de Janeiro slum dweller, a character in a John Updike novel, sums it up with remarkable conciseness and perspicacity: "The world itself is stolen goods. All property is theft, and those who have stolen most of if make the laws for the rest of us."[15]

Imprisonment as Punishment

In addition to producing a large body of "substantive" law that does not stem directly from society's moral values, the various purposes of the law have led to a variety of punitive measures. Of these, the prison is the primary and most destructive form. This punitive mechanism has seen many changes and served many different purposes. Some students of imprisonment have suggested that rulers have used imprisonment for personal rather than the public interest to promote a self-serving political economy, to control the surplus population or the "dangerous classes," and to introduce a form of discipline consistent with the new capitalist mode of production—the factory.[16]

In general, I am persuaded by these arguments. In particular, however, I contend that the recent imprisonment binge and most contemporary forms of imprisonment are the end products of the recent war on crime and its stepchild, the war on drugs. Conservative politicians pursuing self-serving interests first declared the war on crime in the 1960s. The same politicians and the media that supported them fanned the public's fear of crime, citing the rise in street crime in the late 1960s and early 1970s. Public frenzy over this crime wave gave politicians the justification necessary to target the new dangerous class—the poor, mostly nonwhite, young, male, inner-city dwellers. Once politicians had public support to target this population, they were able to jail and imprison them. The purpose of these politicians was mainly the control and disposal of these persons.

Control of the dangerous class is not the "official" purpose of imprisonment. Most criminology or criminal justice texts list retribution for crimes committed, general deterrence of crime in society, the incapacitation of dangerous criminals, and the reformation (or rehabilitation) of criminals as its purposes.[17] Instead, I suggest that key decision makers, those who have had the primary influence in shaping society's penal strategies, have pursued three "unofficial" purposes. The first is class control. These decision makers believe that a new dangerous class constitutes a substantial threat to the lives and property of "honest people" and to social order. The second unofficial purpose is scapegoating, directing public attention to the behavior of the dangerous class to divert attention away from conditions and relationships that benefit decision makers or their patrons and have the potential of being recognized as serious social problems (e.g., the growing disparity in the distribution of wealth in the United States). The third unofficial purpose is to use the threat of the dangerous class as a device to gain political capital and win elections.

Policies driven by these three unofficial but dominant purposes not only have led to the escalation of punishment but also have obtruded into penal practices and greatly affected the conditions of imprisonment. These policies have moved imprisonment away from the more (but not completely) defensible purposes of retribution, general deterrence, incapacitation, and reformation.[18] They influence the types and degree of pain prisoners receive and, therein, the harm they experience.

In addition to these unofficial purposes of imprisonment imposed by persons external to penal organizations, prison administrators and staff pursue purposes that are generated by, and emerge within, the prison bureaucracy itself.[19] These include (1) maintaining moral superiority of the employees over prisoners, (2) avoiding outside criticism, (3) maintaining the autonomy of the prison bureaucracy, and (4) increasing the ease of employees' work. These unofficial purposes stem from the self-serving motivations of the employees; they are not unique to prisons but appear to some degree in all bureaucracies. In prison organizations, however, these unofficial purposes are more extreme than in most other government bureaucracies and have special qualities because of the prison's peculiar assignment, that of controlling lower-caste, potentially dangerous persons.[20]

This complex and shifting mix of official and unofficial purposes has produced a variety of prison regimens through its 200-year history in the United States. Two enduring characteristics, pain and harm, have varied in intensity and form with these shifts. Prisoners' modes of coping with imprisonment have varied with the shifts in prison regimens.

Prisoners do not simply comply with the regimens imposed on them. They actively conspire to survive, to reduce their state of deprivation, to ease their moral condemnation, and to pursue their own self-interests. To the extent that their situation allows, they fully or partly cooperate with other prisoners and form their own social organizations with their own values and rules to achieve their goals. In the next chapter, I examine the major phases in America's prison history with the intention of exploring these variations. My purpose is to reveal and help the reader understand the experience of prisoners in the new prisons and the harm these new prisons cause.

Origins of the Prison

The United States is credited with, or blamed for, making the prison the primary penal response to felonies or serious crimes. Indeed, the history of the prison coincides with U.S. history. One of the world's first such prisons, the Walnut Street Jail, opened in 1790 in Philadelphia. Before that, in the colonies and in Europe, most felons were banished, fined, publicly shamed in stocks and pillories, whipped, mutilated, or executed. Since its introduction, the prison has remained the cornerstone of our criminal justice system. As one student of the prison put it, "Unlike the Wall of Jericho or, more recently the Berlin Wall, the prison edifice stands firm. Indeed, prisons are a more central feature of our criminal justice system than at any time in history."[21] This importance is revealed by the fact that approximately 2.7 percent of the current U.S. population, 5.6 million people, have served time in prison.[22]

Americans did not invent the prison from scratch. Before America's introduction of the "penitentiary" in 1790, several penal practices that led to imprisonment were employed by different European countries. As early as 64 B.C., a prison was built under the sewers of Rome. From the late fifteenth century to the eighteenth century, galley slavery, a precursor of imprisonment, was used extensively in many countries, particularly France and Spain. England's gaols were in wide use from the thirteenth century, and England introduced houses of corrections in 1609. The United States introduced the penitentiary, a new type of prison, which added reformation to the prison's former purposes—punishment, deterrence, and incapacitation (or quarantine).[23]

Development of prison systems in Europe and the United States, particularly as it relates to changes in shifting political economies, has been thoroughly examined.[24] In the next chapter, I provide an overview of this history and identify key elements in its various historical forms, using a large body of close studies of prisons since the 1930s.[25] Information on the earlier phases, 1800 through 1930, is sketchy.

In Chapters 3 through 6, I describe the new forms of imprisonment that have been developed since 1983, during which time the country has experienced unprecedented expansion of its prison population and constructed hundreds of new prisons. In Chapter 7, I examine the problems prisoners face when they are released from the new prisons. In Chapter 8, I step back and more carefully trace the decisions and developments that led to the imprisonment binge. Finally, in Chapter 9, I explore the aftermath of America's disastrous penal experiment.

Endnotes

1. John Irwin and James Austin, *It's About Time: America's Imprisonment Binge* (Belmont, CA: Wadsworth, 1994).

2. Ibid., xiii.

3. See John Irwin, *Prisons in Turmoil* (Boston: Little, Brown, 1980).

4. These began with James Q. Wilson warning us that "wicked people exist," in *Thinking About Crime* (New York: Random House, 1975). They peaked with the railing of his outspoken student, John Dilulio, warning us that "Crime in America: It's Going to Get Worse" *Reader's Digest*, August 1995.

5. James Austin and I evaluated parolees' experiences, and the picture was depressing. Most of those we interviewed were not achieving economic viability or coming close to realizing their life aspirations, and most returned to prison after release. It appeared that most who did stay out were on the edge, many descending into dereliction (*It's About Time*, Chapter 5).

6. For example, very early in the history of prisons, prisoners developed a "convict code," residues of which endure and influence prisoner behavior today.

7. David Garland, *The Culture of Control* (Chicago: University of Chicago Press, 2001), 153.

8. A full discussion of these rates appears in Chapter 8.

9. Garland, *Culture of Control*, 153.

10. See Emile Durkheim, *The Division of Labor* (New York: Macmillan, 1933). For a thorough discussion of Durkheim's ideas on this issue, see David Garland, *Punishment in Modern Society* (Chicago: University of Chicago Press, 1990), Chapter 1.

11. I have selected *purpose* instead of *motive* or *intent* because it does not have restricted legal connotations. I use *purpose* narrowly to mean conscious purpose rather than the function of some process or arrangement as seen by an observer.

12. See Joseph Gusfield, *The Culture of Public Reform: Drinking and the Symbolic Order* (Chicago: University of Chicago Press, 1981) for an examination of class conflict in the "legislation of morality."

13. See Ron Fuller, *The Morality of Law* (New Haven, CT: Yale University Press, 1964), and Edmond Cahn, *The Sense of Injustice* (Bloomington: Indiana University Press, 1975).

14. See John Finnis, *Natural Law and Natural Rights* (New York: Oxford University Press, 1990), and John Rawls, *A Theory of Justice* (Cambridge, MA: Harvard University Press, 1971).

15. John Updike, *Brazil* (New York: Facett Columbine, 1994), 8.

16. See G. Rusche and O. Kirchheimer, *Punishment and Social Structure* (New York: Columbia University Press, 1939), E. B. Pashukanis, *Law*

and Marxism: A General Theory (London: Ink Links, 1978); and Michel Foucault, *Discipline and Punish: The Birth of the Prison* (London: Allen and Unwin, 1977).

17. See, for instance, Edwin H. Sutherland, Donald R. Cressey, and David F. Luckenbill, *Principles of Criminology*, 11th ed. (New York: General Hall, 1992), 477, and Ira J. Silverman and Manuel Vega, *Corrections: A Comprehensive View* (New York: West, 1996) 20.

18. In Working Party for the American Friend's Service Committee, *The Struggle for Justice* (New York: Hill and Wang, 1971), the "working party" critically examined these purposes and agreed that general deterrence and retribution have only limited value. Reformation and incapacitation, they argued, were not accomplishable or acceptable according to contemporary values of justice and humanity.

19. One of the important discoveries by sociologists was the operation of the "informal" social organization within "bureaucracies," which has its unofficial norms, values, and personal relationships and which operates within the formal structure and often conflicts with its official rules and goals. See Milton Dalton, *Men Who Manage* (New York: Wiley, 1959).

20. See John Irwin, "The Trouble With Rehabilitation," *Criminal Justice and Behavior,* no. 2 (1974).

21. Robert Johnson, *Hard Time* (Belmont, CA: Wadsworth, 2002), 1.

22. Bureau of Justice Statistics, as quoted in the *Los Angeles Times,* 18 August 2003, p. A10.

23. At the urging of John Howard, the English critic of penal practices, the English Parliament passed the Penitentiary Act (1779), which called for a regimen of imprisonment that involved (1) humane treatment, (2) governance by formal rules, (3) safety, (4) instruction in morality, (5) isolation, and (6) organized work. This was basically the concept that Americans put into practice in New York and Pennsylvania.

24. See G. Rusche and O. Kirchheimer, *Punishment and Penal Discipline* (New York: Columbia University Press, 1939); Foucault, *Discipline and Punish*; B. McKelvey, *American Prisons: A History of Good Intentions* (Montclair, NJ: Patterson Smith, 1977); Dario Melossi, *The Prison and the Factory: The Origins of the Penitentiary System* (Berkeley: University of California Press, 1980); David Rothman, *The Discovery of the Asylum: Social Order and Disorder in the New Republic* (Boston: Little, Brown, 1980); and David Garland, *Punishment and Welfare: A History of Penal Strategies* (Aldershot, England: Gower, 1985) and *Punishment in Modern Society.*

25. See Donald Clemmer, *The Prison Community* (New York: Holt, Rinehart, and Winston, 1965); Gresham Sykes, *The Society of Captives* (Princeton, NJ: Princeton University Press, 1958); David Ward and

Gene Kassebaum, *Women's Prison: Sex and Social Structure* (Chicago: Aldine-Atherton, 1958); Rose Giallombardo, *Society of Women: A Study of a Women's Prison* (New York: Wiley, 1966); John Irwin, *The Felon* (Englewood Cliffs, NJ: Prentice Hall, 1970) and *Prisons in Turmoil*; Esther Hefferman, *Making It in Prison: The Square, the Cool, and the Life* (New York: Wiley, 1972); Leo Carroll, *Hacks, Blacks, and Others: Race Relations in Maximum Security Prison* (Lexington, MA: Lexington, 1974); James Jacobs, *Stateville: The Penitentiary in Mass Society* (Chicago: University of Chicago Press, 1977); Nicole Rafter, *Partial Justice: Women in State Prisons, 1800–1935* (Boston: Northeastern University Press, 1985); and Barbara Owen, *In the Mix* (New York: State University of New York Press, 1998). ✦

Chapter 2

American Prisons

England's Fatal Experiment

At the beginning of the eighteenth century, the colonies in America set out on their own to address many social and political issues, including the problem of crime. England, which had exported many of its penal practices to the colonies, was in the final stage of its fatal experiment—the excessive and ineffective policy of imposing capital punishment for hundreds of crimes, many of them petty property crimes.[1] English rulers attempted to control the "dangerous classes"—the emerging urban poor—and to protect English property, particularly the forms of property being accumulated by the new wealthy class—the gentry. Without a police force, which we now take for granted, the new English elites, the gentry, tried to impose control through the elevation of the institution of English "justice," which offered a mixture of terror, ceremony, and mercy.[2] As it became apparent that this approach was failing and the urban poor accumulated and increasingly threatened the property and tranquility of the English upper classes, the rulers turned to banishment, first to America and then to Australia.

In the beginning of the nineteenth century, English rulers realized that the excessive use of capital punishment was a failure. Also, banishment was becoming less practicable. After the Revolution, Americans refused to accept the transported felons, while the nonconvict Australian immigrants opposed additional transportation to their colony.[3] The urban poor continued to accumulate and threaten the English elite's property and propriety. Consequently, additional strategies for the control of the dangerous classes were devised. At this juncture, utilitarian philosophers with new theories of crime and crime control stepped forward and offered a "rational" response to crime. According to the utilitarians, individuals commit crime when they perceive that the rewards of crime exceed the punishment received for transgressions. Therefore, control of crime is accomplished by making punishment exceed the reward.[4] Jeremy Bentham, a leading utilitarian, also planned the "panopticon," a circular prison in which all activities of prisoners could be watched and controlled. This ideal punishment scheme for felons had explicit utilitarian purposes and attendant moral justifications. It also had the implicit purpose of control of the lower classes.[5]

The Penitentiary

In America, many immigrants and other poor people were siphoned off to the frontiers. Consequently, in the late seventeenth century and the eighteenth century, fewer unemployed, disenfranchised, lower-class people gathered in American cities than in the growing urban centers in England and Europe. Also, religious groups, such as the Quakers and Puritans, played a major role in planning new American institutions. A spirit of innovation and humanitarianism prevailed.[6] American religious reformers introduced a plan to replace the cruel and ineffective penal practices, particularly corporal punishment and banishment, that America had inherited from England. They were influenced by the various antecedents of imprisonment practiced by Europeans, by Jeremy Bentham's panopticon, and by the Penitentiary Act passed by the English Parliament in 1779.[7]

By 1815, the United States' first two prison experiments—New York's Newgate and Pennsylvania's Walnut Street—were becoming dangerously overcrowded. A riot occurred at Newgate in 1818. After 1815, the states were losing money on convict "cottage industries" in both prisons because of a general economic downturn. Also, reports issued by New York and Pennsylvania inspectors and reform societies indicated that Newgate and Walnut Street prisoners—who mixed freely—gambled, drank, and engaged in general debauchery. In spite of these apparent failures in their first prison experiments, Americans persevered with their plans to develop an innovative response to their crime problem and introduced two types of "penitentiaries." In 1818, the New York Prison

Board Inspector wrote, "a better plan must be devised, not a mere plan of good living and light punishment, but of dread and terror, [and that the] prisoners [were] the most abandoned and profligate of mankind and steeled against virtue."[8]

New York and Pennsylvania followed slightly different penitentiary plans. The basic idea in both states was to avoid prisoner contamination and promote the reformation of felons through separation, discipline, and contemplation. In New York, prisoners were allowed to congregate during the day. In Pennsylvania, prisoners were totally isolated in separate cells.

Auburn

New York built the first penitentiary in the small village of Auburn, 150 miles north of New York City. Auburn Prison was intended to be a harsh, secure facility in which separation of prisoners would be strictly enforced. The main cell block—the "north wing"—had five tiers. Each tier had 45 seven-by-three-and-a-half-foot cells. The cells had no plumbing, heat, lighting, or ventilation. Martin Miller wrote that the official routine had the following features:

1. Though most prisoners worked in "congregation" during the day, silence was enforced in all areas.
2. Every prisoner activity—rising, washing, leaving their cells, eating, lying down on their beds—was regulated by bells and temporal rules.
3. Prisoners moved about the prison in military company, marching in a half-gait shuffle, eyes downward, right hands on the shoulder of the man in front and left hands holding their night buckets, cans of drinking water, or small trays for food.[9]

Prisoners were viewed as unredeemable, untrustworthy individuals who must be broken and disciplined. Elam Lynds, the "deputy keeper" at Auburn, wrote, "Break the spirit and you will have a better maintained prison. Make him kneel, make him fear you and break his spirit. Dominate him."[10] The penitentiary's discipline was enforced with severe, occasionally deadly floggings, which were made legal in 1819.

Auburn authorities also experimented (1821) with holding the most "hardened criminals" in complete physical isolation in small cells, in which they had no visitors, a reduced diet, and no work.

After two years, five of the 80 men held in this manner had died, 11 were deemed insane, 41 were profoundly ill, one had mutilated himself, and another had committed suicide.[11]

As they had in Newgate, prisoners worked in shops and were contracted to private entrepreneurs who supplied material, sold the products, and paid a fee to the state. Shoes and boots were the most common products. In 1825, New York built Sing Sing penitentiary, which, except for minor changes, followed the Auburn plan. Most of the other states soon constructed prisons generally patterned after New York's penitentiaries.

Discipline

Life in these penitentiaries was cruel and arduous. Corporal punishment was delivered regularly. Colonel Levi S. Burr, who served a sentence at Sing Sing in its early years, wrote:

> In truth I have seen [the cudgel] applied daily and almost every hour. . . . Sometimes repeatedly on the same subject several times in the day, and often more than 20 at a time one after the other, until the keeper was exhausted.

> At another time, the same keeper exerted his strength upon a man by the name of Osterhou. . . . He was a novice in that part of discipline that requires the company to keep time by the step and made a mistake while marching to his labor. The keeper felled him to the ground and beat him cruelly.[12]

Many prisoners were flogged to death, and many others died because of the brutal routine. In some of the early penitentiaries, death rates were from two to twelve times those in society outside. In 1829, Sing Sing's rate was double, Maryland's state prison, triple, Virginia's, five times, and Tennessee's, twelve times the rate in the general society.[13]

Social Life

The silent system, the discipline, and the rigorous routine produced an unusual social atmosphere. Gustave de Beaumont and Alexis de Tocqueville, two French emissaries sent to America in 1833 to examine the new penitentiaries, described the silence at Sing Sing:

> In the evening, at the setting of the sun, labor ceases, and the convicts leave the workshops to retire into their cells. Upon rising, going to

sleep, eating, leaving the cells and going back to them, everything passes in the most profound silence, and nothing is heard in the whole prison but the steps of those who march, or sounds proceeding from the workshops. But when the day is finished, and the prisoners have retired to their cells, the silence within these vast walls, which contain so many prisoners, is that of death. We have often trod during night those monotonous and dumb galleries, where a lamp is always burning; we felt as if we traversed catacombs; there were a thousand living beings, and yet it was a desert solitude.[14]

Because of the lack of personal accounts or prison ethnographies (which abounded later), we can only speculate about the social life of prisoners in this type of penitentiary. However, it is certain that considerable and regular communication, unnoticed by Beaumont and Tocqueville, occurred in spite of the rigorous attempts to enforce silence. In fact, convicts doing time in silent systems developed a special style of speech:

Although the prisoners are forbidden to talk, nevertheless they communicate as freely as if the rule did not exist. When I attempted to ask my neighbor a question, he hushed me up with a hissing noise—but he answered my question. His lips did not move, but I could hear him talk in a faint murmur which would have been inaudible ten paces away. . . .

The convicts never glance into the speaker's face or at his lips; they look straight ahead and talk in the manner of ventriloquists, but instead of using a loud and clear tone they whisper in a low murmur.[15]

With this limited communication, we can imagine that convicts formed friendships, exchanged contraband, and planned deviant, even disruptive action, such as escapes. However, we have no evidence of elaborate prisoner subterranean social organizations, such as those that developed in later systems with less restricted communication and mobility.

Pennsylvania

The type of penitentiary introduced in Pennsylvania was a completely solitary system, which hands over the prisoner to all the trials of solitude, leads him through reflection to remorse, through religion to hope; makes him industrious by the burden of idleness, and which, while it inflicts the torment of solitude, makes him find a charm in the converse of pious men.[16]

In Western Penitentiary (1818) and then Eastern Penitentiary (1829), prisoners were held, day and night, in solitary cells (each with a small exercise yard), completely out of contact with anyone except staff and occasional approved visitors. Charles Dickens, who toured the United States in 1842 and visited some of its "innovations," described the procedures at Eastern Penitentiary:

> [H]e is led to the cell from which he never again comes forth, until his whole term of imprisonment has expired. He never hears of wife and children; home or friends; the life or death of any single creature. He sees the prison-officers, but with that exception he never looks upon a human countenance, or hears a human voice. [17]

Again, because of the lack of personal accounts or research reports, we can only construct a partial and speculative rendition of prisoner experiences in this extreme form of imprisonment. Dickens' description of the cell supplies a partial reflection of the prisoner's life:

> Every cell has double doors; the outer one of sturdy oak, the other of grated iron, wherein there is a trap through which his food is handed. He has a Bible, and a slate and pencil, and, under certain restrictions, has sometimes other books, provided for the purpose, and pen and ink and paper. His razor, plate, and can, and basin, hang upon the wall, or shine upon the little shelf. Fresh water is laid on in every cell, and he can draw it at his pleasure. During the day, his bedstead turns up against the wall, and leaves more space for him to work in. His loom, or bench, or wheel, is there; and there he labours, sleeps and wakes, and counts the seasons as they change and he grows old.[18]

Prisoners labored in their cells at weaving, shoemaking, tailoring, and joining. Work was very important to them: "There was another German who had entered the jail but yesterday, and who started from his bed when we looked in, and pleaded, in his broken English, very hard for work."[19] Beaumont and Tocqueville noted that "isolation without labor has been tried, and those prisoners who have not become insane or did not die of despair have returned to society only to commit new crimes," and "there was not a single one among them who did not speak of labor with a kind of gratitude, and who did not express the idea that without the relief of constant occupation, life would be insufferable."[20]

In addition, prisoners in solitary struggled to embellish their cells and lives:

> He wore a paper hat of his own making, and was pleased to have it noticed and commended. He had very ingeniously manufactured a sort of Dutch clock from some disregarded odds and ends; and his vinegar bottle served for the pendulum. . . .

> In another cell, there was a German, sentenced to five years' imprisonment for larceny, two of which had just expired. With colours procured in the same manner, he had painted every inch of the walls and ceiling quite beautifully. . . .

> There was a poet, who after doing two days' work in every four-and-twenty hours, one for himself and one for the prison, wrote verses about ships.[21]

The European observers concluded that there was no communication among prisoners and consequently no prisoner social life.[22] It is certain that prisoners in the Eastern and the Western Penitentiaries in Pennsylvania and in the few other completely solitary prisons devised some system of communication and did have at least a scanty social life. Thomas Cleveland, M.D., warden of the Rhode Island State Prison, described prisoner communication in the Rhode Island Prison in 1844, while it was a solitary system:

> When shut up in the cells, they exercised, under the cravings of the social instinct, which walls and chains cannot repress, every contrivance that ingenuity could suggest, by means of the window, and the pipes passing through the cells, to hold some communication with each other, and they were more frequently successful than would have been supposed possible.[23]

As noted by Dickens, one prisoner had "procured" through "larceny" the "colours" to decorate his cell. This suggests some interaction and clandestine activities among prisoners. In fact, some prisoners were regularly released to perform maintenance work. This indicates that there was some communication and exchange of material among convicts, and this was probably the way the "colours" were procured.

Prisoners in more recent eras have indicated that fantasizing was very important to them, and they were able to vividly relive many episodes of their preprison life. Victor Nelson, who served a prison sentence in the 1920s, described his fantasizing:

> One cannot rest. One can merely escape from the existing drabness. One can merely lie down on the bed and drift off into the dream world; into memories of the past, visions of the future; neither of which is satisfactory except in retrospect or anticipation. One lies in a stupor, shutting out the undignified, unappetizing dullness; deliberately or unconsciously running away from life. This is a bad habit to get into, this flying from reality; but it is a habit into which practically all of us get, mildly or terribly, depending entirely on the length of our sentences, our ages, our intensities of awareness.[24]

We can assume that this activity was particularly important to the prisoners in the early penitentiaries.

Above all, these isolated prisoners despaired, stagnated, and, in many instances, expired:

> [A]nd yet a more dejected, heart-broken, wretched creature, it would be difficult to imagine. I never saw such a picture of forlorn affliction and distress of mind. My heart bled for him; and when the tears ran down his cheeks, and he took one of the visitors aside, to ask, with his trembling hands nervously clutching at his coat to detain him, whether there was no hope of his dismal sentence being commuted, the spectacle was really too painful to witness.[25]

The warden of the Rhode Island State Prison, a doctor, remarked on the psychological impact of the solitary system:

> Of the *forty* prisoners, committed while the strictly solitary system was in operation, ten, or one-fourth of the whole number, (two of whom were blacks), manifested decided symptoms of derangement; seven so much so as to unfit them for labor for a longer or shorter period, and five were discharged insane, two of whom recovered, and three now remain unrestored to a sound state of mind.[26]

After the introduction of these two different types of penitentiaries, arguments over the superiority of Auburn or the Pennsylvania system were waged in journals, newspapers, and public meetings. However, in spite of the fact that many observers believed the Pennsylvania system to be superior, the much greater cost of this system and the greater potential for the exploitation of convict labor of the Auburn system resulted in most states adopting the latter.

Hard Labor

By the middle of the nineteenth century, it appeared that the efforts to reform prisoners through separation, solitude, and contemplation had failed. Consequently, most states began concentrating on keeping prisoners under control, disciplining them, and exploiting their labor.[27] Control was maintained through the use of cruel and bizarre forms of corporal punishment, such as whipping, water torture, and solitary confinement in excessively cruel spaces. Silence and strict discipline systems were continued.

The Prisons

Most of the prisons built in the nineteenth century were patterned after Auburn and Sing Sing and were like fortresses, with huge granite walls and large cell blocks that contained stacks of three, four, or five tiers. These stacks were inside a stone or concrete building. The cells had no lights, heat, or plumbing. For a toilet, prisoners used a "honey bucket," which they carried from their cells every morning to empty in some designated location. In addition to the wall and cell blocks, there were shop or factory buildings, an administration building, a mess hall and kitchen, and perhaps some other buildings containing a laundry, a school, and an infirmary. The other major feature was the "yard"—a large open area within the walls, which might have had some recreational equipment. Overall, these prisons were harsh worlds of steel and stone, of unbearable heat and stench in the summer and chilling cold in the winter, of cramped quarters, and of clanking metal doors.

In addition to these fortress prisons, many of the southern, more rural states had "farms" or "camps," which had dormitories instead of cell blocks and fences instead of walls. Frequently, prisoners wore leg chains so they could not run or walk fast. Armed men guarded prisoners day and night. Often, prisoners were chained to their beds while sleeping:

At night, another long chain was run down alongside of each cot. The prisoner had to set on the cot and hold the iron ring of the upright chain in his hand while the guard ran this chain through the iron ring. This was called the building chain and was securely fastened at each end of the building after being run through the iron ring of each prisoner's upright chain.

Thus each prisoner was securely chained up each night and could only move three feet from his cot. Any movement of the prisoner caused the chains to rattle and a corresponding curse from the guard. If it was necessary to get up to use the toilet, the prisoner must first yell "Getting up" and then wait for the guard's reply "Get up." The whole process was very noisy and was accompanied by the clanking of heavy chains.

The chains the prisoners wore were permanently riveted on them, and were worn every minute of the time. They worked in them, slept in them, were a part of them. The chains could not be taken off unless they were cut off with a hammer and a cold chisel.[28]

Tasks

In the fortress prisons, prisoners worked in shops or factories producing shoes, cloth, "jute," furniture, or other products deemed profitable by the state or a private contractor. In the farms, prisoners worked in the fields, again for the state or a contractor. In the camps, "chain gangs" of prisoners worked on roads and other state projects. Since the state or private contractors were attempting to make a profit and the normal wage incentives were absent, prisoners were forced to complete a certain amount of daily work—a "task"—which typically was difficult.

I know that in this place that most punishments were inflicted because of the demand of the prison contractors because of the reports for not doing tasks. Many men were driven desperate and insane because of these conditions. Columbus at that time had an insane asylum inside the walls containing about 20 convicts most of whom had been driven insane because of abuse inflicted upon them while there and in general as a result of not being able to satisfy the demands of some Contractor.[29]

There was a little Jewish boy working next to me named Bennie Lowenthal. Bennie was tubercular. He couldn't do the task. Meyer was after him all the time. When things broke well with me, when my stock ran well, when I wasn't held up, I could do my task in six hours, and on these days I would help out Bennie so that Meyer wouldn't have him punished for failing to do the task.

I couldn't help Bennie on the day in question. The stock had been bad. I was behind when Meyer took the report of work completed. Bennie was behind. Meyer came along the line with his book. He stopped at Bennie's bench. He began to curse the tubercular convict. Then he hit the kid, who was just nineteen.[30]

In the southern farms and camps, prisoners worked from dawn to dusk, with inadequate food and rest:

We commenced work about 5 A.M.—and were still at it until 11:30 A.M.—when the guard called out "Lay 'em down," (meaning lay down the tools and eat). Dinner came out in a galvanized iron bucket. Tin plates were in a wooden box and another box contained corn pone, cut in six-inch squares. Each convict grabbed a tin plate and a square of corn pone, and one of the convicts, using his plate as a dipper, dished out the contents of the iron bucket as each convict presented his tin plate. The contents of the iron bucket was boiled, dried cow-peas (not eaten anywhere else but in Georgia) and called "red beans." . . .

Dinner eaten, we lay down at full length—right where we happened to be, and rested and smoked if we had anything to smoke. At one o'clock we were roused by the guards calling out "Let's go back." And back to work we'd go. The afternoon was a repetition of the morning—the convicts laboring as hard as they could, the chains clanking, and the guards cursing and finding fault with each convict. Finally, just as the sun was sinking in the West, about 6 P.M., and the prisoners were about sunk also, the guard called out again "Lay 'em down." The days work was over.

Supper consisted of another square of corn pone, another three slices of fried pig fat and another dose of sorghum.[31]

The work in some of the southern state prisons (where the era of hard labor extended far into the 1900s) was so punishing that many prisoners mutilated themselves to avoid it. For example, between 1940 and 1944, 273 Texas prisoners mutilated themselves, and between 1944 and 1948, this number increased to 341. They severed their Achilles tendon (tendons that attach to the back of the knee), which crippled them for an extended period, broke their arms, amputated their hands and feet, and burned themselves with lye.[32]

Control

In prisons of hard labor, there was no pretense of any noble or humanitarian reformative purpose. Prisoners were believed to be wretched, mostly unredeemable, untrustworthy individuals who must be strictly and harshly disciplined, particularly if successful exploitation of their labor was to be accomplished.

Most states continued to impose silence systems and strict regimens on prisoners. The following rules were enforced in Minnesota prisons at the turn of century:

1. Your first duty is strict obedience to the rules and regulations and any orders of the office under whose charge you may be placed.
2. You must observe strict silence in all departments of the prison and while marching through the yard.
3. You must not speak to, give or receive from, visitors anything except by permission of the Warden or Deputy Warden. Gazing at visitors or strangers passing through the prison is strictly forbidden.
4. You are expected to apply yourself diligently to whatever labor you are assigned and after reasonable teaching to perform the same amount of work as would be required of you as a citizen.
5. At every signal to fall in for marching take [your] place in line promptly. March with military step, attend to and promptly obey the orders of your officer.
6. You will be required to keep your person clean and your clothing tidy and in good order. You must not make any alterations in your clothing or cut your shoes, if they do not fit or need repairs report the fact to your officer. You must not carry knives, tools of any kind, pencil, paper or any material whatever from your shop to your cell without permission in writing from the Warden or Deputy Warden. Finding any of these things in your possession will be considered proof that you have violated this rule. Tinkering or writing notes to other convicts or carrying notes from one convict to another is strictly forbidden.

7. You are not allowed to have any money on your person or in your possession, neither are you permitted to trade or purchase any article whatever. All of your business must be done through the Warden.

8. You must approach an officer in a respectful manner. Always salute him before speaking. You must confine your conversation with him strictly to the business in hand. You must not address an officer on matters outside the prison. Insolence in any form to an officer, foreman, or even to a fellow convict will not be tolerated.

9. On entering the cell house, office of the Board of Control, Warden or Deputy Warden, you must uncover unless your duties are such that you have special permission to remain covered.[33]

When prisoners broke the rules, failed to complete their tasks, or aroused the hostility or displeasure of prison staff, they were severely punished. Sometimes they were put on "bread and water" for days or weeks in solitary cells (which were usually cramped, without furniture, dark, and hot or cold). Many were lashed:

> The convict started to speak—to say something in his defense— but it was drowned out. Strong hands grabbed hold of him, pulled down his pants, baring his buttocks, and then laid him face downward on one of the benches. He was held down so that he could not move. A leather strap six feet long, three inches wide, one-quarter inch thick was brought forth. The wielder of this instrument of torture stood off from the convict, judging his distance with a practiced eye. He growled at the convict: "So you won't work, eh? Well, damn you, I'll learn you to work on this chain gang!"

> And with a terrific crash, the heavy strap came down on bare flesh with all the strength of the wielder behind it. The convict let out a yell—pleaded for mercy—promised to work—promised anything, but the strap rose again and descended with a sickening crash, the force of which temporarily shut off the pleadings of the convict. And so it went—one, two, three, four, five, six, seven, eight, nine, ten. Ten licks and the convict, half fainting or perhaps unconscious, was stood up on his feet—blood running down his legs, and one of the guards carried or led him back into the sleeping quarters.[34]

Others received crueler forms of punishment, such as various forms of water torture:

> There was a bathtub in the corner of the bull pen. They filled it with ice-cold water. Then they sat me in it and fastened my arms and hands to the sides of the tub. They also fastened my ankles to the bottom of the tub with iron clamps. The tub, you will please understand, was built for the water cure. They put an iron collar around my neck. Every time I moved, the clamps on my ankles, wrists and neck cut into the skin. But that wasn't all. The worst was yet to come. "Burly Sam" played a hose around my face. The water was cold, it seemed colder than the water in the tub. He kept playing the stream around my nostrils. I was gasping for breath. I opened my mouth. That's why Sam was playing the hose around my nostrils. He wanted me to open my mouth so that he could shoot the stream into my mouth. I felt myself growing dizzy. My lungs and heart and stomach seemed to be freezing. I was numb from head to feet. Suddenly everything turned black. When I woke up I was lying on the stone floor of a dungeon in the bull pen. I didn't know how long I had been there until a guard brought me some bread and water. He said I had been in the dungeon two hours.[35]

Many of the southern states made use of convict trusties to keep control over other prisoners. These trusties were given extreme powers—the power to use corporal punishment, even homicide—in return for special privileges. In Texas, they were called "building tenders" who, according to Crouch and Marquart, "enjoyed near limitless authority to maintain control."[36] For example, in 1922 at Eastham Prison, two building tenders responded to an escape attempt:

> Well they [three inmates] cut a hole in the loft and were making one in the roof when the building tender went and told the night guard, or picket boss. The boss told the building tender to go up and bring the boys down. He went up on top of the bunk rack, about seven feet below the loft, and told the boys the jig was up, that the boss had heard them, and they must come down. They started down, feet first, through the hole they had made. It was barely big enough to squeeze their bodies through, and when they got all but their arms and head through, he [the building tender] stabbed two of them. But the third man saw what was taking place so he dived through head first. The building tenders [there were two of them]

followed him and like to beat him to death. Then when they finished with him they went back up there and pitched the corpses off the top bunk, which was about ten feet high.[37]

When Tom Murton became warden of Arkansas' Tucker Farm in 1967, he discovered that the trusties ran the prison:

> From what I knew of the daily routine at Tucker, it started at sunup when the Longline went out to the fields. The workday usually ended twelve to fourteen hours later, when it was dark.
>
> The Longline was guarded by trusties armed with a variety of weapons ranging from high-powered rifles and shotguns to heavy-caliber side arms. When the Longline left the building for work, the inmate guards moved out to provide perimeter security with a "rider," or foreman, followed by two "high powers"— guards on horseback, carrying carbines. They in turn were followed by two "shotguns," on foot, who kept a distance of fifty to seventy-five yards from the working party. Two more shotguns and a sub-rider (assistant foreman) brought up the rear. Two more high powers stayed farther away from the main body, to back up the shotguns in case they were rushed by the inmates, and to see to it that the shotguns themselves didn't escape or fire on the high powers.[38]

The prisoners accepted the trustee positions to avoid the severe and deprived living conditions:

> So, they offer you a job to beat the other inmates and you take it because there are two types of living conditions: you exist, or you survive.
>
> If you existed, you walked around in the barracks with an army blanket around you—no underwear, no T-shirt, no socks. You wore a pair of rubber boots for house shoes. If it was summer, you wore a pair of brogans and because the blanket was too hot you wrapped a sheet around you.
>
> A trusty had underwear because he took it away from a rank man. A trusty occasionally had milk on the table and salt-meat—a rank man had weevils and beans.
>
> A trusty was surviving; a rank man was existing. So, you became a trusty and were glad to do it.[39]

Social Organization

In spite of the extreme control measures, prisoners commingled, communicated, and developed individual and collective strategies for survival and advancing their own interests. Alexander Berkman, an anarchist imprisoned in the 1890s, commented eloquently on the convict social world:

> A perfected model it is, this prison life, with its apparent uniformity and dull passivity. But beneath the torpid surface smolder the fires of being, now crackling faintly under a [dun-colored] smothering smoke, now blazing forth with the ruthlessness of despair. Hidden by the veil of discipline rages the struggle of fiercely contending wills, and intricate meshes are woven in the quagmire of darkness and suppression.[40]

Berkman recognized a definite hierarchy in the prisoner society. The great bulk, who are "accidental and occasional offenders direct from the field, factory, and the mine,"

> plod along in the shops, in sullen misery and dread. Day in, day out, year after year, they drudge at the monotonous work, dully wondering at the numerous trusties idling about, while their own heavy tasks are constantly increased. From cell to shop and back again, always under the stern eyes of the guards, their days drag in deadening toil.[41]

But other figures—"con men," "politicians," "old timers," "yegg-men," and "guns"—connived, manipulated, and conspired to survive imprisonment and gain some advantage, privilege, and extra commodities.[42]

Significantly, the hard labor prison also had trusties, "pets," or "stools" who, in return for special privileges, cooperated with the authorities:

> The prisoners spy upon each other, and in turn upon the officers. The latter encourage the trusties in unearthing the secret doings of the inmates, and the stools enviously compete with each other in supplying information to the keepers. . .

> The stools and the trusties are an essential element in the government of the prison. With rare exception, every officer has one or more on his staff. They assist him in his duties, perform most of his

work, and make out the reports for the illiterate guards. Occasionally, they are even called upon to help the "clubbing squad." The more intelligent stools enjoy the confidence of the Deputy and his assistants, and thence advance to the favor of the Warden. The latter places more reliance upon his favorite trusties than upon the guards. "I have about a hundred paid officers to keep watch over the prisoners," ... "and two hundred volunteers to watch both."[43]

Administrators believed that promoting informing was necessary to control prisoners who were carrying on clandestine behavior and forming subterranean societies. They have continued to promote it through the successive stages of the prison, even though it has had many unintended and undesirable consequences, such as increased conflict and violence among prisoners.

Big Houses

At the end of the nineteenth century, emerging labor organizations and business owners that competed with those using cheap prisoner labor successfully lobbied to restrict the use of convict labor. Federal laws were passed prohibiting the sale of convict-produced goods across state lines. Most states ceased using convicts to produce goods that were sold on the open market. Subsequently, prisoners only produced goods that would be used by state agencies.

In addition, the reforms of the "progressive era" reached most state prison systems and, except for prisons in southern states, most excessively brutal practices were eliminated. Also, at this stage of the political economy of the United States, new forms of industrial production and new capitalist economic relationships developed, a working-class movement took shape, and the standard of living of the lower classes rose. Because of these changes, fines and probation became more acceptable and, therefore, more prevalent forms of punishment.

Prisons became places where felons were sent to "do time"—to be punished by just being there and to be temporarily incapacitated. I described the Big House in an earlier study:

This granite, steel, cement, and asphalt monstrosity stood as the state's most extreme form of punishment, short of the death penalty. It was San Quentin in California, Sing Sing in New York, Stateville in Illinois, Jackson in Michigan, Jefferson City in Missouri, Cannon City in Colorado, and so on. It was a place of banishment and punishment to which convicts were "sent up." Its major characteristics were isolation, routine, and monotony. Its mood was mean and grim, perforated here and there by ragged-edged vitality and humor.[44]

Without the possibility of making profits, lawmakers and prison administrators lacked a reason to exploit convict labor. Also, the progressive era reforms eliminated a great deal of the cruel punishment of prisoners. In most states, prisoners' general level of material deprivation was also allowed to rise because that of outside lower classes had risen. Prison staff primarily acted to keep prisoners under control and prevent them from escaping. They accomplished the first of these by enforcing a relatively strict routine and within that allowing the prisoners to manage themselves. Consequently, the prisoners in the Big Houses in the East, Midwest, and West, where white prisoners were the great majority, created a solidary convict society: "The Big House was, like all prisons, a place where convicts lived and constructed a world. This world had divisions and strata, special informal rules and meanings, and its own set of enterprises."[45]

The Big House was bounded by a tight official schedule. According to the prescribed routine, prisoners rose early; hurriedly ate breakfast; returned to their cells for one of the four or five daily counts; proceeded to work, school, or the yard for a day of idleness; hurriedly ate lunch; counted; went back to work, school, or idleness; hurriedly ate dinner; and returned to their cells for the night. After count, they read, wrote letters or literary works, pursued hobbies, talked to other prisoners, listened to the radio on their earphones (when this innovation reached the prison), and then went to sleep when the lights were turned off.

The Convict Code

Within this formal routine, a complex, informal prisoner social world operated. This world pivoted around the convict code, a prison adaptation of the thieves' code. Thieves were not the majority, but they were the most sophisticated criminal type. Their strong commitment to thieves' values, their communication network—which extended throughout the thieves' world, inside and outside of prison—and their loyalty to other thieves gave them the upper hand in prisons. The central rule in the thieves' code was "Thou shalt not snitch." In prison, thieves converted this to the dual norm of "Do not rat on another prisoner" and "Do your own time." Thieves also were obliged by their code to be cool and tough, that is, to maintain respect and dignity, not to show weakness, to help other thieves, and to leave most other prisoners alone.

Their code dominated the Big House and generally translated into these rules:

1. Do not inform.
2. Do not openly interact or cooperate with the guards or the administration.
3. Do your own time.

These rules helped to produce a gap of hostility and unfriendliness between prisoners and guards, a hierarchy of prisoners, a system of mutual aid among a minority of prisoners, and patterns of exploitation among others.

The prisoners divided themselves into a variety of prisoner types. In addition to the "yeggs," "Johnsons," "people," "right guys," or "regulars"—various labels for thieves and persons whom they accepted as trustworthy—there were several types more indigenous to the prison. There were prison "politicians," "merchants," and "gamblers," who were involved in supplying, exchanging, and controlling prison resources and commodities.[46] There were prison "queens," who openly presented themselves as homosexuals, and "punks," who were considered to have been "turned out"—that is, made into homosexuals by other prisoners or by the prison experience. There was the "character," who continuously created humorous derision through his dress, language, storytelling ability, or general behavior. There were the "masses," who broke into the subtypes of "assholes" or "hoosiers"—lower- and working-class persons with little or no criminal skills and low respect—and "square johns"—prisoners oriented to conventional society and not viewed as criminals by the rest of the population. There was a variety of "dingbats" considered to be crazy but harmless. Finally, there were "rapos," prisoners serving sentences for sexual acts such as incest and child molesting, which were repulsive to most prisoners, and "stool pigeons," "rats," or "snitches," who supplied information about other prisoners to authorities.

There was also a variety of prison "toughs"; persons who were deeply and openly hostile to the prison administration, the conventional society, and most other prisoners and who displayed a readiness to employ violence against others. These prisoners ranged from the less predictable and less social "crazies" to the more predictable and clique-oriented "hard rocks" or "tush hogs."

These types were arranged in a hierarchy of prestige, power, and privilege. Right guys, through their propensity to cooperate with each other, their prestige as thieves, and their presentation of coolness and toughness, were at the top. Clemmer described the elite of the prison in the following manner: "In the class which we have termed the 'elite' are the more intelligent, urbanized, sophisticated of offenders who, for the most part, do not toady to officials and who set themselves apart, and have their relations chiefly with each other."[47] Very close to the top were the merchants, politicians, and gamblers. They occupied this high position because they largely controlled the scarce prison resources. Characters, when they were accomplished, were awarded a special position with considerable respect and popularity but not much direct power. Down the ladder were the toughs, who had to be respected because they were a constant threat. The cliques of hard rocks occasionally hurt or killed someone, though seldom anyone with prestige and power. The crazies, who were often very dangerous, were treated with extreme caution but were avoided and excluded as much as possible. In the middle were the masses, who were ignored by the leaders, stayed out of the prison's informal world, and restricted their social activities to small friendship groups or remained loners. Below them were the queens, punks, rats, and rapos, the latter being at the very bottom of the pile. On the outside of all informal prisoner activities were the dingbats, who were ignored by all.

Correctional Institutions

A dramatically altered set of conditions took shape in the United States after World War II. After a brief recession, America's industrial apparatus righted itself, and the country entered into an extended period of prosperity. The prewar isolationism and hard-times mentality of the Depression gave way to global activism and an optimistic spirit of American power and efficiency. Though the fear of communism resulted in considerable repression of thought (McCarthyism), the promises of the New Deal made by the Roosevelt administration and continued under President Truman, were reaching fruition. The welfare state was taking shape.

In the field of crime control, the rehabilitative ideal prevailed. This new theory was based on the idea that crime was a result of physiological or psychological pathology, not sin or evilness. In the early 1900s, in the burgeoning fields of psychiatry and psychology, theories of the psychological causes of crime abounded.[48] After World War II, a body of new professionals, steeped in these theories, entered the field of criminal justice and devised a new penal response. In many states, such as California, Wisconsin, New Jersey, and New York, the public mood was receptive, and tax money was available. These and other states entered into the "correctional" era, or, as David Garland put it, penal welfarism:

> 1960s penal-welfarism was by 1970, the established policy framework in both Britain and America. Its basic axiom—that penal measures ought, where possible, to be rehabilitative interventions rather than negative, retributive punishment—gave rise to a whole new network of interlocking principles and practices. These included sentencing laws that allowed indeterminate sentences linked to early release and parole supervision; the juvenile court with its child welfare philosophy; the use of social inquiry and psychiatric reports; the individualization of treatment based upon expert assessment and classification; criminological research focusing upon etiological issues and treatment effectiveness; social work with offenders and their families; and custodial regimes that stressed the re-educative purposes of imprisonment and the importance of re-integrative support upon release.[49]

New laws were passed to change the austere, punitive Big House prisons into "correctional institutions." Indeterminate sentence laws were introduced or expanded. Parole boards were given more power. Prison administrative structures were reorganized with a much greater role for "treatment"-oriented personnel. Most states built new prisons, called correctional institutions, that were

more consistent with the revamped major purpose of imprisonment, that of reformation, now labeled "rehabilitation." Soledad
(where I served five years) was one of California's new correctional
institutions:

> Soledad's physical structure radically departed from that of the
> Big Houses. It had no granite wall; instead, circling the prison was
> a high fence with gun towers situated every few hundred feet and
> nestled in the corners. The nine cell blocks stemmed off a long hall.
> Two relatively pleasant dining rooms with tile floors and octagonal
> oak tables, a spacious library, a well-equipped hospital, a laundry, an
> education building, a gym, several shops, and the administration
> building connected to this hall. In fact, the entire prison commu-
> nity operated in and around the hall, and prisoners could (and
> many of them did) live day after day without ever going outside.
>
> Each cell block (called a "wing") had a "day room" jutting off the
> side at the ground level, and all the inside walls in the prison were
> painted in pastel colors—pale blue, pale green, light yellow, and
> tan. All cell blocks originally had one man cells, though many were
> assigned two occupants later. All cells except those in one small
> wing used for new prisoners and for segregation and isolation (O
> wing) had solid doors with a small, screened inspection window.
> The cells in all cell blocks (except O wing) were in three tiers
> around the outside of the wings, so each cell had an outside win-
> dow. Instead of bars, the windows had small panes with heavy
> metal moldings. All cells originally had a bunk, a desk, and a chair.
> The close security cell blocks also had a sink and toilet. In the five
> medium security cell blocks, the prisoners carried keys to their
> own cells. A row of cells could be locked by a guard's setting a lock-
> ing bar, but in the 1950s, except for regular counts and special
> lockdowns, prisoners in medium-security wings entered and left
> the cells at their own discretion.[50]

The major purposes pursued by the lawmakers, new prison
managerial professionals, and penology "experts," who were planning and implementing this new penal strategy, were rational and
humanitarian. They intended to employ the new techniques developed by social science to reduce crime and convert pathological
criminals into successful, law-abiding citizens. They were also motivated by a desire to operate a humane penal system.[51]

The implementors of the rehabilitative ideal—the academics, penal professionals, and elected officials—introduced three features that were the cornerstones of the correctional institution. The first was the "indeterminate sentencing system," mentioned earlier:

According to the early planners of the rehabilitative prison, prison officials should have the discretionary power to release the prisoner when the administrators or their correctional experts determine that he is cured of criminality. Many early supporters of the rehabilitative ideal, such as Karl Menninger, advocated sentences of zero to life for all offenders so that correctional professionals could concentrate on treating criminals and releasing them when they were cured. In actuality, no prison system in the United States or any other place achieved this extreme, but California, after thirty-five years of developing an indeterminate sentence routine through legislation and administrative policies, came the closest. After 1950, the Adult Authority—the official name of the California board—exercised the power to determine an individual's sentence within statutory limits for a particular crime, to set a parole date before this sentence was finished, and, at any time until the fixed sentence was completed, to restore the sentence back to its statutory maximum or any other length within the margins. It exercised these powers with no requirements for due process or review of decisions.[52]

The second cornerstone was "classification":

An ideal correctional institution primarily organized to rehabilitate prisoners would require an elaborate, systematic diagnostic and planning process that determined the nature of the individual's criminality and prescribed a cure. Through the decades before the 1950s, the creators of the rehabilitative approach steadily developed more complex classification systems, ostensibly to accomplish these ends. Theoretically, the finished version that they incorporated in the new postwar correctional institutions operated as follows. First, a team of professionals—psychologists, case workers, sociologists, vocational counselors, and psychiatrists—tested the criminal, interviewed him, and gathered life history information. Then a team of those correctionalists formed an initial classification committee and reviewed the tests and evaluations, planned the prisoner's therapeutic routine, assigned him to a particular prison, and recommended particular rehabilitative programs for him. In the final stage, classification committees at particular prisons periodically reviewed the prisoner's progress, recommended changes in programs, and sometimes transferred him to another prison.[53]

The final cornerstone was "treatment." The intention of the planners was to devise a variety of effective treatment strategies.

What actually existed in the correctional institution in the 1950s was care and treatment. An administrative branch that coexisted with the custody branch, planned and administered three types of treatment programs—therapeutic, academic, and vocational—and generated reports on prisoners' progress for the institutional classification committees and the parole board.

The most common therapeutic program was group counseling, which because it was led by staff persons with little or no training in clinical procedures, was a weak version of group therapy.[54]

Maintaining control over prisoner populations was never abandoned as a major purpose in the operation of actual prisons. The new administrative structures usually had two branches—custody and treatment. The personnel in each of the branches were at odds in penal philosophy. They frequently came into conflict in decisions, such as the classification of particular prisoners, and competed for supremacy in the operation of the prison. Also, treatment programs had the unstated purpose of maintaining control over prisoners, and they actually operated not to improve prisoners' mental health but to usher them into a life of conformity to mundane, impecunious, lower-class regimens.

Formal Routine

The formal routine in correctional institutions was more relaxed than in the Big Houses:

On a weekday the lights came on at 7:00 A.M., but there was no bell or whistle. The individual "wing officers" released their cell blocks one at a time for breakfast. A person could eat or could sleep another hour before work. The food was slightly better than average prison fare, which is slightly inferior to average institution fare and ranks well below state hospitals and armed services. One pleasant aspect of the dining routine was that prisoners were allowed to linger for ten or twenty minutes and drink unlimited amounts of coffee. After breakfast, prisoners reported to their work or school assignment. Before lunch there was a count, during which all prisoners had to be in their cells or at a designated place where guards counted them, then lunch, a return to work or school, and another count before dinner. During the day the cell blocks were open, and prisoners could roam freely from their blocks, through the hall, to the large yard and its few recreational facilities, and to the library or gym. After dinner the wing officer kept the front door to the cell block locked except at scheduled unlocks for school, gym, library, and, during the summer, "night yard."[55]

Informal Prisoner Social Organization

The correctional institution prisoners' group structures, intergroup relationships, and informal systems of social control were radically different than those in the Big Houses. Some of these differences were a result of the shift in ethnic and racial balance. The percentage of nonwhite prisoners had increased significantly. Latinos (mainly Mexican Americans) and African Americans together made up 40 percent of the population in California prisons. Similar shifts in ethnic and racial composition occurred in most western, northern, and eastern states. As a consequence of the Civil Rights movement and the general shift in the attitudes of minority groups in American society, the nonwhite prisoners were more assertive and militant than they had been before World War II. In addition, new "criminal types," particularly "dope fiends" (heroin addicts), "weedheads" (marijuana users), and "hustlers," appeared in the prisoner mix. The thieves of earlier eras no longer dominated the prison informal social worlds.

African American and the Mexican American prisoners were divided into factions. African Americans raised in Los Angeles or the San Francisco Bay Area were culturally different than and maintained some distance from others who had migrated to California from the South or Southwest. Mexican Americans, or "Chicanos," raised in Los Angeles and San Diego were in conflict with "Tejanos," Chicanos from Texas, mainly El Paso. This mixture interfered with the solidary prisoner social system that had prevailed in most Big Houses.

This subcultural mix of prisoners resisted the establishment of a single overriding convict code or the emergence of a single group of leaders. The convict code did not have the unanimity and force that it had in the Big House. The number of thieves who formerly established and maintained the code was too small, and other criminals—hustlers, dope fiends, heads—with other codes of conduct competed for status and power in the informal realm.[56]

In spite of the more complex mixture of prisoners, Soledad's informal ambience was peaceful and orderly during most of the 1950s. Tolerance and general friendliness prevailed. The races were somewhat hostile toward each other and followed informal patterns of segregation, but there was commingling between all races, and many prisoners maintained close friendships with members of other racial groups.[57]

To a great extent, the prisoner mood stemmed from an initial enthusiasm for the new penal routine that the prisoners entering or returning to prison experienced in those early years of the correctional institution. In the relatively agreeable environment, most prisoners were convinced that many staff members (particularly the "free-men," the nonguard employees) were sincere and were trying to help them. It was implied or stated that these new procedures would locate the prisoners' psychological problems, vocational deficiencies, and physical defects and fix them. The enthusiasm and the new hope continued into the early years of Soledad and the other correctional institutions. The prisoners believed that the new penal approach was producing a much more humane prison routine.[58]

Tips and Cliques

A network of overlapping "cliques" and "tips," through which friendships were formed and maintained, commodities were exchanged, hostilities defused, and disputes settled, promoted peace and order in Soledad. Tips were extended social networks or crowds that were loosely held together by shared subcultural orientations or preprison acquaintances. Most of the tips were intraracial, but they were overlapping and connected. An individual could be involved in more than one tip and usually was related to other tips that connected with his own.

Prisoners formed smaller cliques within or across tips. These cliques were almost identical to the primary and semiprimary groups described by Clemmer in his study of Menard.[59] Clique members worked, "celled," hung around the tier, yard, and dayroom, ate, and engaged in the same leisure activities together. The basis of organization varied greatly. Sometimes the cliques formed out of small groups of prisoners who became acquainted at work or in the cell blocks. More often, they developed among persons who shared interest in some activity in prison, preprison experiences, subcultural orientations, and thereby tip membership. When clique members were also members of the same tip, the cliques were more cooperative, stable, and cohesive.

Rehabilitation and Social Order

The rehabilitative philosophy and its actualizations directly promoted order. When prisoners accepted the rehabilitative viewpoint and the conception of themselves as psychologically abnormal, they directed their attention inward and away from social and prison circumstances. It inhibited them from defining their situation as unfair and from developing critical, perhaps collective, attitudes toward the society and the prison administration. Prisoners were divided psychologically by focusing on their own personalities and searching for cures for their individual pathologies. Also, in attempting to cure themselves, prisoners involved themselves in the programs that grew out of the rehabilitative ideal. The formal policy in Soledad dictated that every prisoner have a full-time work, school, or vocational training assignment. The classification committees and the Adult Authority encouraged prisoners to pursue either academic or vocational training. Prisoners were required by policy to continue school until they tested at the fifth-grade level. A few prisoners refused to work or attend school or vocational training programs, but they were usually transferred or placed in segregation. Most prisoners were busy at work or school whether or not they believed in the rehabilitative ideal, and this, too, promoted peace and stability.

The rehabilitative ideal promoted order directly. The parole board used conformity to the prison routine as a principal indicator of rehabilitation and refused to review a prisoner who had received any serious disciplinary reports within six months. The message was clear: Conform or you will not be paroled. Most prisoners responded to the message.

Dismantling the Rehabilitative Ideal

Much like the failed penitentiary ideal, rehabilitation did not fulfill its promise. In the 1960s, the theories underpinning the correctional institution were called into question. Repeated evaluation of treatment programs produced the discouraging result of "no difference." The prisoners who received treatment were rearrested at the same rate as those who did not.[60] Growing numbers of prisoners, concerned citizens, and prison experts began recognizing that rehabilitation was serving other purposes than the reformation of criminals. In particular, the treatment programs were actually serving more to control prisoners than to rehabilitate them. Also, the critics recognized that the indeterminate sentence system was being used to control prisoners *and* to deliver punishment without due process. Prisoners and outside activists, and many academics, mounted a sustained campaign against the rehabilitative ideal and were successful in dismantling it. A mixture of ex-prisoners, political activists, civil rights lawyers, and professors joined a "working party" for the American Friends Service Committee (AFSC) and produced a report published as a book—*The Struggle for Justice*.[61] This was followed by a series of books, written by other social scientists and legal scholars, which were critical of the operation of the rehabilitative ideal.[62] By the middle of the 1970s, prisoner movement activists succeeded in replacing California's sentencing law with the Uniform Sentencing Act. This act redefined the primary purpose of imprisonment from rehabilitation to punishment and set down a scheme of uniform sentences to be delivered by judges instead of being determined by parole boards.

The law as originally passed in January 1976 called for relatively short sentences. By the time it took effect, six months after its passage in July 1976, lawmakers who were campaigning on "tough on crime" platforms succeeded in lengthening the sentences dramatically. After the changes in law occurred in California, many states followed suit, shifting the official definition of the purpose of imprisonment to punishment and increasing the length of sentences.

The body of reformers who led the crusade against the operation of the rehabilitative prison regimen and who succeeded in changing the law in California were pursuing humanitarian and utilitarian purposes. These reformers had come to believe that the rehabilitative system was based on unsound social scientific theories and that its operation had resulted in arbitrary and inconsistent sentencing patterns and inhumane imprisonment routines. Their intention was for people to recognize that the basic purpose of imprisonment was punishment and then to put into place a system that used punishment *with restraint.* Sentences should be short and the conditions of confinement should be humane with minimal deprivation. They also envisioned that "helping" resources would be made available to prisoners. However, at the juncture at which their reform activities were culminating in actual changes in the law, the fear of crime had been stirred up, and a punitive reaction was taking shape among the general public. Consequently, the laws and programs that actually took form after 1975 were fashioned mostly by politicians who fomented and exploited the public's fear of crime and steadily escalated the punitive response of the law. They were attempting (1) to divert attention away from other social and economic developments, such as "stagflation" (unemployment and inflation), and the growing wealth disparity in the United States; (2) to control a new dangerous class of nonwhite, young, unemployed ghetto dwellers; and (3) to advance or protect their political careers. (These developments are fully examined in Chapter 8.)

Community Corrections

Shortly after 1965, while the critique of the effectiveness of prison rehabilitative programs was emerging, "correctional experts" began planning a new direction for "corrections." At this time President Lyndon Johnson appointed the President's Commission on Law Enforcement and Administration of Justice to study the U.S. crime problem. Within the Commission, there was a Task Force on Corrections. Eight of the 63 consultants were employees of the California Department of Corrections, and seven more were California academics who had worked closely with that department in planning the new treatment strategies. The Task

Force came to the conclusion that the failure of rehabilitation was mainly due to the nature of the "fortress prison." They argued that a major problem with these fortresses was that they were remote from urban communities:

> Although most inmates of American correctional institutions come from metropolitan areas, the institutions themselves often are located away from urban areas and even primary transportation routes.... Remoteness interferes with efforts to reintegrate inmates into their communities and makes it hard to recruit correctional staff, particularly professionals.[63]

The Task Force offered a new rehabilitative strategy called "community corrections":

> The general underlying premise for the new directions in corrections is that crime and delinquency are symptoms of failures and disorganization of the community as well as of individual offenders. In particular, these failures are seen as depriving offenders of contact with the institutions that are basically responsible for assuring development of law-abiding conduct: sound family life, good schools, employment, recreational opportunities and desirable companions, to name only some of the more direct influences. . . .
>
> The task of corrections, therefore, includes building or rebuilding solid ties between offenders and community, integrating or reintegrating the offender into community life-restoring family ties, obtaining employment and education, securing in the larger sense a place for the offender in the routine functioning of society. This requires not only efforts directed toward changing the individual offender, which has been almost the exclusive focus of rehabilitation, but also mobilization and change of the community and its institutions.[64]

To implement community corrections, the Task Force recommended new small institutions in urban settings. From the late 1960s through the early 1970s, considerable planning and a small measure of actual implementation of community corrections was accomplished. In 1975, I evaluated Eagle River, a community corrections institution that was built and operated in Alaska. Soon after it opened, this prison encountered intense negative public attention, mainly precipitated by ongoing criticism directed at the institution by an Anchorage television newscaster. This attention caused most of the community aspects, including the school and work release programs the institution had been operating, to be discontinued and the general security of the institution to be greatly increased. These events revealed the vulnerability of the new directions in corrections. By 1977, the new experiment—community corrections—was for all intents and purposes dead. In fact, it never got off the ground. No prisons that consummated the community corrections plan presented by the Task Force on Corrections were ever built. Because of resistance from citizens and civic leaders in Anchorage, Eagle River was located in a rural area 25 miles outside Anchorage, the only place the Alaska Department of Corrections could find to place it. Moreover, it never fulfilled the substantive goals of community corrections, that is, the full range of relationships and connections with community resources and organizations.

Prisons in Turmoil

In the late 1960s, California prisons entered a period of extreme turmoil. The disruptions, changes in prisoner relationships, and prison administrators' reactions that occurred first in California spread out from there to many other states, and a period of turmoil unfolded.

The turmoil was set off by changing racial relationships in the prisons. In California, the racial balance had swung over to a majority of nonwhite prisoners. African American prisoners were transformed by the Civil Rights movement. Many affiliated with radical religious and political organizations, such as the Black Muslims and the Black Panther Party. Prisoners divided on racial lines. Groups of white and black prisoners in Soledad, San Quentin, and Folsom increasingly engaged in planned or spontaneous assaults against each other. The homicide rate in several prisons leapt up.

A self-help movement began among nonwhite prisoners. Mexican Americans organized a race-based self-help group called EMPELO (El Mexicano, Preparado, Educado, Listo, & Organizado). African Americans followed with SATE (Self Advancement Through Education). Many outside political activists became interested in prison issues. They began organizing a "prisoner movement" and supported prisoners in a series of strikes, demonstrations, riots, and escapes.[65]

In response to these new upheavals, prison administrations practiced severe repression of prisoner activities. The "custody" branch of the administration shoved aside the "treatment" branch and introduced new forms of control. The underlying conflict that had been festering within many prison administrations ever since the serious experimentation with rehabilitation added force to the reaction. In all treatment-oriented state systems, custody had had its power and prestige reduced by the ascendant "treatment" faction; but the old guard never stopped struggling to maintain its integrity and hold on to power. When the prisoner movement created new problems, custody returned to full power, with renewed strength and considerable vengeance.

The custody branch introduced new methods of segregation of "troublemakers." (In Chapter 5, I discuss at length the history of this development.) Many of the leaders of the militant religious, political, and self-help groups were identified as troublemakers and were transferred to other prisons or placed in segregation. This removed many of the prisoner leaders and paved the way for the emergence of new power structures: the gangs.

Lowriders

Prisons have always contained violence-prone individuals, who were formerly kept in check by the code enforced by the prisoner elders. In the 1950s and 1960s, small cliques of young hoodlums—lowriders—hung around the yard and other public places; talked shit (loudly bragged); played the prison dozens (verbal sparring); occasionally insulted, threatened, attacked, and robbed unprotected weaker prisoners; and squabbled with other lowrider groups, particularly those of other races. Billy "Hands" Robinson, a prison writer, characterized a group of these youngsters in an Illinois prison:

> There were four other dudes in the hole cell they put him in when he first got there, all of them young, what Tank called gangbangers. He didn't like or understand the youngsters but the joint was full of them now and he couldn't avoid them. They were like a herd of animals, he thought. They wolf-packed people and were nothing as individuals.[66]

Most of these early lowriders were young juvenile-prison graduates and young "fuck-ups" (unskilled, lower- and working-class criminals) who were disrespected by older, "solid" criminals and regular convicts. They were a constant threat to the other prisoners, who were trying to maintain peace. For most of the 1950s and 1960s, other prisoners disparaged, ignored, and avoided the lowriders, whose activities were kept in check by the consensus against them and the belief (accepted by lowriders and most other prisoners) that if the lowriders went too far, the older prison regulars would use force to control them.

Lowriders steadily increased in numbers. In the states with large cities, whose ghettos bulged during the 1950s and 1960s, the youth prison systems expanded to accommodate the increase in youth crime. The adult prisons began to receive growing numbers of youth prison graduates and criminally unskilled, more openly aggressive young urban "thugs." They could no longer be controlled. These tough youths entered the growing racial melee and stepped up their attacks and robberies on other prisoners. When there were no successful countermoves against them, they took over the convict world and particularly one of its most important activities: the sub-rosa economic enterprises.[67]

In different states, the young hoodlums arrived at the adult prisons with different backgrounds and consequently formed different types of groups in the prisons. In California, the takeover began in 1967 in San Quentin, when a clique of young Chicanos, who had known each other on the streets of Los Angeles and in other prisons, began to take drugs forcefully from other prisoners, mostly Chicano.[68] The clique gained a reputation for toughness and the label "Mexican Mafia." Other aspiring young Chicano hoodlums became interested in affiliating with the Mafia, and the word went out that Mafia members insisted that initiates murder another prisoner before being admitted into the Mafia. This rumor and the actual attacks aroused and consolidated large numbers of "independent" Chicanos, who planned to eliminate the Mafia members. On a planned day, the independent Chicanos pursued known Mafia members through San Quentin, attempting to assassinate them. Several dozen prisoners were seriously wounded and one was killed in this daylong battle, but the Mafia held its ground, won many of the knife fights, and was not eliminated. After this unsuccessful attempt, some of the formerly independent

Chicanos, particularly those from Texas and the small towns in California who had been in conflict with Los Angeles Chicanos for decades, formed a countergroup—La Nuestra Familia. In the ensuing years, the conflict between the two Chicano gangs increased and spread to other prisons and even to the outside, where the gangs tried to penetrate drug trafficking.[69] The attacks and counterattacks between members of the two gangs became so frequent that prison administrators attempted to segregate the gangs, designating two prisons, San Quentin and Folsom, for the Mafia and two prisons, Soledad and Tracy, for La Nuestra Familia. When Chicanos entered the California prison system, they were asked their gang affiliation; if they were to be sent to any of those four prisons (which are the medium- to maximum-security prisons), they were sent to one dominated by their gang.

The Chicano gangs' escalation of robbery, assault, and murder also consolidated and expanded black and white lowrider groups, some of which had already been involved in similar violent and rapacious activities but on a smaller scale. Two gangs, the Aryan Brotherhood and the Black Guerrilla Family, rose in prominence and increased their violent activities. Eventually, the Aryan Brotherhood formed an alliance with the Mafia, and the Black Guerrilla Family became allied with La Nuestra Familia. While a hostile and tentative stalemate prevailed, peace did not return. Other racist cliques among the black and white prisoners occasionally attacked other prisoners, the Chicano gangs continued to fight each other, and there seemed to be factions within the Chicano gangs themselves.

In Illinois, black Chicago street gangs—the Blackstone Rangers (changed later to Black P Stone Nation), the Devil's Disciples, and the Vice Lords—and a Latin street gang, named the Latin Kings, spread into Stateville and finally took over the convict world. According to James Jacobs,

> When the gangs emerged at Stateville in 1969, they placed the old con power structure in physical and financial jeopardy. For the first time, those convicts with good jobs were not necessarily protected in their dealings, legitimate or illegitimate. Seeing strength in numbers, the gang members attempted to take what they wanted by force. They seemed unconcerned about doing fifteen days in the hole (the limit imposed by the courts). When they went

to the hole, they were thrown in a cell with five or six fellow gang members. For the first time in history, the old cons who "knew how to do time" found their lives disrupted and in danger. Gang members moved in to take over the "rackets." One informant described an instance where a half dozen "gang bangers" simultaneously put knives to his throat. Rather than cut the gangs in, many of the dealers went out of business.[70]

By 1974, the aggressive black and Latino gangs had precipitated counterorganizations among white prisoners, who, in their reduced numbers, had been extremely vulnerable to assault, robbery, rape, and murder by the other gangs.[71]

The activities of these violent groups who, in the pursuit of loot, sex, respect, or revenge, would attack any outsider completely unraveled any remnants of the old codes of honor and tip networks that formerly helped to maintain order. In a limited, closed space such as a prison, threats of attacks like those posed by these groups could not be ignored. Prisoners felt compelled to prepare to protect themselves or get out of the way. Those who chose to continue to circulate in public, with few exceptions, formed or joined a clique or gang for their own protection. Consequently, violence-oriented groups dominated many, if not most, large men's prisons.

The emergence of the gangs produced a new prisoner leader—the "tough convict" or "hog" who replaced the "right guy." The upsurge of rapacious and murderous groups all but eliminated the right guy and drastically altered the identity of the convict, the remaining hero of the prison world. Most of all, toughness pushed out most other attributes, particularly the norms of tolerance, mutual aid, and loyalty to a large number of other regulars.

Stiff and divisive administrative opposition weakened convict unity, and the attacks of violent racial groups obliterated it. When the lowrider or "gangbanger" cliques turned on the remaining convict leaders (many of whom had been removed from the prison mainline because of their political activities) and the elders were not able to drive the lowriders back into a position of subordination or otherwise to control them, the ancient regime fell, and with it, the old convict identity.

Toughness in the violent men's prisons meant several things. First, it meant being able to take care of oneself in the prison world, where people would attack others with little or no provocation.

Second, it meant having the guts to take from the weak. Leo Carroll described the view of manhood shared by a clique of young "wise guys" who formed one of the most powerful groups in the prison that he studied and who preyed on other unorganized prisoners:

> Prison, in their eyes, is the ultimate test of manhood. A man in prison is able to secure what he wants and protect what he had: "In here, a man gets what he can," "nobody can force a man to do something he don't want to," are key elements of their belief system. Any prisoner who does not meet these standards is not a man, "has no respect for himself" and is therefore not entitled to respect from others.[72]

Loyalty to other prisoners shrank to loyalty to one's clique or gang. In Illinois, James Jacobs found that

> gang members simply see nothing wrong with "ripping off" independents. The fact that they occupy adjoining cells does not seem to offer a basis for solidarity. While at one time inmates may have endorsed the principle of "doing your own time," the gangs endorsed the morality of "doing gang time."[73]

In addition to threats of robbery, assaults, and murder, the threat of being raped and physically forced into the role of the insertee (punk or kid) increased in the violent prison: "Fuck it. It's none of my business. If a sucker is weak, he's got to fall around here. I came when I was eighteen and nobody turned me out. I didn't even smile for two years."[74]

After the appearance of the gangs and the development of the new convict orientation, prisoners in most of the medium and higher custody prisons in California and other eastern, midwestern, and western states had to orient themselves to new forms of violence. They either joined or affiliated with one of the gangs, formed their own clique or gang for protection, or did as most prisoners had done—withdrew from prison public life. They disassociated themselves from the violent cliques and gangs, spent as little time as possible in the yard and other public places where gangs hung out, and avoided gang members, even though they may have been friends with some of them in earlier years. They stuck to a few friends whom they would meet in the cell blocks, at work, through shared interests, in other prisons, or on the outside (home boys). With their friends they ate, worked, attended meetings of the various clubs and formal organizations that abounded in the prison, and participated in leisure-time activities together. Collectively, they withdrew from the convict world and left it to the rapacious younger prisoners.

At the end of the 1980s, in most of the large men's prisons, a state of dangerous and tentative order prevailed. For decades, the potentially obstreperous and conflictive population was held in a tentative peace by prisoner leaders, a code, and the constant threat of extreme force. When the informal system of peace disintegrated, the formal force was brought in, used (in fact, misused), withstood by the prisoners, and dissipated. Administrators continued to apply old formulas to restore order. Mostly, they attempted to divide and segregate the masses and to crush the more obdurate prisoners. In California, for instance, the Department of Corrections continued to search for gang leaders and other troublemakers, transferred those who were so labeled to the maximum-security prisons, and segregated them there in special units. The growing numbers of segregated prisoners became more vicious and uncontrollable. (These developments are thoroughly examined in Chapter 5.)

The Punitive Swing

Several developments after 1975 led to an era of excessive punitive penology in the United States. First, the widespread fear of crime that had been aroused several times in the preceding decade was stirred up dramatically after 1980. The second development was the rejection of the "liberal" theories of the causes of crime and the nature of criminals, which had informed "corrections," as penal practices were called during the era dominated by liberal ideas. Third, prison practitioners suffered a decade of turmoil, during which prisoner-to-prisoner and prisoner-to-staff violence skyrocketed and demonstrations, riots, and escapes, some aided or planned by outside prisoner movement activists, completely disrupted practitioners' work settings and sometimes threatened their lives. In the late 1970s, these practitioners set about to design new prisons, which they were forced to plan and quickly build because of the rapidly escalating prison populations. They planned and built two new types of prisons: a warehouse prison, which is a large, secure prison built to house and control the bulk of the new prisoners, and the "supermax," a highly secure prison designed to hold the most difficult-to-manage prisoners. The next three chapters examine these two types of prisons.

Endnotes

1. David Rothman, in *The Discovery of the Asylum,* argued that to a great extent American penal policymakers were reacting to the excessive, punitive English forms of punishment when they devised their own penal forms.

2. Douglas Hay, "Property, Authority, and the Criminal Law," in D. Hay et al. eds., *Albion's Fatal Tree* (New York: Pantheon, 1975), convincingly made this argument.

3. See Robert Hughes, *The Fatal Shore: The Epic of Australia's Founding* (New York: Vintage, 1988).

4. See especially Jeremy Bentham, *An Introduction to the Principles of Morals and Legislation* ([London, 1789] Oxford: Claredon Books).

5. See Foucault, *Discipline and Punish.*

6. See Rothman, *Discovery of the Asylum.*

7. This act set out in theory the outline for a penitentiary like those that were actually introduced in America.

8. Prison Board of Inspectors of New York, *Report,* quoted in Ralph S. Herre, "A History of Auburn Prison From the Beginning to About 1867" (D.Ed. diss., Pennsylvania State University, 1950), 37.

9. See Martin B. Miller, "Dread and Terror: The Creation of State Penitentiaries in New York and Pennsylvania, 1788 to 1833" (D.Crim. diss., University of California, Berkeley, 1980), 284–288.

10. W. D. Lewis, *From Newgate to Dannemora: The Rise of the Penitentiary in New York, 1796–1848* (Ithaca, NY: Cornell University Press, 1965), 121.

11. Greshom Powers, *A Brief Account of the Construction, Management and Discipline of the New York State Prison at Auburn* (Auburn, NY, 1826) 35–36.

12. Colonel Levi S. Burr, "Voice From Sing Sing, Giving a General Description of the State Prison," addressed to the Honorable, the Senate and Assembly of the State of New York, (Albany, NY 1833) 17, n.1.

13. See Miller, "Dread and Terror," 341.

14. Gustave de Beaumont and Alexis de Tocqueville, *On the Penitentiary System in the United States and Its Application in France* (Carbondale and Edwardsville: Southern Illinois University Press, 1964), 65.

15. Carlo De Fornaro, *A Modern Purgatory* (New York: Mitchell Kennerley, 1917), 51.

16. Beaumont and Tocqueville, *On the Penitentiary System,* 84.

17. Charles Dickens, *American Notes for General Circulation* (London: Penguin Books, 1972), 100–101..

18. Ibid., 148.

19. Ibid., 150.

20. Beaumont and Tocqueville, *On the Penitentiary System,* 56 and 57.

21. Dickens, *American Notes,* 148, 149, and 150.

22. A description of a modern instance of complete solitary confinement throws doubt on this conclusion. Phillip Butler, a captured American pilot, was held with other captured pilots in total isolation in a North Vietnam prison for several years. Though he and the other captured pilots never saw or heard each other, they communicated by tapping on their cell walls. They used a tap code that they had to teach each new prisoner after convincing the newcomer that they were also Americans. They began by repeatedly tapping out the beats to "shave and a haircut" and waited for the responding two beats: "six bits." Then they used a simple code by assigning one tap for A, two for B, and so on and tapped "hi" (eight taps, pause, nine taps) until the newcomer answered "hi." Then they taught him a more complex code. See Phillip Butler, "Tap Codes: Ascribed Meaning in Prisoner Communication," *Urban Life* 5, no. 4 (1977): 399–416.

23. Thomas Cleveland, *Sixth Annual Report of the Warden of the State Prison, to the Honorable General Assembly of the State of Rhode-Island, October Session, A.D. 1844,* p. 26.

24. Victor Nelson, *Prison Days and Nights* (New York: Grove, 1933), 14.

25. Dickens, *American Notes,* 148.

26. Cleveland, *Sixth Annual Report of the Warden of the State Prison,* 23.

27. Rothman, *Discovery of the Asylum,* 237–240, and Enoc C. Wines and Theodore Dwight, *Report on the Prisons and Reformatories of the United States and Canada* (New York, 1867).

28. Robert E. Burns, *I Am a Fugitive From a Georgia Chain Gang!* (New York: Vanguard, 1932), 48.

29. Charles L. Clark, *Lockstep and Corridor* (Cincinnati: The University of Ohio Press, 1927), 70.

30. Jack Callahan, *Man's Grim Justice, My Life Outside the Law* (New York: J. Sears, 1928), 150.

31. Burns, *I Am a Fugitive,* 51–53.

32. Ben M. Crouch and James W. Marquart, *An Appeal to Justice* (Austin: University of Texas Press, 1989), 23.

33. George L. Bartlett, *Thru the Mill by '4342'* (St. Paul, MN: McGill-Warner, 1915), 28–29.

34. Burns, *I Am a Fugitive,* 14.

35. Callahan, *Man's Grim Justice* 151.

36. Crouch and Marquart, *An Appeal to Justice*, 98.
37. Ibid., 88.
38. Tom Murton and Joe Hyams, *Accomplices to the Crime* (New York: Grove, 1979), 24.
39. Ibid., 25.
40. Alexander Berkman, *Prison Memoirs of an Anarchist* (New York: Mother Earth Publishing, 1912), 273.
41. Ibid., 278.
42. Ibid., 273–278.
43. Ibid., 273–274.
44. Irwin, *Prisons in Turmoil*, 5.
45. Ibid., 9.
46. The recognition of particular prisoner roles started in the mid-1930s, when Hans Riemer, a criminology student, arranged with a judge to be incarcerated as a felon in a state prison. He identified "politicians" and "right guys" as leaders in the prison community. See Hans Riemer, "Socialization in the Prison Community," *Proceedings of the American Prison Association* (1937), 151–155. Clarence Schrag, in "Social Types in a Prison Community" (Master's thesis, University of Washington, 1944), and Gresham Sykes, in *Society of Captives*, elaborated the description of prisoner roles.
47. Clemmer, *The Prison Community*, 107.
48. See Karl Menninger, *The Crime of Punishment* (New York: Viking, 1968).
49. Garland, *Culture of Control*, 34–35.
50. Irwin, *Prisons in Turmoil*, 48.
51. In the early 1970s, when many of us were developing our criticisms of and campaigning against the rehabilitative ideal, I had several conversations with Donald Cressey, who, with several other leading criminologists, was active in the early 1950s in planning rehabilitative penal strategies. He emphasized that he and the others were not completely convinced of the approaches' efficacy but supported them because they resulted in a more humane penal routine.
52. Irwin, *Prisons in Turmoil*, 40–41.
53. Ibid., 43.
54. Ibid., 44.
55. Ibid., 49.
56. Ibid., 55.
57. During my five years at Soledad, there were only a few knife fights, two murders, and one suicide.
58. Irwin, *Prisons in Turmoil*, 56–57.
59. Clemmer, *Prison Community*, 135.

60. Robert Martinson, "What Works? Questions and Answers About Prison Reform," *The Public Interest* 35 (1974): 22–54.

61. Working Party for the American Friends Service Committee, *The Struggle for Justice.*

62. See especially Norval Morris, *The Future of Imprisonment* (Chicago: University of Chicago Press, 1974), David Fogel, *The Living Proof: The Justice Model of Corrections* (Cincinnati, OH: Anderson, 1975), and Andrew Von Hirsch, *Doing Justice* (New York: Hill and Wang, 1976).

63. The President's Commission on Law Enforcement and Administration of Justice, *Task Force Report: Corrections* (Washington, DC: Government Printing Office, 1967), 4.

64. Ibid.

65. This turbulent period, which was complex and pivotal, has been written about extensively. In *Prisons in Turmoil,* I dealt with it in three chapters: "Division," "Revolution," and "Reaction." Here I offer only these few major descriptive points, which prepare for the examination of the phase in the prison social organization that I call "Prisons in Turmoil."

66. Billy Robinson, "Love: A Hard-Legged Triangle," *Black Scholar,* September 1971, p. 39.

67. Virgil Williams and Mary Fish use this label in the best study to appear on prisoner economic systems. See *Convicts, Codes, and Contraband* (Cambridge, MA: Ballinger, 1974).

68. I have put this account together from many sources. To start, I was visiting San Quentin regularly and meeting with a group of convict "experts" when the Mexican Mafia was taking shape and when the "shoot-out at the OK Corral," the name used for the daylong fight between the Chicano factions, occurred. I have read dozens of accounts of the Chicano gangs written by journalists and prisoners, some of them the original members of the two gangs. Also, through the years, I have interviewed hundreds of prisoners and ex-prisoners about these activities. Needless to say, the versions differ. I have tried to distill out the most reliable account.

69. The prison and police agencies in California argued and produced some evidence that activities of the prison gangs splashed out of the prisons. The gangs, it was believed, struggled with each other, with factions within the gangs, and against other drug dealers. Many outside assassinations were blamed on the gangs. "Pierce [a police lieutenant] said authorities believed a feud between two gangs, the Mexican Mafia and La Nuestra Familia, to be responsible for a chain of crimes in the area," *San Francisco Chronicle,* 7 March 1977, p. 20.

70. Jacobs, *Stateville,* 157–158.

71. Ibid., 159.

72. Carroll, *Hacks, Blacks, and Others*, 69.
73. Jacobs, *Stateville*, 157.
74. Edward Bunker, *Animal Factory* (New York: Viking, 1977), 32. ✦

Chapter 3

The Warehouse Prison

For decades, prisons were referred to as warehouses, but this label was inaccurate. It masked the existence of the complex social organizations that existed in earlier institutions. Since 1980, many prisons in states such as California and Texas that rapidly expanded their prison populations have become true human warehouses. In these warehouses, prisoners endure deeply reduced mobility, activities, and involvement in prison programs and are merely stored to serve out their sentences.

As I discussed in Chapter 1, warehouse prisons were the product of the war on crime earnestly waged from the middle 1970s through the 1990s. They were built to contain and control new "dangerous criminals," whose image was developed by law-and-order politicians, sensationalizing media personnel, and conservative social scientists. In response to this new criminal, lawmakers and penal practitioners passed punitive laws and established new penal policies. These ideas about the criminal dominated new laws and policies: (1) criminals are permanently committed to predatory crime; (2) criminals do not respond to rehabilitative efforts; (3) criminals need to be punished severely and held in very secure places of imprisonment; and (4) only the threat of harsh punishment will deter other potential criminals from committing crime. A prisoner "locked down" in a Virginia prison in 1997 described the philosophy behind the new criminal justice policy:

> I understand the philosophy behind the increased use of long sentences and harsh incarceration. The idea is to make prison a secular hell on earth—a place where the young potential felon will fear to go, where the ex-con will fear to return. But an underlying theme is that "these people" are irredeemable "predators" (i.e., "animals"),

who are without worth. Why, then, provide them with the opportunity to rehabilitate—or give them any hope?[1]

With these ideas setting the parameters for new prisons and prison programs, planners went to work. In the 20-year period from 1980 to 2000, hundreds of new prisons were built, more than had been built before in the entire history of prisons in the United States. California added 22 prisons to its 11 that existed in 1975.

The Structure of the New Prisons

The rapid expansion of prison systems across the country gave rise to a huge prison-industrial complex. Architecture schools created prison design specialties. Prison hardware manufacturers and construction companies specializing in prison construction sprang up, expanded, and prospered.

> The "war on crime" (including the "war on drugs") has become a booming business, with literally hundreds of companies, large and small, eager for a share of the growing profits. Employment in this industry offers careers for thousands of young men and women, with college degrees in "criminal justice" now available at more than 3,000 colleges and universities. The criminal justice system provides a steady supply of career possibilities (police officers, correctional officers, etc.) with good starting pay and benefits, along with job security. Many of these occupations now have powerful unions.[2]

The planners of the new prisons had decades of experimentation in prison construction and prison regimens from which to learn. They had at their disposal a wealth of new technology, electronic and other forms. Unlike the designers of prisons in earlier periods of rapid construction (such as the first decades of the nineteenth century), these planners worked under a clear and simple mandate: Build secure, efficient prisons as economically as possible. The war on crime and the theories of the causes of crime that underpinned the war demanded secure, no-frills prisons. Space and facilities for purposes other than security, such as rehabilitation, were not considered.

Architectural Plan

Security, efficiency, and economy dominated the planning and construction of most new prisons. Security was the primary consideration in the new prison design. Instructed by the failures and flaws of the Big House fortresses, such as San Quentin, Sing Sing, and Jackson, and the specialized, early forms of maximum security prisons, such as the federal prisons Alcatraz and Marion, penologists developed a new prison model.

The new model incorporates housing units, known variably as "cell blocks," "wings," and "buildings," that hold about 200 prisoners. In the Big Houses some of the cell blocks housed over 1,000 prisoners each. In the new model, smaller units are laid out to enable the guards to observe all activities in the building and to control all movement in and out of the cells and the units from an enclosed, secure location. High-security prisoners are held in units in which the prisoners can be "locked down" (kept in their cells) for long periods. The cells have extremely small windows to the outside, and the cell fronts are solid so that nothing can be thrown out of, or weapons used from, the cells.

The second most important consideration in prison design is efficiency. Using electronic devices and strategically located, well-protected control rooms and control towers, the flow of prisoners through doors and gates from one location to another (e.g., from the cell blocks to exercise yards, to the visiting area, to the mess hall, to work sites, or to other prison locations such as the law library, classrooms, and interview rooms) is controlled with minimum personnel and maximum staff protection.

Economy is the third consideration of prison design. The chunky, plain buildings—cell blocks, mess halls, and other buildings inside the compound—are built of prefabricated, steel-reenforced, unpainted concrete slabs. Doors are solid metal. Yards are plain, unlandscaped asphalt, concrete, or dirt. Double steel-wire fences topped with rolls of razor wire circle the institutions. There are no grand, granite walls, massive gates, decorations, or frills of any kind. The new prisons are monocolored, plain, large compounds. Without the gun towers and double fences, they could easily be mistaken for industrial warehouses sitting out in rural sites, where most of these prisons are located.

Warehouse prisons are located in remote areas because the land is less expensive and more available there. Also, pressure from citizens' groups to *not* locate a prison close to their communities is minimized if not eliminated completely. In fact, in rural areas near proposed sites, the townspeople often welcome the prisons, because they believe that the prisons will provide jobs and bring money into their communities.[3] The housing units are built with minimal space for cells, dorm beds, or recreation. Most cells, which are the minimum size stipulated by federal standards, house two prisoners. Dormitory beds are crowded into small alcoves, sometimes three high. The result is that the housing units are very crowded. Only "holding tanks" in county jails are more crowded. In most California warehouse prisons, the gymnasiums have been converted into dormitories that are still more crowded than even county jail holding tanks.

Administrative Regimens

The rapid expansion of prison systems resulted in some significant changes in administrative regimens that profoundly affected prisoners. In the radical reorganization of the 1970s, authoritarian structures, in which each prison or the entire prison system was autocratically "ruled" by a warden or director, were replaced by bureaucracies headed by professionals restricted or guided by a vast system of rules and regulations, many of which were imposed by the courts in their decisions in federal lawsuits.[4] In this same period, the prison treatment branch, which had been founded on the ideals of rehabilitation and was staffed by college graduates with degrees in the social sciences, was greatly demoted or eliminated.

Conflict and Divisions

Though the mandate for the new prison systems has been simplified and the contradictory purposes of punishment and rehabilitation have been virtually eliminated, the new administrative systems are complex and rife with internal divisions, dissension, conflict, and deviance. These issues greatly influence the relationships between prison staff and prisoners. Though I will not engage in a lengthy discussion of contemporary prison administrative systems, I will briefly review the major divisions and sources of conflict relevant to "serving time" in the warehouse prison.

First of all, though there has been considerable effort to establish orderly bureaucracies governed by rules, prison systems have grown so rapidly and are so large that it has been difficult to achieve cohesion and a high degree of conformity to the rules. Also, the sheer number of rules is extraordinary—the *Operations*

Manual for the California Department of Corrections has 827 pages of double column, fine print.

Further complicating things, each employee in the prison staff hierarchy has different and conflicting concerns, which leads to different interpretations of and different degrees of compliance to the rules. In addition to the pressing managerial issues involved in running a prison, the top administrators are greatly motivated to avoid criticism from outsiders—the press, the governor's office, the legislature—all of whom have some form of influence over the prison operation. The directors and wardens are also mindful of the actions of members of the courts, who have made decisions that greatly affect prison operations.[5] The line staff are less sensitive to these issues, being primarily interested in their immediate work situation: personal safety, working conditions, and pay. They feel the top administrators are unsympathetic and do not fully understand their needs. "They don't walk the tiers." The conflicts stemming from these differences in interests have spawned guards' unions, which have become a powerful force in the prison regime. These unions have made it more difficult for top management to discipline guards for poor behavior, which in turn enables individual guards and groups of guards to get away with rule violations, even illegal activities.[6]

Besides these typical sources of conflict characteristic of large, complex bureaucratic organizations, prison systems have experienced the influx of new classes of employees—women and minorities. These two populations have markedly different orientations than white male employees, who dominated prison employee ranks in the past.[7] At first, women were a source of considerable conflict within the staff ranks. Lynn Zimmer, who studied women guarding men in the middle 1980s, described the conflict:

> Nearly all members of the prison community initially opposed the hiring of women to guard male inmates. A great deal of this opposition has been translated into actions that create obstacles to women's adjustment. For female guards, remaining on the job means coping with continual opposition and harassment from male co-workers, discriminatory assignment policies of male supervisors, and some explicit sexual misconduct [by] inmates.[8]

When women entered the prison workforce, male guards believed women were neither strong nor tough enough to guard male prisoners. Further, the male guards believed the female guards were more sympathetic to the male prisoners, with whom it was believed they fraternized too much. However, as time passed, the women adjusted to prison work, acquired the dominant guard culture, and blended into the informal guards' social world.[9]

Issues related to the male/female conflict were not limited to female and male guards. Many male prisoners were uncomfortable with female guards circulating in the cell blocks because prisoners used the toilets and showers in plain view. Sexual harassment of female guards became an important disciplinary issue. Catcalls or other sexual expressions made by prisoners could result in disciplinary action. Even "reckless eyeballing" by a prisoner of a female guard could be interpreted as "disrespect to an officer" and result in disciplinary action.

In today's prison environment, prisoners view female and male guards equally in respect to fairness, arbitrariness, and empathy. However, prisoners must exercise caution when they interact with female guards. Certain verbal expressions or placing a hand on a female guard is very likely to result in disciplinary action. "You can smell 'em, see 'em, but you can't touch 'em."[10] Finally, female guards in male prisons have changed the general prison atmosphere, which formerly was almost completely monosexual.[11] There are positives and negatives to this change. On one hand, prisoners are not so completely isolated from females. On the other hand, having women around with whom "sexual" interaction is strictly forbidden (but not completely restricted in actual practice) is frustrating for the male prisoners.

Nonwhites, particularly African Americans, began entering guard forces at about the same time as women. As was the case with women, there was considerable resentment of African American guards by the white male guards, many of whom came from rural backgrounds. The white guards believed that the minority guards, particularly black guards, were more sympathetic to prisoners in general and urban black prisoners in particular. During the 1970s, a period of intense racial hostility among prisoners of different races, there was some cooperation between guards and groups of prisoners of the same race. However, as was the case with black police officers adjusting to police organizations, black and Latino officers were eventually absorbed into the general society of guards and inculcated into guard culture. From the prisoners' viewpoint, there is presently little difference between white and nonwhite guards.

In addition to the racial and gender subgroups, there are other categories of lower-level employees who have very different interests and, therefore, different performance styles. Some line officers are ambitious and career oriented and have their sights set on rising up through the ranks to become top administrators. This leads them to more conformity to the formal rules. In addition, cliques of guards have special, somewhat devious "agendas." Some, such as the "goon squad" members, are dedicated to trying to "bust" prisoners. Others, such as "The Sharks" at Corcoran and other gung-ho guard cliques, are oriented toward brutally punishing prisoners:

> On June 21, 1995, nearly a year into the FBI investigation, three-dozen officers—including a group known as "The Sharks" for their reputation for attacking without warning—waited for a busload of black inmates from Calipatria prison. Some donned black leather gloves and placed tape over their name tags.
>
> According to a Department of Corrections inquiry, the greeting party wanted to teach the new arrivals a lesson. Associate Warden Farris and Capt. Lee Fouch had allowed false rumors to circulate that the 36 Calipatria inmates assaulted guards and were hiding weapons in the braided dreadlocks, the state inquiry found.
>
> As the bus pulled into Corcoran, witnesses saw the Sharks doing warmup exercises and stretching. The shackled inmates were pushed off the bus one by one, and run through a gauntlet of fists, batons, and combat boots. Some were poked in the eyes and pulled by the testicles as guards shouted racial epithets. Others were rammed into windows and walls.[12]

These differences in orientations to guards' work lead to widely different approaches to obeying and enforcing the formal rules. And this results in, at least, great inconsistencies and arbitrariness in rule enforcement—the major complaints of prisoners—and, at worst, excessive brutality toward prisoners.

Guard Culture

Though the guard world is heterogeneous and somewhat divided, there are some common attitudes held by most guards and staff. The most important of these for our purposes is their shared derogatory attitude toward prisoners; generally, they perceive prisoners as worthless, untrustworthy, manipulative, and disreputable deviants. A guard at the U.S. Penitentiary, Leavenworth explained why he had not tried to stop a fight between two prisoners: "Most of us have wives and kids or grandkids. You tell me: Are you going to risk your life by stepping in front of a knife when you have one lousy piece of shit trying to kill another lousy piece of shit?"[13]

The keepers' negative view of prisoners has existed since the inception of imprisonment. It has roots in the class divisions in the societies that invented imprisonment. Most prisoners came from the "disreputable poor" or the "dangerous classes." The members of the higher classes believed that the lower classes were morally, mentally, and physically inferior. These distinctions extend into modern times. The conservative politicians who promoted the current penal measures emphasized the distinction between "decent people" and the new dangerous classes.

In addition to this societal class invidiousness, an internal class or caste division in the prison hierarchy intensifies the negative attitudes toward prisoners. In a previous article, I described this tension and its resolution in the attitude of moral superiority over prisoners of the staff, particularly the guards:

> Maintaining moral superiority over the clients in a sense is a special case of the general organizational characteristic of establishing hierarchies of status distinctions. In the case of correctional systems, two factors intensify this general process and give it unique contours. First, there is a large, inherent distinction between the prisoner and the employee in this organization. This is true even though the prisoner is involved full-time and fulfills many staff functions. Second, the prisoner is suspended in a state of extreme deprivation. This introduces an important moral problem for the employees, who associate regularly with the prisoners. They (the employees) must cope with their feelings of injustice, sympathy, or pity for other human beings who are living in a reduced state. If this problem does not enter their consciousness from their own sensibilities, it is regularly brought to their attention by the prisoners, who are making supplications for increased privileges or who are objecting to their state of deprivation. The employees, in order to solve this potential threat to their moral integrity, tend to firmly

embrace the view that the prisoners are moral inferiors who deserve their state of reduced circumstances.[14, 15]

This conflict between prisoners and guards was greatly magnified in the tumultuous 1970s and '80s, when open and violent hostility between prisoners and guards raged, resulting in hundreds of assaults and some homicides of guards by prisoners and prisoners by guards. In this period, the general sense of moral superiority, hate, and disgust toward prisoners reached new heights.

The violence toward guards by prisoners has declined since the 1970s, but guards' and other staff's negative attitudes toward prisoners continue.[16] The reason for this begins with cultural differences between the two categories. In the past, prison staff, particularly guard forces, were more likely to be white and from rural areas; prisoners were mostly nonwhite and urban. In the 1980s and '90s, with the great increase in the number of prisons and the shrinking of other occupational opportunities for middle- and working-class persons, many more urban and better-educated persons entered prison work. Further, affirmative action policies brought more nonwhites and woman into prison work. While rural-white versus urban-nonwhite differences between staff and prisoners still exist in some states, these differences have been reduced greatly in the large, more urban states such as California.

The gulf between staff and prisoners is still wide. The culture of guards, as the culture of police, with its negative images of the "criminal," persists. In the contemporary prison, this gulf is more a function of the particular institutional arrangement than the personal values and meanings that employees bring to the workplace. Controlling persons who are in a position of extreme deprivation and who are antagonistic toward their overseers promotes negative attitudes. In their job training, new staff members are taught to mistrust prisoners. The outcome of new employees' inculcation with the existing informal guard culture and their interactions with prisoners—most of whom hate the guards and many of whom attempt to manipulate them to increase their levels of privilege and material means—results in guards and staff distrusting, demeaning, and often hating prisoners.[17] A prisoner who worked as a clerk in an office with a new female staff person related her change in attitude after she went through the staff orientation:

When she first came to work, we got along real well. She was real pleasant to me. Then she went to staff training and came back with a different attitude. She would hardly talk to me. I know they fed her a lot of bullshit about how you can't trust any cons. And she believed all of it.[18]

Prisoners' Views of Guards

Prisoners intensely dislike their overseers. This is partly a result of the immediate institutional arrangement. But prisoners' dislike of "cops," or the "man," is rooted in their preprison experiences.[19] Prisoners from urban, lower-class settings learn to hate and distrust cops from their early childhood. These negative attitudes are further developed in the prison setting.

There are some exceptions. Prisoners, upon getting to know particular guards, may remove them from the general despised category.

I would also meet some good guards and some bad ones. Some guards would come to work there and realize that it's only a job. It will be as you make it, just as is life. Others came to work simply to make a convict's day hard—they were guards who believed that convicts had no rights. They would write you unjust misconduct reports and would lie to ensure you were found guilty.[20]

A guard may be removed from the despised category if prisoners believe that the guard possesses exceptional qualities and define him or her as "all right," that is, "a good guy who is fair and can be trusted, who will not fuck you over or bust you for some chicken shit beef."[21] In other situations, deviant guards are given good-guy status because they have entered into some special or illegal arrangement with some prisoners.[22] For example, some guards smuggle drugs or a few enter into sexual alliances with prisoners, while others team up with prisoners to help punish other prisoners.[23] However, in general, prisoners harbor a deep dislike for and distrust of their guards.

Prisoners evaluate guards on the basis of the following four characteristics: (1) fairness, (2) consistency, (3) stringency, and (4) empathy. The most important characteristic is fairness. Fairness means uniform application of the rules. In the contemporary rule-laden prison setting, it also means "nonpettiness." Fair guards are those who tend to overlook the enforcement of many petty rules. A prisoner at California State Prison, Solano, talks about the "all right" cops he encountered at the maximum security prison where he was previously incarcerated:

> Most of the guards at New Folsom (a maximum security prison) were all right. They didn't bother with the petty shit. They were just glad when you weren't sticking somebody and getting in their face. They'd even give you a pass when [you] were high on wine, as long as you weren't causing any trouble. You knew where you stood with those guys.[24]

Next to fairness, and blending with it, is consistency. The prisoner quoted above also addressed consistency as well as pettiness: "Here, man [Solano State Prison], you don't [know] what's gonna happen. They change the rules every day. They bust you for smoking in the building sometimes, let you go others. This place is chicken shit."[25]

The third characteristic, stringency, refers to the intensity of supervision. Some guards are more relaxed in their supervisory duties, while others are active and strict. The more relaxed guards do not circulate in the buildings as frequently and are more lenient in enforcing the rules. Of course, prisoners prefer the more lenient guards.

In the case of the fourth characteristic, empathy, a minority of guards empathize with prisoners and treat them with respect. This is more likely to be true of guards who are generally tolerant of others or those whose earlier life experiences familiarized them with criminal or deviant worlds. However, the majority of guards do not empathize with or respect prisoners as credible and decent human beings. They reveal this disrespect by the manner in which they address prisoners, give them orders, and respond to their requests. This pervasive "disrespect" is one of the more psychologically painful and infuriating features of imprisonment.

Guarding Styles

These guarding characteristics appear in different combinations in several dominant types of guards. Experienced prisoners recognize and respond differently to these various types. Their favorites are guards who are "all right." Above all, "all right cops" are fair in both senses of fairness. They enforce rules uniformly but do not bother with petty matters, that is, they give prisoners a lot of slack. They are also consistent. They may or may not be empathic; many guards who are respected by prisoners do not particularly like prisoners and prisoners know this. But these guards still operate with fairness and consistency. Barbara Owen, in her study of guards in San Quentin, described the "all right officer":

> A type generally represented by old-timers, this approach is characterized by the ability to balance and reconcile the conflicts of the institution and the daily routine. These types of workers have developed the common sense to do the job but also recognize the limits of their authority over the prisoners and other workers.[26]

Prisoners employ a broad guard category they designate "assholes." The most common category is "chicken shit" assholes, who are petty, inconsistent, unfair, and nonempathic. Gung-ho or mean assholes go out of their way to bust prisoners. Finally, there are dumb, "wishy-washy" assholes, who are not believed to be mean but are persons prisoners cannot trust because they are believed to be stupid and unpredictable. Barbara Owen described this type from the other staff members' point of view:

> This [wishy-washy] is a dangerous approach due to its unpredictab[le], discretionary, and inconsistent nature. These are workers seen as being afraid of the inmates and the ones who have not learned to say no. Often newcomers will be labeled this type because they have not yet devised appropriate strategies for dealing with the conflicts and the contradictions of prisoner relationships.[27]

Prisoners also recognize professional or career-oriented guards who, because they are ambitious, are strict yet consistent and fair rule enforcers. Also, career guards tend to be aloof and less empathic. Barbara Owen identified the professional correctional officer:

> With the advent of new job titles, an emphasis on increased training, and an occupational awareness fostered by the unions, this approach to the job is pursued by those with higher levels of education, and who desire to make a career within the Department of Corrections.[28]

Some female guards perform like den mothers and some male guards like scoutmasters. In these comparable styles, the guards act with considerable empathy and fairness. They work closely with prisoners, usually in their capacity as the officer in charge of a housing unit. In this post, they get to know a large number of prisoners and play a maternal or paternal role, mixing authority and help. This style is similar to the "inventive role" of women guards described by Lynn Zimmer:

> I know the guys in this unit so well that when I come on duty I can tell right away who is mad at whom, who is upset, who got a bad letter from home, etc. Instead of letting them go at each other, I can usually stop trouble before it begins by giving them a chance to talk these things out.
>
> These guys may be locked up, but they're still men. You get a few troublemakers, of course, but not too many, really. Just because someone has committed a crime doesn't mean he's forgotten how to act around a lady.[29]

Though this inventive role is more often a female style, many male guards act like scoutmasters. They tend to see prisoners as redeemable bad boys rather than worthless criminals and approach them with a paternalistic style, similar to that of the inventive woman guard.

Most guards, however, are neutral in empathy, not strict and not petty. They are the majority who are just putting in their time. Theirs is just a job, and they are trying to get by with as little hassle as possible. If the prisoners do not cause them trouble, they will not go out of their way to bother them. From the prisoners' point of view, they are just nine-to-fivers who sit around a lot. "You can't count on them, but they are not going to fuck with you too much if you stay out of their face."[30]

Solano

We have been examining the warehouse prison as a general type. Now we will focus on Solano as an "exemplar" of the warehouse prisons. Solano, a California middle-level prison, is one of the 22 California prisons built in the 1980s and '90s. It houses both Level II and Level III prisoners, middle-range classifications, while Level IV prisoners, the state's highest classification, are held in the new supermax prisons. Solano is typical of many of the new prisons built nationwide in that period of rapid expansion of prison populations.

Solano is not an excessively cruel prison like many of the ones in southern states that have been opened or reorganized since 1980. In response to the public punitive mode, some of the southern states' prison systems have reintroduced chain gangs, breaking rocks, striped prison uniforms, silence systems, corporal punishment, and other cruel practices of earlier eras. In contrast, Solano's administration is comparatively benign. Its planning, construction, and operation have been guided by the three principles of design discussed earlier: security, efficiency, and economy. Intentional cruelty is not part of the plan.

Solano was built according to a new California architectural plan that was followed, with slight modifications, in 15 other prisons built in California in that period. Like the others, it was intended to hold from 3,000 to 5,000 prisoners. However, its

Figure 3.1
Solano State Prison

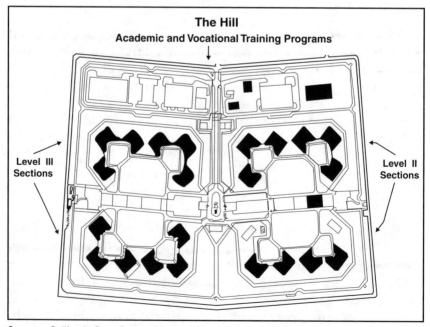

Source: California State Prison, Solano, Mission Summary, 1999

population swelled to just under 6,000 in 2000. Solano is divided into four sections—two Level II and two Level III. Level II and Level III sections are separated by double fences. (See Figure 3.1). Passage between the two is controlled electronically from a tower in the center of the compound. There is no prisoner flow from Level II to Level III. The two Level II sections and the two Level III sections are separated by a row of buildings containing education services, mess halls, a medical clinic, gyms (converted to dorms), and administration offices. There is a complex of workshops "on the hill" adjacent to main compound and visiting rooms on the south and north sides of the prison—one for Level II prisoners, the other for Level III.

The buildings that house the prisoners are built according to a 270-degree plan. Looking at them from above, they form a square with a triangle cut into one side (See Figure 3.2).

The two tiers of cells, or "alcoves," containing dorm beds are built into the three straight sides of the square. The entrance and elevated control booth are at the apex of the triangle. With this design, the officer in the control booth can observe the flow in and out of the entrance, scan the entire dayroom, and look at all the cell fronts and into all the alcoves.

Each of the 12 Level III buildings has two tiers with 100 two-man cells surrounding a large, open dayroom. The cells, which are 6 by 12 feet, have a small, stainless steel sink and a toilet, a small steel cabinet, two steel bunks, a steel desk, and a steel stool. The prisoners are allowed to have two of the following: small TV, guitar, radio, or CD or cassette tape player. The cells are almost completely filled by these furnishings and personal items, and there is barely space to move around. Each of the eight Level II buildings has 24 alcoves with 10 to 16 double- or triple-deck bunks with metal lockers on the side. These are crowded into a 15-by-20-foot space. The Level II buildings have four bathrooms with toilets and sinks. Both the Level III and Level II buildings have two shower rooms with nine shower heads each. Because there are many female officers in the buildings, these have waist-high, oilcloth screens across the entrances.

In Level II buildings, the dayroom has three large televisions: one watched mostly by African American prisoners, one by Spanish-speaking prisoners, and one mostly by white prisoners. In addition, there are 26 stainless steel tables, each with four

Figure 3.2
Diagram of Prisoner Housing

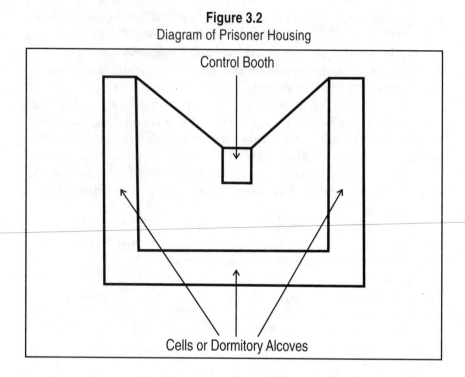

Cells or Dormitory Alcoves

attached stools. The Level III buildings, since prisoners have
TVs in their cells, have one TV in the dayroom. They also have
fewer tables (10), because Level III prisoners spend much more
time in their cells. Two small, enclosed rooms used by officers
and counselors are located below the elevated control room, one
on each side of the tunnel entrance. In front of one of these rooms
are a table, chairs, and filing cabinets, which are used by the
guards.

Dayrooms are large, high-ceilinged, well-lighted, poorly ven-
tilated areas. They are very hot in the summer. In the Level II buildings, during the days and evenings, prisoners are free to venture
out of their alcoves to go to the toilets, showers, and the dayroom
anytime except for the regular counts and the occasional lockdowns. In the Level II buildings, the dayrooms are usually filled,
busy, and noisy. Sound bounces off the concrete floors, walls, and
ceilings. In the Level III buildings, access to the dayroom is more
restricted, and more prisoners choose to stay in their cells, even

during unlock periods. The dayrooms in the Level III buildings are less busy, crowded, and noisy.

Prisoners are served breakfast and dinner in the eight mess halls, two for each section of the prison. Private caterers supply "franchise" food, most of which is prepared off-site. The meals are repetitious, bland, and skimpy. The prisoners are given a sack lunch with a sandwich and fruit. The food is ordinary institutional fare—better than county jails, worse than most hospitals. It will sustain minimum health but, over the long haul, becomes more and more unsatisfying. Prisoners who have money "on the books" augment their eating pleasure and dietary needs with food commodities—mostly "junk foods"—purchased through the canteen. Many prisoners occasionally or regularly avoid the mess halls and prepare their own meals from food commodities they purchase from the canteen or prisoner "merchants," who sell food pilfered from the kitchen. They have hot plates, or "stingers," for heating food.

Prisoners have relatively open access to the recreation yards, where basketball, handball, tennis courts, and exercise equipment are available. Weight lifting, which once was a popular exercise, has been eliminated. Prisoners have limited access to a small library that is open five days a week; an education department, where reentry and health education classes are given on a voluntary basis; a chapel; two visiting rooms, where they may visit with approved relatives or friends on Thursday through Sunday; and a medical clinic, where they may *try* to obtain medical treatment. Also, there is a canteen open on Thursday through Saturday, where prisoners pick up the commodities they have ordered, such as beverages, canned foods, "condiments" such as ketchup, soy sauce, and peanut butter, sodas, groceries such as oatmeal, instant noodle soup (a favorite), salami, tortillas, crackers, chips, snacks, ice cream, candy, rolling tobacco, cigars, pipe tobacco, tobacco accessories, and batteries. Most of the time, however, prisoners are restricted to their buildings and, in Level III, to their the small cells.

During the week, about 2,500 Solano prisoners proceed "up to the hill" to the adjoining section, where academic education, vocational training, and prison industries take place. These activities on the hill are suspended on foggy days, which are frequent in winter, and during lockdowns because of prisoner melees or other control problems.

Programs at Solano

Education

Current prison educational programs have shrunk considerably and changed dramatically from those that existed during the "correctional" era of the 1950s and '60s. This change is reflected at Solano. Slightly fewer than 1,000 prisoners, about 17 percent of the population, attend school, generally adult basic education classes. Fewer than 100 are in the GED program, and there is no college program. From the 1950s through the 1970s, California prisoners were required to attend school until they tested at ninth-grade level. Such schools were operated by local city and county academic administrations, and classes structured like those in outside public schools were taught by instructors hired by the local school districts. Correspondence courses offered by the University of California, Berkeley Extension Division, were made available to California prisoners in the 1950s.[31] At the end of the 1960s, the federal Office of Economic Opportunity funded college programs in four states—Oregon, Pennsylvania, Minnesota, and New Mexico. Throughout the 1970s, college programs were introduced in prisons across the country. Many prisons, including several in California, had college programs that offered associate's degrees. Other states' programs offered bachelor's degrees in the liberal arts.

With the advent of the punitive spirit in penology and the abandonment of rehabilitation as an official goal of imprisonment, college programs virtually disappeared. In California, the current educational emphasis is on English as a second language and elementary-level education. The students are taught using "workbooks," and have little instructor-directed material. A prisoner who worked as a clerk for the education director described education at Solano:

> The education program is a joke. You have to attend school if you test below the 6th grade. You are encouraged to attend if you test below the 9th grade. The classes are not like outside schools. Everyone is working at their own level. People are starting and leaving all the time. There is one class with about 16 guys aimed at GED. They work on their own with study books. You can't get any college classes. You have to pay for correspondence courses yourself. They canceled the Pell grants and that ended college programs.[32]

Vocational Training

Slightly fewer than 1,000 Solano prisoners (again, about 17 percent of the population) are involved in vocational training programs. Available programs are auto body repair, automotive technician, carpentry, computer refurbishing and repair, drafting, eyewear manufacturing, horticulture, industrial and electrical skills, machine shop, masonry, mill and cabinet installation, office services, refrigeration and air conditioning, silk screening, small engine repair, upholstering, and welding.

Several conditions greatly weaken the efficacy of these vocational training programs, most important, the lack of funds and resources. Instructors report that they have great difficulty obtaining needed equipment and materials. For example, in the fall of 2001, the office services program had been waiting for months for updated computer programs. All the instructors interviewed indicated that it was very difficult to keep operating because of the serious lack of resources. The welding shop instructor reported that to effectively teach welding, he had to solicit supplies from private industries. He claimed, "The CDC [California Department of Corrections] doesn't give a damn about the program." Most of the instructors I interviewed believed that the administration does not support vocational training programs:

> CDC doesn't care if we train these guys or not. They just want us to fill out the paper and get them under control.

> I'm frustrated and disappointed. They don't let me teach what I want and they don't give a damn about these guys.

> I have to go out on my own and get the material I need. Sometimes I have to pay for it. I have to contact the unions to get these guys jobs. It's a joke. They don't give a rat's ass what happens to these guys.[33]

Instructors are fired, or they quit and are not replaced. In the Fall of 2001, 11 out of 44 vocational staff positions were vacant. Further, the training programs are regularly interrupted by lockdowns and fog periods, during which prisoners cannot be released to the hill for vocational training.

Even with available programs, funding, supplies, and instructors, many programs do not adequately prepare prisoners for well-paying jobs, because prisoners are not trained in up-to-date methods or there is no market for the particular job skills for which they are trained. Prisoners who have passed through the various vocational training programs stated that training for computer refurbishing and repair, mill and cabinet installation, painting, and small engine repair programs was outdated and insufficient to meet current industry requirements. Consequently, few prisoners are adequately trained for a skill for which there is an opportunity to earn a living wage. Adequately trained prisoners who succeed in securing a good job directly from the prison usually do so through the special efforts of the vocational instructors who go beyond their job requirements to train prisoners and secure jobs for them.

Voluntary Programs

In addition to education and vocational training programs, Solano permits regular religious services for Catholics, Protestants, Muslims, Jews, and Native Americans. In addition, there are a number of voluntary groups and associations in which prisoners may participate. By and large, the programs permitted by the administration operate with a basic philosophy that is consistent with prevailing conservative ideas on crime and criminals, particularly, the idea that the prisoner is a moral inferior, a pathological or disreputable being who is in need of redemption, reformation, or salvation. Programs that proceed from this premise and are therefore permitted at Solano are Narcotics Anonymous, Alcoholics Anonymous (AA), Men Against Violence, Prisoners' Outreach Program (POP), Victims and Offenders Reconciliation Group (VORG), and Men's Violence Prevention.

There are some exceptions. There are programs in art and in music, both organized by civilian teachers. Once there even was a book study group, organized by one of the correctional counselors, which met for two years. In general, however, the administration does not permit prisoners to organize personal interest groups unless these conform to the principle stated earlier, that is, the group proceeds from the idea that the convict is a "criminal" or a defective being, and the group's activity is directed toward redemption or salvation.

The problem with this restriction is that many, perhaps most, convicts do not think of themselves as moral inferiors or criminals in the sense society defines the category. Prisoners employ a variety of explanations for the events or acts that led to their incarceration and conceptions of themselves that are different than the public's view. Some prisoners believe their crime or crimes resulted from unusual contextual or life circumstances and do not accurately represent their actual characters. They were drunk, high, under unusual stress, or disadvantaged because of their social circumstances or minority status. Others believe that they were just unlucky to be caught or were singled out because of their race or social status. Many have a critical view of conventional society and believe that the acts that led to their incarceration were not much more reprehensible than those of most other people. Alan Mobley, an ex-convict who recently received a Ph.D. in sociology, discusses how convicts see through "idealized" versions of conventional society:

> [T]he incarcerated often have more than a passing interest in news from the outside world. They know enough about politics and justice issues to suspect that those who so readily condemn them are not so "clean" themselves. Prison inmates are not cloistered academics, nor are they justice system practitioners whose vision is clouded by the veil of legal legitimacy and the thin blue line. Convicted and incarcerated felons have experienced life at ground zero, a place where the messiness of actual procedures meets the more hypothetical policy road. Prisoners are the possessors— whether they like it or not—of an arsenal of finely calibrated "bullshit" detectors. Any idealized notion of society presented to them as real is discredited and rejected—just as quickly, I might add, as their own demonized caricatures are accepted and even embellished.[34]

In earlier eras, particularly that of the correctional institution, convicts were allowed to organize groups based on a wide variety of personal interests. In California prisons in the 1950s through the 1970s, there were a number of organized groups not allowed in today's prisons: for example, the Gavel Club, the Squires, a theater group, a classical music appreciation group, a slot car club, as well as several self-help organizations, such as EMPELO, organized by Chicano prisoners, and SATE, organized by black prisoners. The experiences of one prisoner who participated in this research is revealing. In 1989, while he was imprisoned at another Level III prison, he organized a study group of black prisoners to learn black history and to prepare themselves for life after prison through self-improvement activities, mainly reading and academic courses. He wrote a formal constitution and bylaws for the group, in which he specified acceptable self-help activities in which members must be engaged. To advertise the group, he wrote a one-page flyer describing the group. The administration was alerted to the group through this flyer, placed the prisoner in segregation, confiscated all of his written material about the group, and then transferred him to Lancaster, a Level IV prison.

Substance Abuse Programs

In 1997, the California state government authorized the California Department of Corrections (CDC) to implement a 1,000-bed expansion of substance abuse programs (SAPs). Solano contracted with Center Point, a private drug treatment program, and established a special housing unit for "substance abusers," which was intended to

> reduce the incidence of both substance abuse and relapse and criminal recidivism among participants and to promote prosocial behavior that will enable the participants to exhibit satisfactory conduct within the facility and upon parole, leading to successful reintegration back into the community. To achieve this end, the SAP shall offer services which are comprehensive in scope, spanning both incarceration and parole, and of a sufficient duration and intensity that participants are prepared for release, supported in the community, and develop the skills, knowledge, and ability to avoid substance abuse relapse and recidivism.[35]

Two hundred SAP participants are housed in a Level III building in which they attend daily group sessions led by employees of Center Point. These employees are all ex-addicts and mostly ex-convicts, who passed through treatment programs and remained drug free for a length of time. The group sessions' format is derived from AA and Synanon methods (two of the most influential alcohol and drug treatment programs). In these sessions, participants write biographies in which they analyze their personal problems as they relate to their drug or alcohol use. They meet in 30-to-40 person groups for daily sessions, which are led by the Center Point staff. One at a time, the participants become the focus of the group's attention. After the larger group session, they break into smaller groups to discuss specific issues. Their Center Point staff evaluate their performance, and they are passed through stages and given certificates of completion in public ceremonies. Upon successful completion of the program and their prison sentence, they are eligible to enter live-in programs, where they are supported and assisted in making a transition to living outside.

Reliable and convincing evidence of the success of this particular program (and prison drug treatment programs in general) is not available. I have attended many sessions of drug treatment programs in prisons, and I am not convinced of their efficacy. Much of the participation in the group sessions appears to be unenthusiastic. Informal participant comments suggest a range of commitment and enthusiasm to SAPs. Most are very critical and cynical:

> This program is bullshit. I'm only here because they make me attend 'cause I got drugs on my record.

> This in here is bogus shit. But the halfway house is a good thing. That's why I'm here. I know I'm going need a lot of help on the outside.[36]

However, there are program advocates. One young prisoner, upon graduation from the program, made the following comment: "I've really benefitted by the program. I'm going to school. I've learned a lot about myself. It's going to make difference for me when I get out."[37]

Prison Industry Authority

The CDC conducts industrial activities through the Prison Industry Authority (PIA), which produces several commodities for use by the CDC and other state institutions. PIA supplies laundry services for the Solano prison, California Medical Facility, and Sonoma State Hospital; optical products for CDC institutions, state agencies, and Medi-Cal; bookbinding for CDC files; DMV-disabled-persons placards and Cal-Trans signs; and metal furniture for CDC institutions and county jails. About 400 Solano prisoners are assigned to these industries and the maintenance and administrative activities of PIA. On weekdays, they work for eight hours on the hill (that is, when there are no fog or control problems), and they are paid up to 85 cents an hour.

Conclusions

The warehouse prison—as exemplified by California State Prison, Solano—efficiently and securely manages very large prisoner populations (up to 6,000). This is accomplished through its technologically sophisticated architectural design and an extensive, restrictive, and relatively rigidly enforced set of formal rules and procedures. The prison administration, which is a large and complex bureaucracy, is divided with internal conflicts among staff and between staff and prisoners. Consequently, the rules are enforced with considerable inconsistency, arbitrariness, and hostility.

The physical design of the Solano warehouse prison results in hundreds of prisoners being crowded into limited space. The higher-security housing (Level III in California's classification system) has buildings with approximately a hundred, 6-by-12-foot, two-man cells. The Level II buildings have 24 alcoves, measuring 15 by 20 feet, with 14 double-decker beds. The prison has four recreation yards, each serving about 1,200 men. The gymnasiums were converted to temporary dorms, which have become permanent. These are even more crowded than the other buildings.

All in all, the imprisonment routine at Solano is not brutal, dangerous, or excessively cruel. It *is* tightly controlled, limited, monotonous, and lacking in opportunities for self-improvement. The routine contains several irritating or infuriating qualities, the most significant of which is the strict and arbitrary nature of the routine. How prisoners cope with this inconsistent and restricted routine and the consequences of doing time in the warehouse prison are explored in Chapter 4.

Endnotes

1. Evans D. Hopkins, "Lockdown: Life Inside Is Getting Harder," *New Yorker*, 24 February 1997.
2. Randall G. Sheldon and William B. Brown, "The Crime Control Industry and the Management of the Surplus Population," *Critical Criminology* 9 (Autumn 2000): 39–40.
3. This pattern of locating prisons in remote areas is in direct conflict with the penal concepts that emerged in the reform era of the 1960s. At that time, it was believed that prisons should be located close to the urban centers from which most of the prisoners came to encourage more family contact and use of community resources. This idea

was superceded by the "not in my backyard" sentiment and the desire to banish convicts to remote locations. Convict isolation has greatly increased as a result of these remote prisons.

4. See James Jacobs, *Stateville* (Chicago: University of Chicago Press, 1977). Beginning in 1970, a series of "totality of conditions" lawsuits were filed against various states' prison systems, which resulted in dramatic changes in prison routines: *Holt v. Sarver* (Arkansas, 1970), *Pugh v. Locke* (Alabama, 1976), *Palmigiano v. Garrahy* (Rhode Island, 1977), and *Ruiz v. Estelle* (Texas, 1980). See Leo Carroll, *Lawful Order* (New York: Garland, 1998) for a thorough "case study" of the impact of the federal court's rulings in a "totality of conditions" lawsuit (*Palmigiano v. Garrahy*) filed against Rhode Island's prisons in 1977.

5. The federal courts have intervened in the operation of state prison systems in a series of "In Total" cases.

6. Events at Corcoran Prison in California in the early 1990s demonstrated this power. Beatings and homicides of prisoners by guards resulted in the indictment of eight guards, who were tried in federal court. The guards' union—the CCPOA—greatly impeded the investigation and was ready to pay for the defendants' defense when the state stepped in. They were acquitted in the trial. See Robert B. Gunnison and Greg Lucus, "Guard Union's Clout Impeding Prison Investigation, Critics Say," *San Francisco Chronicle*, 18 March 1998, pp. A1, A13.

7. According to the 2000 Staffing Profile included in the Solano Mission Statement, 30 percent of the staff were female, and 19 percent were black, 13 percent Hispanic, and about 10 percent other nonwhites.

8. Lynn Zimmer, *Women Guarding Men* (Chicago: University of Chicago Press, 1986), 107.

9. Zimmer (ibid.) identified three modes of women's adjustment to guard work, which she labeled institutional, modified, and inventive. In the institutional mode, women tried to perform like the male guards. In the modified mode, they believed that they could not perform on an equal basis as men and elected to work at posts that entailed little or no contact with male prisoners. In the inventive mode, they worked closely with prisoners to establish closer relationships and therefore to govern more successfully.

10. Prisoner statement, Solano, Spring 2000.

11. In an unpublished autobiography, I wrote about the rare intrusion of a woman into Soledad Prison's milieu: "Once in awhile, you would get a peek at some women who worked on the other side of the gates in the administration building. After I had been in Soledad a couple of years, the captain's wife, a nurse, started working in the hospital, and she would enter through the gate in the administration building and walk down the hall to the hospital. Every convict around would

get himself into position to witness her trek. We would just stand there, staring at her, trying to imagine what her body looked like under her rustling, white nurse's uniform and to feel her up and devour her with our eyes. Looking back, I figure she was an average looking woman, a little heavy, not a bad face, but certainly no beauty. But she was ravishing to us then" (John Irwin, "Rogue," manuscript, 2000, pp. 273–274).

12. Mark Arax, "Tales of Brutality Behind Bars," *Los Angeles Times*, 21 August 1996, p. A1.

13. Pete Earley, *The Hot House* (New York: Bantam, 1992), 247.

14. John Irwin, "The Trouble With Rehabilitation," *Criminal Justice and Behavior 1*, no. 2 (1974): 141–142.

15. Harvey Powelson, who was employed as a prison psychiatrist at San Quentin in the 1940s, identified this process. See Harvey Powelson and Reinhard Bendix, "Psychiatry in Prison," *Psychiatry* 14 (1951).

16. In California, 14 staff members were murdered by prisoners from 1970 to 1981. There have been no staff fatalities since 1981.

17. Often, when I was entering Solano, the guard controlling the front gate, upon reading my identification card, which designated my status as a "reseacher," would ask, "What kind of research are you doing?" When I responded, "Interviewing prisoners," he or she would usually ask, "Do you believe them?"

18. Prisoner interview, Solano, July 2000.

19. The new term for guards—"cops"—reveals that contemporary prisoners carry their attitudes toward law enforcement officers into the prison from the streets. Convicts formerly referred to guards as "bulls" or "screws," which were names indigenous and exclusive to the prison. Now they use the same label they use to refer to police officers on the outside.

20. Joseph A. Johnson, "A Career Statement," in Robert Johnson and Hans Toch, eds., *Crime and Punishment: Inside Views* (Los Angeles: Roxbury, 2000), 167.

21. Solano prisoner's statement, fall 2001.

22. Barbara Owen, in her study of guards in a California prison, uses this label to refer to guards who "pack" for prisoners. It is the label guards use, not convicts. See B. Owen, *The Reproduction of Social Control* (New York: Preager, 1988).

23. In the late 1990s, at California State Prison at Pelican Bay, a maximum security prison, a clique of guards was "setting up" prisoners believed to be "child molesters" for other prisoners to beat up. This eventually caused an investigation and indictment of several guards.

24. Prisoner interview, Solano, March 2001.

25. Ibid.

26. Owen, *The Reproduction of Social Control*, 95.
27. Ibid., 94.
28. Ibid., 95.
29. Zimmer, *Women Guarding Men*, 130, 131.
30. Statement from a Solano prisoner, October 2000.
31. I earned 24 units from extension courses while in prison.
32. Prisoner interview, Solano, fall 2001.
33. Interview of vocational instructors, Solano, spring 2001.
34. Alan Mobley, "Guess Who's Coming to Dinner? A Prisoner Perspective on the Possibilities of Reentry," manuscript, November 2001, p. 8.
35. California Department of Corrections (CDC), "California State Prison, Solano, Mission Summary" (Sacramento: CDC, 1999), 29.
36. Field notes, fall 2001.
37. Ibid. ✦

Chapter 4

Doing Time in Solano

Solano is a large, crowded, and rigidly controlled warehouse prison. Solano prisoners have greatly restricted mobility and limited access to helping programs and activities in general. In this chapter, I examine how male prisoners do time in this new type of prison.

The Prisoners

Race

Who is in Solano? This question is particularly important because prisoners' experiences in prison and prisoner social worlds are greatly affected by prisoners' preprison orientations.[1] Race has been and continues to be one of the most salient influences on prisoner behavior. As discussed in Chapter 2, violence among the races—particularly among whites, African Americans, and Chicanos—was the most disruptive ingredient in the 1970s' "prisons in turmoil." In Solano, the three major racial categories—blacks, whites, and Latinos—are relatively balanced: 33.9 percent, 33.6 percent, and 26.1 percent, respectively, with 6.4 percent "others." The others are mostly Chinese, Vietnamese, Filipinos, and Native Americans. Latinos are divided into two ethnically different groups: Mexican Americans, or Chicanos, and foreign-born Latinos, who are mostly from Mexico but include Latinos from other Central and South American countries. Foreign-born Latinos constitute a separate racial category called "Border Brothers" or *Paisas* (from *paisano*, meaning countryman).

Criminal Identity

Prisoner behavior and relationships are also significantly influenced by their involvement in contemporary criminal behavior systems. As I suggested, in an earlier study, "The first stage of the criminal career is the person's involvement with a criminal behavior system and the acquisition of a criminal perspective and identity."[2] Many prisoners had contact with and thus had taken on the values and behavior patterns of these various systems. In California prisons in the 1960s, "thieves," "heads," "dope fiends," "hustlers," "state-raised youth," "lower-class men," "square johns," and disorganized criminals were the prevailing criminal identity types.[3] In the 1970s, these criminal types were superceded by racial identities and gang and clique memberships. In the new warehouse prisons, the intensity and importance of racial identities and gang affiliations has diminished somewhat, while criminal identities are regaining power and influence. However, the many criminal behavior systems that flourished in earlier eras have disappeared. This is particularly true of those that were related to traditional criminal behavior systems with their relatively unique subcultures, such as those of the thief and the hustler. In contemporary society, new identities and criminal lifestyles have emerged. Three of these—"thugs," "gangbangers," and "outlaws"—are somewhat overlapping identities of young, mostly male, working- and lower-class members.[4]

Thugs. In cities and small towns, large numbers of contemporary, lower-class, young males are unemployed and unattached to virtually all conventional educational, political, social, and religious organizations. They swirl loosely about their social worlds, struggling to survive while seeking excitement and respect. At this stage of their lives, their physical energies, sexual drives, and desire for esteem are intense. They are prime candidates for deviant endeavors. Many present themselves as thugs, act tough, and are available for whatever criminal pursuits they believe might fulfill their need for money, goods, excitement, reputation, and sex. Instead of being introduced into crime by the carriers of criminal traditions, as was the case in earlier, more stable urban neighborhoods, they gather their ideas about living and committing crime from their criminally unskilled and socially unsophisticated peers and distorted media presentations, particularly movies, TV beer commercials, and rap music. They are the contemporary version of the "disorganized criminals" described in *The Felon*.[5] They engage in a variety of petty criminal activities, some of them involving violence. Though they may not be full-fledged addicts, they are often high or drunk when they get into trouble. They get arrested with some regularity and, though their crimes are usually petty, unskilled, and unprofitable, they are frequently sent to prison.[6]

Gangbangers. Within the same social segment—the unattached, urban or rural young male from the lower and working classes—hundreds join together in gangs. Most of these gangs evolve from groups of urban youths—"the boys from the barrio"—who hang, party, and socialize together.[7] These gangs, based mostly on race and territory, vary greatly in size, degree of cohesiveness, and purpose. Some gangs originated in California prisons and spread to outside communities.[8] Others, such as the Bloods and Crips, migrated from Los Angeles to other cities across the state and country. Still other gangs are confined to a small neighborhood or isolated communities.

Many street gangs have elaborate rules, oaths, signs, tattoos, and organizational hierarchies. Others merely consist of loosely affiliated youngsters who grew up together or are organized for particular criminal pursuits, such as drug dealing, or who convene just to increase member safety in their home territory.

Since the 1970s, the conflict and violence between gangs has escalated. A substantial increase in murder, particularly drive-by shootings committed by gang members, has aroused the fear and concern of the public, resulted in new laws, and precipitated increased police activity. Joan Moore, who has studied Chicano gangs in East Los Angeles for the last 30 years, wrote about the "moral panic" aroused by Los Angeles gang activities in the 1980s:

> The second moral panic centered on minority gangs of the 1980s. More narrowly, in Los Angeles a series of particularly brutal street shootings by black gangs began a long and intense reaction. The impact was very sharp. In 1977 the *Los Angeles Times* printed only thirty-six stories about gangs; only fifteen were printed in 1978. In 1987 sixty-nine articles appeared and in 1988 an amazing 267, nearly all of them dealing with police sweeps, revenge shootings, murder trials, and other matters.[9]

Thousands of gang members have been imprisoned over the last three decades and, as such, have become an important part of the prison mix.

Outlaws. A few prisoners seriously and intentionally pursued lives of monetary crime and viewed themselves as committed outlaws. These outlaws are usually younger, working- and lower-class men. Many were arrested as juveniles and served time in juvenile institutions. In earlier periods, they would have been drawn into the more sophisticated criminal behavior systems and engaged in safe burglary, big "heists" (armed robberies), check forgery schemes, or merchandise hijacking. The development of new technologies and systems to protect money and the disappearance of the more developed "thief" subcultures have shut off these options. Today, these outlaws deal crack, steal cars, burglarize houses, rob mom-and-pop grocery stores, mug people on the street, or hijack cars. Their crimes are more impulsive, less profitable, and more frequently violent than those of the thieves or professionals of other decades. A gang of these outlaws, which demonstrated these characteristics, was recently arrested by Oakland police.

> Led by two brothers, 18 and 20 years old, and their 17-year-old cousin, the group terrorized the city from its base in the Brookfield Village neighborhood of East Oakland—an area associated with a turf gang known as "Nut Case," police said.
>
> Police believe they held up as many as 100 victims from East Oakland to Berkeley, hitting neighborhoods both wealthy and poor, flatlands and hills.
>
> One of their victims was Sunny Thach, a young father killed and robbed of $70 on Jan. 6 as he carried laundry from his car to his home. The gang allegedly sought Asian victims because they believed Asians carried more cash than others, police said.[10]

State-raised prisoners. Many adult prisoners have been in the custody of state institutions for a significant portion of their juvenile years. Some were made wards of the state at an early age and went from foster homes to boys' schools, and then on to juvenile prisons. Others were arrested at a young age and spent many years in various Youth Authority institutions. They learned to survive in mean, juvenile institutions and were imbued with prisoner values and behavior patterns that obtain in youth prisons. In particular, they learned to be tough and to form cliques for protection. When they reached adulthood, many of them experienced great difficulty living as adults on the outside and were sent to adult prisons, usually for very unsophisticated, impulsive crimes. Prisoners with the state-raised identity are comfortable in prison, where they have a large network of fellow state-raised acquaintances. Dallas Scott, a prisoner at Leavenworth, described his career as a state-raised prisoner:

> I've never really had much concept of life outside jail. I was twelve years old the first time I went in and I haven't really been out long enough since to know anything else but this life. . . . Prisons are full of guys like me. . . . You start out doing small things, you know, bucking authority, and the next thing you know you are in juvenile hall or jail, and that is where you form your basic personality.[11]

Corner boys. Many male prisoners grew up in lower-class neighborhoods where street crime was a normal occurrence, but they themselves were not regularly involved in crime and do not view themselves as criminals. They were at risk of being arrested because they were on the streets for many hours, and police regularly patrol those lower-class neighborhoods looking for street criminals. Corner boys are occasionally arrested and imprisoned because they just happen to be present when crimes are committed by friends or relatives and, under special circumstances, such as when they are in the company of more criminally oriented acquaintances, saving face in front of peers, intoxicated, or trying to take advantage of an unanticipated opportunity for financial gain, they are drawn into the commission of a crime.

Dope fiends, crackheads, and other druggies. Although patterns of addiction are constantly changing, there is a constant population, mostly lower class or working class, who pursue a life of drug use that gets them into consistent trouble with the law for which they are sent to prison, either for crimes they commit to sustain their drug use or for dealing drugs. In the 1950s, they were mostly heroin users. In the 1960s, heroin users were joined by users of speed and "poly-drug abusers." In the late 1960s through the 1970s, cocaine "abusers" joined the ranks, and then finally "crackheads" appeared. Currently, about one fifth of the Solano Prison population is incarcerated for drug crimes. Not all of these persons are addicts, but many addicts are in prison for other crimes. So a large proportion of the Solano Prison population is abusing or addicted to one drug or another.

Derelicts and crazies. Some prisoners, usually after many years of serving time in jail and prison, have lost their capacity to live outside the prison. When outside, they teetered on the edge of physical survival. They avoided committing serious crimes, but they occasionally committed some petty crime, such as petty theft, and were sent to prison. Before the mid-1960s and changes in the law that permitted involuntary hospitalization of people judged to be psychotic or mentally incompetent, many of them would have been hospitalized in state mental health institutions. Since the states have ceased involuntary commitments, most "crazies" are left to wander on the streets. The state prison has become the institution of last resort for these denizens.

Sex offenders. Slightly more than 10 percent of the Solano Prison population are incarcerated for sex offenses. Most of these prisoners do not view themselves as criminals. Instead, they view their crimes as manifestations of inner characteristics, propensities, or impulses that overwhelmed them. They are divided into two main categories, rapists and molesters, both of which are dishonored statuses in the prisoner world.

Square johns. Many state prisoners have had little or no contact with criminal behavior systems and have never viewed themselves as criminals. These prisoners were sent to prison for involvement in atypical acts. They murdered someone in a fit of rage or while drunk, embezzled money from their employer, or made a large cocaine deal or committed some other serious crime while in unusual or extraordinary circumstances. Many of them are serving life sentences for murder.

Sentence Length

Prisoners adapt differently to the prison and to each other according to the length of their sentences. The modern warehouse prison contains prisoners with greatly varying sentence lengths. On the one hand, many persons convicted of very petty crimes, which formerly would have resulted in county jail sentences, are being sent to prison for short sentences—one or two years. With credit for time served in the county jail, they may serve less than one year in prison. On the other hand, many persons are being sent to prison for *very* long prison terms—life or longer. In 2001, there were 46 prisoners in Solano serving terms from 40 to 150 years.

It is useful to categorize Solano prisoners by their sentence lengths into "churners," "summer campers," middle-rangers, long-termers, and lifers. Prisoners in these categories tend to adjust to prison differently.[12] Churners, who as of April 2001 represented about 4 percent or 230 of the 5,778 Solano prisoners, were serving less than two years.[13] Summer campers constituted 16 percent (926) and were serving sentences of two to three years. Middle-rangers were 40 percent (2,314) with sentences of three to nine years. Long-termers were 20 percent (1,157) and were serving sentences of more than nine years. Last, Solano held 1,150 (20 percent) lifers.[14] The prisoners in these different categories are handled by the administration, adapt to prison, and relate to each other differently. I discuss these differences in the sections that follow.

Prisoner Social Organization

How does this mix of prisoners cope with the general circumstances of imprisonment and the particular arrangements in the new warehouse prison? First of all, they must cope with the "pains of imprisonment" inherent in all forms of imprisonment, that is, the loss of freedom, sexual and material deprivations, degradation, and lack of privacy and autonomy. Since the 1960s, intense intraprisoner conflict escalated, and the threat of physical violence was added. Beyond these, there are the special circumstances of the warehouse prisons—rigidity, overcrowding, lack of mobility, and absence of "program" options.

Researchers recognized early in the study of prisons that prisoners develop unique social organizations to help them establish a more secure environment for themselves and to help them cope with the pains of imprisonment.[15] Throughout the 1950s and '60s, prison scholars constructed an elaborate theory of prisoner social organization. They suggested that prisoners participated in a relatively solidary and integrated social system that was based on a special value system—the "convict code." Through this system, with its special prisoner "roles," prisoners regulated conflict among themselves and acquired and distributed the scarce prison commodities, services, and privileges.[16] However, as pointed out in Chapter 2, this solidary system was blown apart by hostile and violent prisoner divisions, a revolutionary prisoner movement, and the repressive, counterproductive reaction of prison administrations. Administrators and planners developed the warehouse prison partially in response to this period of turmoil and violence.

Détente

Solano, as most other midrange prisons in California, lacks intense intergroup conflict.[17] There is little openly expressed hostility and almost no actual physical violence among the members of different racial groups. As one Solano prisoner put it, "I can't remember when there was a stabbing here. The most you get is a couple of guys slapping at each other and cops break it right up. It's nothing like the '70s and '80s when guys were sticking each other regularly."[18]

There is one exception to this general ongoing peaceful state. This is the relationship between two categories of Mexican Americans, Norteños and Sureños, which is violent and disruptive. (I discuss this conflict further on.)

There are several reasons prison violence, prevalent in the 1960s through the 1980s, has subsided. The most important of these is that prison planners and prison administrators have succeeded in developing a prison operation that greatly reduces the potential for violence. In the new California prisons, the layout of the housing units, the yards, and the entire prison compound facilitates surveillance and rapid response to any disturbance. But more important, the existence of supermax prisons with Segregated Housing Units (SHUs), in which 10,000 prisoners can be kept in secure lockup, has greatly reduced violence in the lower-custody prisons. California prison administrators transfer prisoners who have been involved in several violent events or have a high violence potential (because of gang affiliation or some other characteristic) to supermax prisons. This and the fact that prisoners in the lower-custody prisons know that if they cause too much trouble, they will be transferred to the harsher supermax prisons have reduced violence. A Solano prisoner commented: "The minute they opened New Folsom [a supermax prison] things settled down in Old Folsom."[19]

Housing so many prisoners in the high-custody, isolated, and austere supermax prisons has introduced some serious new problems that are discussed in the next chapter. However, it appears that their existence has reduced violence in the lower-custody prisons in California.

The racial prejudice and mostly informal racial segregation that characterized prison social organizations in the 1960s, '70s, and '80s continues, though at a greatly reduced level. Though prisoners are friendly with some individuals of a different race, they almost exclusively "hang" with, and restrict their close friendships to, their own race. In the dayrooms, the clumps of prisoners sitting around tables playing dominoes, cards, or some other board game, or just "bullshitting," are usually of the same race. In the Level II buildings, which have three TVs in the dayrooms, black prisoners occupy the tables and watch TV on one side of the dayroom, whites on the other, and Spanish-speaking Latinos in the middle. On the yard, prisoners gather around a bench, walk the yard, and engage in some sport, such as handball, soccer, or basketball, with members of their own race. Likewise, when they fan out through the mess hall to sit and eat their meals, the prisoners divide into racial groups. However, there is some mixing. In some of the athletic activities, particularly basketball and soccer, there is a racial mixture. Here and there, clumps of prisoners of different races interact on the yard or in the dayrooms.

Young California Mexican American prisoners, who are divided into north and south factions, do some mixing with white and black prisoners. However, northerners tend to mix more with blacks and southerners with whites. This pattern originated in the 1970s, when the Mexican Mafia, the powerful southern gang, affiliated with young white racist prisoners, such as the Aryan Brotherhood, and La Nuestra Familia, the northern gang, affiliated with black prisoners, particularly the Black Guerrilla Family. Now, while watching television or playing games, southern Mexicans will occasionally mingle with white prisoners and northern Mexicans with black prisoners.

Prisoner Groups

Within the races, friendship groups form on the basis of a variety of characteristics, the most important of which is where the prisoners came from or where they were raised—the town, neighborhood, section of the state (e.g., north or south), or country. Other characteristics are their criminal identities, gang affiliation, religion (particularly Muslims and born-again Christians), age, and special, in-prison interests. Most friendship groups are relatively loose and unstructured. The two exceptions are known as cars and gangs.

Cars. Cars, which are the most obvious and prevalent of the identified groups, are usually homies, persons who come from the same neighborhood and are of the same race. However, some cars form on the basis of some other commonality such as religion. In Solano, there are Christian cars, Muslim cars, and Asian cars.

Cars are not organized like gangs. They do not have designated leaders and codes. They are just a bunch of guys who share some commonality and hang together. They offer each other support, even some protection. They may have a member they respect and look up to—a "shot-caller"—but not a formal leader. They are the contemporary replacement of the cliques and tips prevalent in the prisoner social world in the 1950s and 1960s.[20]

Gangs. Gangs are social organizations with some degree of definite organization. Many of them have names, some a definite sense of membership, designated leaders, hierarchies, codes (often written), and insignia (sometimes tattooed on members' bodies). Many gang members were state raised or gangbangers on the outside. Gangs are usually organized for particular purposes such as drug dealing or defense of a particular social group, for example, Valley Mexicans or white supremacists. When they appeared in the California prisons in the late 1960s and then became prominent in the 1970s and 1980s, all prisoners had to make adjustments to the threat of violence they presented. The existence of gangs completely altered prisoner social relationships. In general, prisoners "cliqued up" for protection or withdrew from prison public life as much as possible.

For years, prison administrators have vigorously attempted to control gangs and eliminate gang behavior. Their primary strategy has been to identify gang members, particularly leaders, and place them in administrative segregation. In fact, the supermax prisons were primarily constructed to control gangs and their violent behavior.

The 1999 "Mission Summary," circulated by the Solano administration, identified 17 gangs at Solano: Four-One-Five, Crips, Bloods,

Black Guerrilla Family (BGF), Fresno Bulldogs, Vanguard, Nuestra Familia (NF), Sureños, Norteños, Aryan Brotherhood, Skinheads, Nazi Low Riders, Misfits, Black Gangster Disciples, CoCo County Boys, Sacramaniacs, and Southside Government. My interviews with dozens of prisoners at Solano suggest that none of these 17 gangs are presently active at Solano. Most gang members have either matured out of this activity, which tends to be a young man's game, or have been transferred to Level IV prisons. Solano prisoners who still consider themselves gang members must act with extreme secrecy and caution to avoid being transferred to a supermax prison. In effect, gangs at Solano are inactive.

Norteños and sureños. Most young Mexican American prisoners affiliate with other Chicanos who were raised either north or south of Los Angeles and who are identified by the administration, themselves, and other Mexican Americans as Norteños or Sureños. Hostility built upon older divisions among Chicanos continues between them. The hostility started when many El Paso Mexicans migrated to Los Angeles in the 1940s, and the younger males, many of whom were addicted to heroin, came into conflict in the jails and prisons with Los Angeles Chicanos. It worsened when an L.A.-based gang, the Mexican Mafia (the EME), emerged in San Quentin and spawned the Nuestra Familia, a gang composed mostly of San Joaquin Valley Chicanos. These two groups have battled for two decades. When the prison administrators successfully isolated most of the active members of these two powerful and murderous factions by sending them to supermax prisons, young Chicano prisoners organized new gangs, mostly based on the towns or sections of the state from which they came. As the administration identified these new groups and placed their members in supermax prisons, hostilities between north and south continued. During the 1980s, prison authorities questioned new Mexican prisoners to determine whether they were Norteños or Sureños. Incoming prisoners had to chose one affiliation or the other. Then the administration segregated Mexican American prisoners on the basis of north or south origins or affiliations.

Today, it is a war game played by young California Chicano prisoners. All young Chicanos are pressured by their peers to align themselves with one side or the other. Some young Chicanos and many older ones avoid affiliation by insisting on their independence and evading the activities of the two factions. Many former affiliates, upon aging, respectably and safely move away from active participation in the affairs of the factions. However, most young California Chicanos choose to affiliate with one of the two factions.

Affiliation means that one hangs with members of his faction, remains ready for any violent actions against the enemy faction, and in general follows the commands of the "shotcaller" of their particular clique within the faction. Groups from the two different factions often skirmish when they have access to each other, usually on the recreation yard or in the dayrooms. Because of the tight security in new prisons, there are many fewer deadly weapons, such as the metal "shivs" that prisoners fabricated in earlier eras. Consequently, the skirmishes—melees, as they are called by the administration—are mostly fistfights.

Several factors explain the persistent, internecine conflict among Mexican Americans, which has been present in California cities and towns and in its prisons for decades. Since the 1930s, most young Chicanos have been excluded from, or have dropped out of, conventional pursuits, particularly educational and occupational paths. Between age 14 and early adulthood, a period when their physical capacities, sexual desires, and identity confusions are peaking, they have been viewed with disrespect as "greasers," or "beaners," and have been barred from most promising occupational careers. They also have been segregated in their barrios, where they mill about. As many urban youngsters have done, they formed gangs[21]:

> Most barrios have a type of gang, and the barrio gang uniquely reflects the multiple pressure and conflicts of Mexican Americans.... It thus has become an institutionalized entity that provides many poor, barrio youths with human support networks and a source of personal ego identity that are unavailable to them elsewhere.[22]

The barrio gangs provided the young Chicano males (and some females) identity, protection, and *carnalidad* (Mexican slang for "brotherhood"). But the gangs required something in return— "toughness":

> "Toughness" is a requirement for group membership that is proven in the ritual of gang initiation. Comments on acting and being tough show a concern about this type of behavior. A few cases

illustrate this point. A 22-year-old male from South Fontana repeated his brother's habits and joined the barrio clique. He mentioned that "if anybody threatens a member we had to get together and beat the guys near to death. That's when you show how tough you are, because you have to be tough to make it in this world. We have to get them before they get us."[23]

They also respect the *vato loco* ("crazy guy") and *locura* in general:

> Locura is a state of mind where various actions bordering on "craziness" take place. A loco exhibits this mind set by alternately acting tough, fearless, and daring and by exhibiting other spontaneous types of behavior, such as getting "loco" on drugs and alcohol. Some manage this role with authority, while others do so with reputation and only when peer or situational pressures are overwhelming. This psycho-social role-set developed over a long period of time and has become a requisite for street survival; additionally, it is an acting and thinking pattern for identification and emulation. There are important advantages to having a loco in your circle. Such locos help the most when rival barrios are mounting "driveby" campaigns against a barrio.[24]

From the outset, the Chicano gangs were firmly attached to neighborhoods, or barrios. It was a Los Angeles barrio clique that was the basis of the first violent gang, the EME, in San Quentin. Some of the barrio gangs go back many generations.[25] When population changes occurred in a neighborhood, some gangs were absorbed into others, but the attachment to geography remained. When the auto became a major cultural object in Cholo (young Mexican American, tough and hip) culture, the warfare, including drive-by shootings, extended over larger territories. These trends—the long-enduring tradition of territorial gangs, the importance of gang membership for identity, protection, and *carnalidad,* the elevation of toughness, and *locura*—have promoted the ongoing territorial warfare between northerners and southerners in California prisons. The fact that these Mexican Americans readily resort to violence has meant that all other members of their social worlds must take them seriously and either avoid them or prepare to meet their violence.

Currently, any prisoner known or believed to be an active member of one of the identified prison gangs is segregated by administrative classification. However, the hostility and combat

between young Chicanos who identify with the Norteños or
Sureños continues. Intense conflict among older Mexican gangs
persists in the maxi-prisons and now on San Quentin's death row,
which houses 600 prisoners, many of whom are gang members.
The *New York Times* reported on a "Rash of Violence" at San
Quentin's death row:

> In the last 18 months, in what San Quentin officials and advocates
> for prisoners call an unprecedented breach of conduct, a group of
> death row inmates have become increasingly hostile and violent.
> Classified as Grade B's for their unruly behavior and gang affilia-
> tions and housed apart from other death row prisoners in a three-
> story building, the Adjustment Center, these inmates have at-
> tacked guards 67 times in a year and a half, triple the rate of attacks
> by Grade B prisoners just a few years ago, say officials at San
> Quentin. [26]

Paisas. Mexican nationals—*Paisas* or Border Brothers—make
up about 20 percent the of prisoner population. *Paisas* are a distinct,
somewhat isolated group in the Solano prisoner society. Most of
them speak little or poor English and are bound by their Spanish language and ethnic identity. Their orientation is to Mexico, and most
of them will be returned to Mexico when they complete their sentence.

Within the prison, they have their own community, stay mostly
to themselves, and are left alone by other prisoners. In the
dayrooms, they control one of the TVs on which they watch Span-
ish-language programs. On yard, they hang, and play handball,
soccer, and basketball, mostly with other *Paisas.* Some Chicano
prisoners who speak Spanish well and want to avoid being pressured to affiliate with the California Mexican factions identify and
hang with the *Paisas.*

Some *Paisas* had been involved in drug trafficking on the outside and have connections with drug dealers. Consequently, they
get involved in drug smuggling and dealing in prison. This brings
them into interaction, and sometimes conflict, with other prisoners.

The administration recognizes and manages *Paisas* as a separate social group. For example, whenever there is a race conflict
and the administration must temporarily segregate or move racial
categories of prisoners, they deal with Border Brothers separately.[27]

Lifers. A growing number of lifers are accumulating in the prisons, and they constitute a social group and an active force in prisoner public affairs. Their numbers have increased because the California courts, guided by the dictates of new punitive laws, such as "three strikes, you're out," and the punitive spirit of the general population are sending more people to prison with life sentences. These lifers, who have sentences of 15 years to life, 25 years to life, life with possibility of parole, and life without possibility of parole (LWOP), are serving *much* more time than during any previous period. For example, before the current punitive era, which started in 1976, prisoners sentenced for first degree murder in California (as well as most other states) served an average of 13 years. Only one person with a life sentence for murder was released from 1999 to 2002. Many contemporary lifers have served 20 years or more. Consequently, the percentage of lifers in the prison population is steadily increasing. Short termers come and go, but lifers remain and accumulate in the prisons.

In 2001, approximately 20 percent of Solano prisoners were lifers. Most lifers have an indeterminate sentence, seven to life, 15 to life, or 25 to life. A minority are LWOPs. Those with the possibility of parole are serving time for first and second degree murder, kidnapping with bodily injury or robbery, and a "third strike," that is, a third felony conviction after two convictions for "serious felonies."[28]

As their numbers have increased, lifers have become an important force in the informal social organization of prisoners. Lifers have always been relatively less troublesome for management. In earlier periods, when the number of lifers was smaller, most other prisoners, who were serving *much* shorter sentences, usually respected lifers, left them alone but shoved them aside as unimportant actors in the prison social order. However, now that they constitute one-fifth of the prison population, they are too prominent to ignore.

Lifers know the law, the prison rules, and the ropes better than anyone else. Some of them have become convict legal experts—"writ writers"—who file petitions and lawsuits for themselves and help other prisoners with theirs. They know and are known by many of the staff, particularly the sergeants, lieutenants, and even the wardens, some of whom they have been around for years. In regard to prisoner relationships to individual staff members, lifers, compared with other prisoners, have a better idea of what to watch

out for, what they can get away with, and what special consider-
ations they can obtain.

In addition, as the years go by, lifers become more acquainted
with each other and increasingly pull together, forming a social
network. This friendship network extends across racial and age
boundaries. Lifers don't necessarily hang together like cars of
homeboys. But they do know, respect, and to some extent cooperate with each other. Consequently, they are an important presence
in the convict world and constitute a body of elder statesmen. They
are sought out for advice and relied upon as go-betweens in conflicts between prisoners and between prisoners and staff.

Prison Adaptive Modes

Time in prison passes no matter what a prisoner does, but only
the most passive or mentally deficient prisoners let time just pass.
They *do* time. Most set goals, make plans, lay out strategies. First,
however, they must cope with the prison, which to most entering
prisoners is a strange, threatening world.[29] In the first several
weeks or months of their imprisonment, prisoners focus on getting
settled into the prison routine. A lifer looked back 16 years to his
first days in Folsom, where he began his sentence:

> I was a young guy and I didn't have *any* experience with criminals
> and convicts. They put me in the fish row in Folsom. I was there for
> about a week, in my orange jump suit. I would look out my cell and
> see all these guys who looked pretty menacing to me. I was scared
> shitless. I didn't know what was going to happen.[30]

Even new prisoners with considerable previous experience with
jails and other lockup situations worry about how they will get by in
prison. Edward Bunker, who had been in many youth institutions,
was intimidated by San Quentin when he started his first adult sentence there:

> The last time I had gone to school, I was ten years old. In reform
> school we were supposed to go to school for a half day, but I was al-
> ways in lockup for one thing or another, fighting another kid or the
> Man. I couldn't do that here. The walls had eaten tougher men than
> me.... Without anyone telling me, I knew that anyone too tough to
> handle would simply be killed.[31]

Each time prisoners return to prison or are transferred to another prison—which, in the new large prison systems, happens frequently—they face some difficulties fitting into the new setting.

The fish's (new prisoner) first concern is the other people he has to deal with—the guards and convicts. I wrote about my initial concerns about getting along with other convicts:

> [F]irst of all I had to deal with the world of convicts. This was different than entering high school or moving to a new town or neighborhood, even different than going to jail. In fact it is different than any other world. It contains a distinct and distorted sample of the general population. More than anything else, more than an asylum for criminals, it is a receptacle for society's most bothersome misfits. Most of the prisoners are a collection of unskilled, disorganized poor slobs who stumbled around in their communities or through the country, causing minor problems, bothering or menacing people with a variety of petty crimes and finally getting into enough trouble to get "sent up." But mixed in with this mass of "hoosiers" (as they were derogatorily labeled by hipper convicts) were a lot [of] cons you would really want to stay clear of—rank assholes, stool pigeons, punks, predators, 33rd degree weirdos, real lunatics, shit eaters (I mean literally, guys who eat shit), and a few bona fide killers. Balancing out this sorry melange were some of the most interesting, creative and intelligent individuals one could find anywhere. So along with the expected social trash, the prison receives and holds a lot of special, even in many ways admirable, people whose energies are so intense, though perhaps warped, conventional people won't allow them in their midst. If they were around today, heroes from former times, such as Daniel Boone, Davy Crocket, Jeramiah Johnson, with no frontier to stomp around in, would probably have to be kept in prison.[32]

In addition to the other cons and guards, the fish has to deal with the rules and the informal norms and patterns. Prisons are small, isolated societies with unique social mores, status systems, taboos, and idiosyncrasies. "Learning the ropes" in prison is as difficult as integrating into a foreign country.

> The way I had learned to proceed in this strange land was play it cool and move out into the prison society with great caution. Don't

jump into new friendships. Confine your interaction to your homies, if any were available, or guys you had already got to know in jail or the guidance center. Then after you had time to get the full "drawings" on a guy and had thoroughly tested him for the intolerable personal attributes—being an informer, an untrustworthy slime, a predator, or a homosexual—then you might make a new friend. It was alright to be friendly with some of the well-respected homosexuals—usually queens, who were open, more audacious, and therefore more interesting than the punks, who most prisoners believed were just weak individuals who had been forced into homosexuality in prison. But you wouldn't want to hang with one, because you would certainly get a "jacket" (label) as a homosexual yourself and this would be bothersome in that guys would be hitting on you all the time and you would probably get into a lot of fights because of it.[33]

Once prisoners are settled in, they tend to follow one of several dominant modes of adapting to prison life. Some plunge into "the mix."[34] Others settle down and just do their time in a manner that maximizes their comfort and safety (particularly from the danger of violence from other prisoners) and keeps them out of trouble with prison staff. A few withdraw as much as possible, avoid interaction with other prisoners, and stay to themselves. A minority of prisoners become seriously involved in self-improvement activities.

The Mix

A sizable number of prisoners, up to one-third of the population, actively participate in prisoner "public" activities—the mix. This is especially true of state-raised prisoners, gangbangers, and thugs. Their particular criminal orientation leads them to this style of prison adaptation. It is also more true of short-termers—"summer campers" and "churners." "These short-termers, all they do is fuck around all day, get into shit. They think they're at summer camp. They know they're going home soon, so they're just having a good time. They're young and dumb. They don't know any better."[35]

Some long-termers, and even lifers, will, at the start of their prison sentence, engage in the mix. However, they usually eventually steer away from the prison public life and take up one of the other modes, that is, if they have not gotten heavily involved in a gang or developed a highly visible and esteemed position in the prison public social organizations. "When I first came to the joint I was into a lot shit, gambling, banging a little. I didn't realize how much time I had to do and I was young, just off the streets. After a couple of years I starting realizing I was going to be here awhile and I better get my shit together."[36]

In general, when prisoners in the mix are not in their cells or at work assignments, they spend most of the hours in the dayrooms or on the yard, hanging, playing games, working out, "jiving," scheming, hustling, gambling, or conniving with their prisoner partners, buddies, or homies. Their activities are mostly uncomplicated and benign. They watch TV, play games, engage in sports, walk the yard, or sit or stand around with their friends—their car—and bullshit. A few persist in "banging"—organizing or joining gangs. As I mentioned earlier, most gang activity has been quashed by transfers or the threat of transfers of gang members to the supermax prisons. However, many younger, state-raised prisoners, thugs, and gangbangers persist in attempting to carry on gang activities in middle-range prisons such as Solano. "They still got gangs here, but they have to stay underground. They can't be open with it or they'll get rolled up. Some of the older guys, ABs and EMEs, still keep their affiliation, but they have to be real careful if they want to stay here."[37]

If the administration identifies a prisoner as a gang member and believes that he has engaged in serious rule breaking, such as attacking other prisoners or smuggling drugs, the prisoner will be "locked up" for a period of time, placed in the local segregation unit, or transferred to a supermax prison. On one of my visits to Solano, one of the Level III sections was locked down. When I asked members of my study group what happened, they informed me that some "Nazi skinheads started some shit." A few young, white prisoners who were identified as members of a new gang, Nazi skinheads, were bunched up on the yard and threatening to gang up on some black prisoners. They were rounded up and placed in segregation.

Most persons in the mix are involved in some rule breaking and illegal activities. Many gamble; a few take bets. Some persistently make prison wine, which they produce with any liquid containing sugar by letting it ferment for a few days. In every housing unit, there are one or a few persons who regularly trade commodities for profit. The commodities are generally items bought from the canteen and stored up by "merchants." Some are contraband items, such as food from the kitchen, ingredients for making wine, or material for tattooing. A few prisoner tattoo artists, using homemade devices, tattoo other prisoners. Consequently, many prisoners, particularly thugs, corner boys, state-raised, and gangbangers, have elaborate, "joint" tattoos over large areas of their torsos. The craft and artfulness of these tattoos are much improved over the prison tattoos in earlier periods.

Same-sex practices are very subdued and covert. A few queens (overt homosexuals) circulate freely in the population and are tolerated by the administration and other prisoners. Sexual assaults are extremely rare, and the open pairing of jockers and punks, which was prevalent in earlier periods, has virtually disappeared. One lifer, who served time at San Quentin and Folsom before coming to Solano six years ago, thinks that AIDS changed sexual practices in the prison: "I think AIDS made guys leery. As soon as it appeared you stopped seeing cons with their kids walking around. I think guys who used to fuck a punk once in awhile got worried."[38] Before AIDS, a small percentage of convicts, perhaps 15 percent, engaged in homosexual practices. Now it is even less.[39]

Other prisoners, many of them addicts or drug abusers, attempt to get drugs smuggled into the prison for their own use or to sell. Drugs, mostly crank (methamphetamine), cocaine, and heroin (because they are less bulky than marijuana), are hidden in packages mailed to prisoners by friends or family members, smuggled in by visitors, or carried in by officers and other staff. The prison administration vigilantly attempts to prevent drug smuggling, and when it discovers a source, it eliminates it. Some prisoners who have a strong urge to use drugs, time on their hands, and a willingness to take risks constantly invent new methods to obtain drugs.

To obtain drugs, prisoners sometimes use cash, usually obtained from their visitors. More often, though, they make cash transactions through outsiders, who purchase drugs directly, pay smugglers, or deposit money in the prisoners' prison accounts. Those prisoners who deal with cash, usually $20 bills, must hide their money in some secure place to which the prisoner has access. Some prisoners hide money in "keister stashes," that is, in their rectum. If the drug is heroin, hypodermic needles must be

[handwritten margin note: Don't agree w/ this. Men won't usually report rape.]

obtained and hidden, again sometimes in the rectum. Because of staff vigilance and the vulnerability of being detected while high, the chances of getting caught are more than slight.[40] Being caught often results in transfers to higher, and therefore more punitive, custody, sometimes with new charges and more time to serve.

Because of the difficulty of smuggling drugs into the prison, the supply is very irregular. Further, prolonged availability of drugs quickly drains most of the prisoner clientele's cash or funds in their accounts. Many regular drug users go into debt, which greatly increases the threat of violence toward the indebted. Moreover, injecting drugs, which usually involves sharing needles, introduces the risk of HIV and hepatitis C infection, both of which are present in prison populations. Because of the risk and difficulties associated with obtaining and using drugs, most prisoners, even many who were regular drug users on the outside, avoid drugs on the inside.

Prisoners who enjoy "tripping" (verbal reminiscing, perhaps with a touch of mendacity or exaggeration) about drug use and many outside observers, particularly those with some investment in drug use (e.g., people in the drug treatment industry and prison staff), are prone to exaggerate the prevalence of drugs in prison. In a federally funded study of drug use in several California prisons, urine analysis of randomly selected prisoners was conducted at three Level III prisons, and only 3 percent of those sampled tested positive for drug use.[40] *Drug use in prison may not be as prevelant as we are lead to believe.*

Doing Time

Many prisoners see their sentence as something they must pass through, which they try to accomplish with the least amount of suffering and the greatest amount of comfort. But they keep their sights on their life on the streets after their release. To do their time, they (1) avoid trouble, (2) find activities that occupy their time, (3) secure a few luxuries, (4) form friendships with small groups of other prisoners while staying away from the mix, and (5) do what they think is necessary to get out as soon as possible.

To occupy their time, "time-doers" work, read, work on hobbies, play cards, chess, and dominoes, engage in sports, watch TV, and idle away hours tripping with friends. Though they may engage in a sport, such as handball, tennis, running, or body building, they tend not to hang out on the yard, where most of the prisoners in the mix congregate and most of "the shit happens."

They seek extra luxuries through prison jobs, such as those in the kitchen, which offer extra food, privacy, and increased mobility. Time-doers purchase goods legally or illegally in the prison market. If they have money on the books, if they have a job that pays a small salary, or if they earn money at a hobby, prisoners can draw up to $180 a month, which may be spent for foodstuffs, coffee, cocoa, stationery, toiletries, tobacco, and cigarettes. Or using canteen items, such as cans of soup or tuna, as currency, they may purchase stolen food from the kitchen or a few other contraband items that are traded in the prisoner sub-rosa economic system. Most important, they stay out of debt and away from other relationships that bring prisoners danger and "trouble." "That's me, man, I'm a time doer. I stay out of trouble. I got my job in PIA, I stay out of shit, stay in my cell a lot, keep my contacts down to my close partners. Work out, play a few games with my friends in the dayroom, and draw my canteen."[41]

Withdrawal

Throughout prison history, some prisoners have coped with their imprisonment by withdrawing. They shy away from public settings and avoid the activities of those prisoners involved in the mix, particularly the deviant, rule-breaking activities. They stay in their cells, confine their relationships to a few friends, and avoid the yard and the dayroom as much as possible. Some withdraw completely and isolate themselves from others. A few descend into psychosis or commit suicide.

In the past, prison administrators, fearing organized prisoner activities, encouraged withdrawal:

> The strategy of withdrawal has been encouraged and facilitated by prisoner administrations, which have always feared and hindered prisoner unity. The history of American prisons, in a sense, is a history of shifting techniques of separating prisoners. The original Pennsylvania prisons completely isolated prisoners. The Auburn system, which prevailed in the initial era of imprisonment in the United States because of cheap costs, employed the "silence system" to reduce interaction between prisoners and to forestall unity.[42]

During the 1960s and '70s, prison planners and administrators moved toward holding prisoners in smaller prisons and smaller units within these prisons. They also provided activities and channels to allow prisoners to escape "mainline" activities, such as clubs, self-help activities, and housing arrangements such as honor blocks. However, in the warehouse prison, with its emphasis on economy and security, prisoners are cut off from these historical escape routes. Withdrawal, particularly in Level II sections of the prison, with the crowded, open dormitories, is much more difficult.

> Man, I try to do a little writing and there is all this shit going on, constantly. Guys all over the place, making noise, slamming dominos down yelling "count this motherfucker." Cops shouting over the loud speakers. The TVs blaring. I can't concentrate. There's no place I can go to get away from it.[43]

Even when faced with the challenge of crowding in the warehouse prison, many prisoners still withdraw as much as possible. If they are in Solano's Level III sections, they go to work or stay in their cells. In the Level II sections, in which prisoners bunk in crowded dormitory-style alcoves, they avoid mixing with others as much as possible. If they are persons who feel extremely threatened, they seek assignment to protective custody sections, where most of the prisoners are pursuing a withdrawal strategy.

Sex offenders and square johns are among those most likely to withdraw. Long-termers, perhaps after many years of participation in the prisoner public activities, also withdraw. So do derelicts and crazies, who are mostly avoided by other prisoners. In writing about my own prison experiences, I commented on prisoners' attitudes toward crazies:

> In the case of most crazies, the other convicts just left them alone, maybe joking about them a little behind their backs, but generally being tolerant and passive toward them. There was one con in this category on my tier at Soledad when I first got there. He was a medium-sized black guy who never talked to anybody and nobody ever talked to him. In fact, you hardly ever saw him. But at mealtimes, when the wing bull pulled the bar and we filed out to go to meals, he darted out of his cell and came down the tier walking twice as fast as everyone else. He had little wire rim glasses that sat crooked on his face, and he stared straight ahead. If you were in his

way, he bumped you aside. Now, if a noncrazy did this, the fight would start, but with him, everyone just moved out of his way. "Pay the motherfucker no mind," was the attitude.[44]

Self-Improvement

An increasing number of prisoners choose to radically change their lives and follow a sometimes carefully devised plan to "better themselves," "improve their mind," or "find themselves" while in prison. Improving oneself may start on a small scale, perhaps as an attempt to overcome educational or intellectual deficiencies. The initial, perfunctory steps in self-improvement often spring the trap. Self-improvement activities have an intrinsic attraction and often instill motivation that was originally lacking in the prisoner.

In trying to improve themselves, prisoners glean from every prison source available. They read philosophy, history, art, science, and fiction. Besides this informal education, they often pursue formal education. Convicts can complete grammar school and obtain a GED in the prison educational facilities. They can attempt to learn a trade through vocational training programs or prison job assignments, augmented by studying trade books, correspondence courses, or journals. They study painting, writing, music, and other creative arts. There are some options for these self-improvement pursuits sponsored by the prison administration, but these are limited.

In the last several decades, a growing number of prisoners have turned to religion to find an alternative to their past life and a new identity for themselves. While Christian contingencies, some of them fundamentalist, Bible-thumping born-agains, have always existed in American prisons, other religions have appeared and gained popularity since the 1960s. The Black Muslims penetrated the prisons in the 1950s. (They enlisted the famous Muslim leader, Macolm X, while he was in a New York prison in the early 1950s.) The Black Muslim groups grew, then divided, and at present, there are several active Muslim factions in most large prisons. Native Americans have established themselves as having a viable and officially recognized religion. There are wired-off areas with "sweat lodges" on each of the four yards in Solano. The administration at Solano recognizes the following religious denominations: Protestant, Catholic, Jewish, Muslim, Native American,

Jehovah's Witnesses, Seventh Day Adventist, Church of Jesus Christ of Latter-day Saints, and Buddhist.

Hundreds of Solano prisoners have seriously embraced one or another of these religions and have greatly altered their prison behavior, self-image, and future plans according to the precepts of their new religious beliefs. Further, many of them associate with others on the basis of their shared religious beliefs and commitments. Religious conversion is a very important self-improvement mode in prison. A prisoner whose essay is included in Johnson and Toch's *Crime and Punishment: Inside Views* wrote of his religious conversion:

> Twenty-four months have come and gone since that evening when I cried out in desperation and asked the Lord to come into my life, and much has transpired. I have traveled very far in my spiritual journey, and with God's love I'm at peace with Him, as well as with myself. The growth and healing is ongoing as I continually strive for the mark. It is by God's mercy and grace that I sit here and type this essay, remaining firm in my witness.[45]

Religious conversion is consistent with prison administrators' perspective regarding the criminals' character and acceptable paths for their conversion into honest citizens and is, therefore, greatly supported by them. Of course, religious conversion requires a person to believe in religious dogmas. Many, perhaps most, prisoners do not and cannot accept these dogmas. Other versions of rehabilitation more acceptable to and consistent with prisoners' views of themselves and which promise them a successful future based on a mixture of self-determination, self-respect, and pleasure are not made available or encouraged by prison authorities.

Conclusions

Solano contains almost 6,000 prisoners, 27 percent of whom are serving 15 years or more. This population consists of persons with very different criminal orientations and who belong to different and often hostile racial groups. This heterogenous population is crammed together in crowded housing units and limited recreational areas. Their activities are greatly curtailed. The potential for conflict and violence among them is large. The type of solidary prisoner social organization that prevailed in earlier American prisons is precluded because of the divisions among prisoners. In the 1970s and '80s, prisoners had become violent and unmanageable. In the warehouse prison, as represented by Solano, there is still considerable intergroup hostility, but overall, there is a general détente among hostile groups. This tentative calm has been achieved because of the warehouse prison's design and the management strategy, which involves close scrutiny, rapid response to prisoner disturbances, and the threat of transfer to supermax prisons. Most prisoners withdraw, do their time, or pursue self-improvement. Some prisoners do participate in the mix, which entails some, but manageable, deviance, such as wine making and drug use, and the formation of cars and gangs. Though an ongoing warfare among Chicano factions continues, most of the disruptive and lethal gang activities of the 1970s and '80s have been curtailed. This peace has its price. The price is the supermax and the harm that this new high-security prison and the warehouse prison, itself, inflict on prisoners. I discuss these matters in the next two chapters.

Endnotes

1. With Donald Cressey, I argued in "Thieves, Convicts, and the Inmate Culture" (*Social Problems,* Fall 1963, pp. 144–145) that prisoners, particularly the criminally oriented "thief," carry preprison orientations that greatly influence their behavior in prison and the social organization of prisoners. This set off the debate over the "importation" or "indigenous" origins of prisoner social organizations.

2. Irwin, *Felon,* 7.

3. Ibid., Chapter 1.

4. I formed these criminal categories through interviews conducted in research over the last 15 years and in the present study of Solano. At Solano, I formed two groups of prisoner "experts," met with them regularly, and discussed these types over an extended time period.

5. Irwin, *Felon,* 23.

6. In an earlier study, James Austin and I interviewed random samples from intake populations in three states and categorized the new prisoners according to the seriousness of the crimes they had committed. We discovered that over 50 percent were sent to prison for petty crimes, that is, crimes that did not involve any significant amount of money, injury, or any other feature than would cause the ordinary cit-

izen to view the crime as particularly serious. See Irwin and Austin, *It's About Time*, 32–36.

7. Joan W. Moore and James Diego Vigil, both of whom have studied Los Angeles Chicano gangs, emphasize the social, pseudofamily, territorial character of the Chicano gangs. See Joan W. Moore, *Going Down to the Barrio*, (Philadelphia: Temple University Press, 1991), and James Diego Vigil, *Barrio Gangs* (Austin: University of Texas Press, 1988).

8. See Joan W. Moore, *Homeboys: Gangs, Drugs, and Prison in the Barrios of Los Angeles* (Philadelphia: Temple University Press, 1978), for a description of the interaction between prison and barrio gangs.

9. Moore, *Going Down to the Barrrio*, 3.

10. Rick Delvecchio, "Gang of Killers Stopped, Oakland Police Say," *San Francisco Chronicle*, 1 February 2003, p. A17.

11. Earley, *Hot House*, 76–77.

12. The first two categories, churners and summer campers, are seen as one category, short-termers, by most prisoners I interviewed. I divided them into the two, which were used as a useful distinction by some prisoners.

13. These percentages were calculated from data supplied by the California Department of Corrections Research Division, 2000.

14. The last three California governors have had a policy of not paroling persons serving sentences for murder, who are the majority of lifers. The parole boards have been correspondingly punitive. With few exceptions, lifers are not being released, though many have served more than 20 years.

15. These studies started in the 1930s with Hans Riemer's identification of the "right guys" and "politicians" as leaders of a prison community ("Socialization in the Prison Community"). Then Clarence Schrag identified more roles in the prison community ("Social Types in a Prison Community"). Gresham Sykes elaborated this type of analysis and described a "social system" with a variety of "argot roles" (*Society of Captives*).

16. See especially Sykes, *Society of Captives*, and Irwin and Cressey, "Thieves, Convicts, and the Inmate Culture."

17. The number of prisoners killed in violent incidents has declined from a high of 35 in 1972 (when the prison population was about 20,000) to 9 in 2000 (when the prison population was over 150,000). Solano has had no prisoner fatalities in the last 12 years.

18. Prisoner interview, Solano, April 2001.

19. Prisoner interview, Solano, April 2001.

20. In *Prisons in Turmoil* (pp. 58–60), I described the main prisoner groups in the 1970s prisoner social organizations as "tips" and "cliques." Tips were extended affiliations, like "crowds" in high school social

worlds. There were tips of people who were from the same location, who had been involved in the same type of criminal behavior, such as dope fiend tips, or who shared the same interests in prison, such as the handball tip. Cliques were groups of prisoners who hung out together. "Cars" are the new form of cliques. The concept of tip has faded. "Homies," prisoners from the same town or neighborhood, has replaced it somewhat.

21. There is a long sociological tradition of theorizing on why boys organize into gangs. See Frederic Thrasher, *The Gang* (Chicago: University of Chicago Press, 1963); H. A. Bloch and A. Niederhoffer, *The Gang: A Study of Adolescent Behavior* (New York: Philosophical Library, 1958); Albert Cohen, *Delinquent Boys* (Glencoe, IL: Free Press, 1955); Richard Cloward and Lloyd Ohlin, *Delinquency and Opportunity* (New York: Free Press, 1960); and Lewis Yablonsky, *The Violent Gang* (London: Macmillan, 1962). The indisputable fact is, idle young boys form gangs.

22. Vigil, *Barrio Gangs*, p. 39.

23. Ibid., 165.

24. Ibid., 166.

25. See Moore, *Going Down to the Barrio*, for the long history of the two major Los Angeles gangs—White Fence and El Hoyo Maravilla.

26. Evelyn Nieves, "Rash of Violence Disrupts San Quentin's Death Row," *New York Times*, 22 May 2001, p. A10.

27. In September 2001, there was a melee between Sureños and Norteños on one of Solano's four yards. The order "yard down" came over the loudspeakers. All the prisoners not involved in the fighting immediately sat on the ground. Officers rushed to the location of the fight and broke it up. After removing all the prisoners who were fighting and reestablishing calm on the yard, which took about an hour, the remaining prisoners were ordered to return to their buildings one race at a time—blacks, whites, Hispanics, and finally, Border Brothers.

28. A list of felonies are designated "serious" in the California Penal Code.

29. Robert Johnson and his mentor, Hans Toch, who have studied imprisonment for many years, begin their examination of prisoner adjustment with the question of how prisoners cope. See Johnson, *Hard Time*; Hans Toch, *Living in Prison: The Ecology of Survival* (New York: Free Press, 1977); and Hans Toch, K. Adams, and J. D. Grant, *Coping: Maladaptation in Prisons* (New Brunswick, NJ: Transaction, 1989). Johnson and Toch have in mind a set of ideals they summarize under the rubric of "mature coping." As stated by Johnson (*Hard Time*), mature coping is "(1) dealing directly with one's problems, using the resources legitimately at one's disposal; (2) refusing to employ deceit or violence other than in self-defense; and (3) building mutual and supportive relationships with others" (p. 13). Their analysis of pris-

oner behavior is mostly about how prisoners conform or depart from these ideals. I believe that individual prisoners would benefit if they achieved the ideals of mature coping. But to understand prisoner behavior, it is not enough to just evaluate their performance according to these standards. We must examine their cultural orientations, their group memberships, and the "packages" of ideas on how to adjust to prison that are carried by groups of prisoners with whom they interact and from whom they learn. For example, there are mature criminals who cope well within the prison but in a different style than mature square johns. Also, there Christian and Muslim proselytizers who teach their forms of coping. So, to understand how prisoners cope, we must examine these social and cultural phenomena.

30. Prisoner interview, Solano, 2001.

31. Edward Bunker, *The Education of a Felon* (New York: St. Martin's, 2000), 142.

32. Irwin, "Rogue," 210.

33. Ibid., 212–213.

34. Barbara Owen, in her study of a woman's prison (*In the Mix*), discovered this label used by women prisoners to denote the actively "public" adaptive style. Male prisoners have not adopted a single term or metaphor to describe the activities and relationships that the women refer to as "the mix." I have appropriated the term for both male and female prisoner activities, however, because it is convenient and suitable.

35. Interview with a lifer at Solano, fall 2001.

36. Interview with a lifer at Solano, fall 2001.

37. Prisoner interview, Solano, spring 2001.

38. Prisoner interview, Solano, spring 2000.

39. Over the years I have interviewed prisoners both in open, informal talks and using questionnaires. Estimates of from 10 to 20 percent involvement in homosexual activities are consistently reported.

40. In the year 2000, there were 42 "incidents," that is, official actions taken involving "controlled substances," at Solano. Fourteen of those were for opiates, 25 for marijuana (Department of Corrections Data Analysis Unit).

41. Response of a lifer at Solano after reading a draft of this chapter, spring 2002.

42. Irwin, *Prisons in Turmoil*, 202.

43. Prisoner interview, March 2001.

44. Irwin, "Rogue," 243.

45. Johnson and Toch, eds., *Crime and Punishment*, 118. ✦

Chapter 5

The Supermax

Since 1985, California has built four supermax prisons, three with Segregated Housing Units (SHUs).[1] These new prisons are the culmination of a long history of placing troublesome prisoners in special, high-security units within prisons. Solitary and segregation, previous prisoner control methods, actually increased control problems, which resulted in their increased use. The architects of new supermaxs were greatly informed by some of the custodial flaws of the earlier "lockup" methods. An examination of the history of solitary and segregation is necessary to understand the contemporary maximum security prison.

Solitary and Segregation

Solitary, along with many other, extremely cruel methods (such as flogging, water torture, and shackling prisoners to cell walls) for punishing and controlling the more recalcitrant prisoners, has been practiced by American prison systems since the beginning of the nineteenth century. After 1900, most prison systems outside the South eliminated the crueler forms of punishment but continued to confine prisoners in solitary—the hole—as a major form of punishment for rule breaking. In his 1940 study of a "prison community," Donald Clemmer described solitary confinement:

> The 24 solitary cells are in a small building known as the yard office. It is set off by itself and is heavily barred and isolated. The cells themselves contain no furniture. The one window is small, and the iron bars of the door have another wooden door which keeps the light from entering. The cells are cold in winter and hot in summer. The inmate is given one blanket and must sleep on a wooden slab

raised about two inches from the cement flooring. One piece of bread and a necessary amount of water is allowed each day.[2]

During the first half of the twentieth century, all walled prisons had solitaries. Some, such as the sweat boxes in southern work camps or the "dungeons" in San Quentin, were extremely brutal places. The unit Clemmer studied at Menard in Illinois was typical.

During that time, many prisons set aside sections for segregation of individuals whom the administration believed could not be allowed to circulate freely within the prison. This included open homosexuals and prisoners who persistently broke the rules or needed protection from other prisoners. Prisoners were usually sentenced to solitary for definite periods but "assigned" to segregation for longer periods, sometimes years.

As discussed in Chapter 2, the social order that was based on a cohesive prisoner social organization, backed up by the indeterminate sentence system, broke down in the late 1960s. New problems of disorder, particularly ethnic and racial militancy and interracial violence, increased, and prison administrators began developing new forms of administrative segregation to control an increasingly disruptive prisoner population. By 1970, California had established high-security "adjustment centers" at three of its major prisons—San Quentin, Folsom, and Soledad. When these failed to reduce the turmoil and violence, more sections of several prisons were converted into new segregation units—SHUs and "Management Control Units." By 1980, 10 percent of California's prisoner population was assigned to some form of lockup.[3] Illinois followed California's lead and established special program units (SPUs) at Joliet, Stateville, and Pontiac prisons in 1972. Other states soon followed California and Illinois in their efforts to isolate and control the most disruptive segments of the prisoner population.[4]

In the early years, California prisoners were assigned (not sentenced) to administrative segregation for their perceived status, such as being a persistent threat to prison stability, staff, and other prisoners. These prisoners were not necessarily charged with any specific rule violations. Although there were administrative procedures regulating the transfer of prisoners to such units, these procedures were often not followed or the assignments were based on subjective criteria. Administrators exercised virtually unrestricted discretion in assigning prisoners to lockup

briefly
discusses the history
of segregation Chapter 5 ✦ *The Supermax* **117**
and solitary confinement.

units. The lack of due process or the arbitrary way in which prisoners were assigned to segregation was not viewed as a problem because, officially, segregation was not intended as a form of punishment.

It was true that the prison administrators initially planned the physical structure of and routines in the segregation units so that they would not have any special punitive aspects. The cells in the first segregation units had the same furnishings as mainline cells—a bunk, mattress, toilet, washbowl, and sometimes a small desk—and prisoners were not intentionally denied other privileges beyond those that were impractical to deliver because the prisoners were restricted to their cells. Lockup prisoners could receive and keep about the same range of material and commodities as mainline prisoners. They either were allowed TV sets in their cells or could watch the television mounted in the unit. Their mail was not restricted. They received and kept books, although their access to the prison library was greatly restricted because of their lockup status.

In actuality, the new lockup units, even in the early stage when they were first introduced, were highly punitive. Prisoners were typically confined to their cell almost 24 hours a day. The official procedures called for them to be released for one or two hours twice a week to a small exercise yard adjacent to their unit, which had limited recreational equipment. In actual practice, prisoners were frequently denied these periods. Lockup prisoners were also occasionally escorted, sometimes by two to four guards, to other parts of the prison to go to the hospital, for a visit, or for other special functions, such as disciplinary hearings. Otherwise, they stayed in their cells.

Segregated prisoners lost access to the extensive programs and activities—schooling, vocational training, movies, libraries, and recreational activities—available to other prisoners in most prisons. They were prevented from socializing with other prisoners during work, dining, on the yard, and in the dayrooms and from engaging in a multitude of games, hustles, rackets, and other cooperative enterprises that prisoners undertook. They talked to each other through their barred cell fronts and even played games such as chess on the walkway directly in front of their cells. But by and large, prisoners in lockup units were cut off from the general, relatively full social life of the prison world.

Prisoners in administrative segregation were often ineligible to receive good-time credits either because of disciplinary violations or because they could not participate in the programs that rewarded prisoners with such credits. Because of good-time credits, most general population prisoners served about 50 percent of their sentences. However, being placed in administrative segregation greatly extended many prisoners' prison sentences. It is now common for some prisoners to spend virtually all of their prison sentence in administrative segregation and to be released directly to the streets from "ad seg."

It is true that prisoners held in segregation were somewhat protected from hostilities and assaults that were increasingly occurring among mainline prisoners. Their sacrifice for this increased safety, however, was tremendous. Moreover, hostility and violence eventually became more intense in the lockup units than in the general population.

Turmoil in Lockup

During the 1970s and early 1980s, the segregation units became extremely tumultuous and violent. This was primarily a result of concentrating the most recalcitrant prisoners in a situation of relatively severe deprivation. Many of these troublemakers had not conformed to the rules in the much less restrictive mainline and were even less willing to do so in segregation.

Since the 1960s, California prison administrators as well as those of other states locked up suspected members of any organization believed to be a threat to prison order. Suspected leaders of the Black Muslims were the first to be segregated, followed by other leaders of black religious and political organizations, such as the Black Panther Party. When gangs of Chicanos, African Americans, whites, and Puerto Ricans appeared, the suspected leaders of these organizations were also assigned to segregation.

As the use of segregation increased, more and more prisoners believed that they had been unfairly placed and held in the segregation units. Placement in segregation was an administrative decision made by a "classification committee." This decision involved minimal due process and, at best, a pro forma appearance by the prisoner at the classification hearing. When Illinois began using its SPUs in 1972, for example, hundreds of prisoners were " reclassified" for the Joliet SPU during a single weekend.[5] Prisoners were "heard" in hearings that lasted less than a minute. Frequently, the classification committee based its decision on hearsay information. Much information was supplied by informers, sometimes anonymously, or appeared in staff memos after staff persons had witnessed a prisoner interacting with known gang members. Even if a prisoner had not been involved in an action warranting discipline, he could remain in the units simply because of staff suspicions.

Racial hostilities ran high in these units, since they were filled with prisoners representing most of the prison gangs. In Illinois, the dominant prison gangs—the Black P. Stone Rangers, Black Disciples, Vice Lords, and Latin Kings—were constantly warring with one another for control. In California, the Aryan Brotherhood, Black Guerrilla Family, Mexican Mafia, and La Nuestra Familia were strongly committed to attacking members of rival groups. When the opportunity presented itself, such as when members of opposing groups were released together to the exercise yard, prisoners fought, knifed, and killed each other. In 1970, a fight between several white and African American prisoners housed in Soledad's Adjustment Center broke out as soon as the African Americans and whites in the section were released to the exercise yard together. A gun tower guard fired at the prisoners and killed three African American prisoners.

As lockup units increasingly became populated by gang members, they also became centers of turmoil. Prisoners engaged each other and guards in constant verbal attacks. A prisoner described his experiences on entering one of the first adjustment centers in California:

> [We] were transferred to Soledad Correctional Facility from "X" Prison. We were placed in the Max Row section, O wing. Immediately entering the sallyport area of this section I could hear inmates shouting and making remarks such as, "Nigger is a scum low-down dog," etc. I couldn't believe my ears at first because I know that if I could hear these things the officers beside me could too, and I started wondering what was going on. Then I fixed my eyes on the wing sergeant and I began to see the clear picture of why those inmates didn't care if the officials heard them instigating racial conflict. The sergeant was, and still is, Mr. M., a known

prejudiced character towards blacks. I was placed in a cell, and since that moment up 'till now, I have had no peace of mind. The white inmates make it a 24-hour job of cursing black inmates just for kicks, and the officials harass us with consistency also.[6]

In the San Quentin adjustment center, prisoners frequently rioted and broke up their cell furnishings, the beds, cabinets, and toilets. On these occasions, water ran out of the cells down the tiers onto the floors. The cell floors were often littered with trash thrown from other cells, and water ran out of them. To regain order, staff shot tear gas into the units and used stun guns or Tasers to subdue prisoners. In return, prisoners in lockup units constantly taunted and vilified their guards. They regularly threw any liquid material, sometimes urine and feces, on passing guards and occasionally assaulted and murdered them.

Not surprisingly, as these conditions worsened in the segregation units, guards grew more hostile toward the prisoners. They were deeply offended and angered by the revolutionary rhetoric delivered by some of the more politically oriented prisoners, in which guards ("pigs" or "the police") were excoriated. George Jackson was held in adjustment centers most of his 20 years in California prisons. In his widely read book, *Soledad Brother*, he wrote,

> The great majority of Soledad pigs are southern migrants who do not want to work in the fields and farms of the area, who can't sell cars or insurance, and who couldn't tolerate the discipline of the army. And, of course, prisons attract sadists pigs come here to feed on the garbage heap for two reasons really, the first half because they can do no other work, frustrated men soon to develop sadistic mannerisms; and the second half, sadists out front, suffering under the restraints placed upon them by an equally sadistic, vindictive society. The sadist knows that to practice his religion upon the society at large will bring down upon his head their sadistic reaction.[7]

Guards frequently responded by punishing and harassing lockup prisoners in every way they could. They delivered their own taunts and vilifications, occasionally beat prisoners, and regularly shortened, disrupted, or denied their authorized privileges, such as correspondence, exercise, and visits. Evidence of these practices was obtained in 1975 by the Federal District Court investigating the conditions in lockup units:

Two guards who used to work in the AC [adjustment center] testified in support of plaintiffs' allegations that guards have beaten, threatened, and harassed plaintiffs and other first tier AC prisoners, that prisoner reports are at times altered, and that AC guards have a stereotyped view of plaintiffs and treat them in a dehumanizing fashion.[8]

Some guards entered into conflicts between prisoner factions by aiding one group of prisoners against another or by setting up individual prisoners. For example, a white prisoner who was identified as being affiliated with the Aryan Brotherhood described his setup by a black guard:

> This black bull was escorting me back to my cell in Max B [a section of the adjustment center] and he stopped and handcuffed me to the rail on the row housing black prisoners and said he would be right back. Then he went and unlocked the row to let all the black dudes out to exercise. As they passed by me, they kicked me, spit on me and punched me. Then he came back and put me in my cell.[9]

Sometimes guards set up prisoners to be killed or even participated in their homicides. In the 1970 fight and killings in the Soledad adjustment center yard, in which three black prisoners were shot to death, a Salinas, California, jury found that eight Soledad staff members had willfully and unjustifiably conspired to kill the prisoners. The staff had intentionally released prisoners into the yard who were expected to begin fighting. The gun tower guard, who some prisoners reported was leaning out of his tower aiming at the prisoners when the fight began, fired five shots, hitting each of the three black prisoners in the middle of their torsos. After the shootings, the guards took more than 30 minutes to carry one mortally wounded prisoner to the hospital even though it was adjacent to the adjustment center.[10]

As the turmoil continued through the late 1970s and early 1980s, guards and the administration steadily reduced the privileges in the adjustment centers until the distinction between the former punitive solitary units and the nonpunitive adjustment centers had all but disappeared. A psychiatrist, appointed in 1980 by the Northern California federal district court to examine the adjustment center unit in San Quentin, commented on the conditions he found there:

When I walked through Security Housing Unit 2 at San Quentin
and heard constant angry screaming and saw garbage flung an-
grily from so many cells, I felt like I was in a pre-1793 mental asylum, and the excessive security itself was creating the madness.
While the mainline playing fields at San Quentin are large and
grassy, the various security units are small and paved. Prisoners
are not allowed any furniture (desks, chairs, etc.) and are prevented by regulations from even draping their cells with blankets
to improve insulation against cold winds. Deprived of most
expectable human means of expressing self, prisoners are left with
a meager token of wall decorations.[11]

Rather than locations where prisoners were incapacitated and
pacified in a controlled but humane setting, lockup units became the
most dangerous (for both prisoners and staff), punitive, and deleterious settings in American prisons. In 1986, a California Department
of Corrections Task Force examining the effectiveness of measures
to control gang violence in California special housing units reported
the high rates of violence in Folsom and San Quentin lockup units:

> A closer look at two of the three institutions with the highest rates
> of assault incidents in 1984 (San Quentin State Prison and Folsom
> State Prison) demonstrates that the institutional rate is strongly im-
> pacted by high rates of violence in special housing (lockup) units.
> Folsom State Prison, for example, had an institutional rate in 1984 of
> 7.26 assault incidents, this being the adjusted rate of its mainline
> units (5.8) and lockup units (17.5). In that year, the rate of assaults
> in Folsom's lockup units [was] almost three times greater than in its
> mainline units. Similarly, rates of assaults were much higher in San
> Quentin's lockup units (18.7) than in its mainline units (10.0).[12]

Robert Slater, who worked at San Quentin as a psychiatrist between 1982 and 1984, described the violence in that prison's adjustment center:

> Periodically, bursts of gunfire serve as unpleasant reminders of
> where we are. Occasionally, a prisoner is killed, maimed, or blinded
> by gunshot. Crude but effective spears, bombs, hot or corrosive liq-
> uids can, and are, hurled through the bars in either direction. In the
> summer of 1984, during a particularly violent period, the authori-
> ties in one of the lockup units brought together a Mexican leader
> and a Black leader, asking them to walk the tiers together to help

cool things down. They agreed to do this. While walking the tiers, a Mexican inmate threw a knife through the bars to the Mexican leader, who proceeded to kill the Black leader.[13]

New Supermax Prisons

The apparent failure of administrative segregation units to pacify prisoners and restore order to the prisons during the 1970s and early 1980s did not cause penologists to abandon the policy of concentrating troublesome prisoners in permanent lockup units. Instead, planners designed and constructed supermax prisons in an attempt to eliminate the features believed to have contributed to the breakdown of order.

The Federal Bureau of Prisons (BOP) first attempted to construct a high-security prison to house the most dangerous and troublesome prisoners in 1934 at Alcatraz Island, the site of an old army prison. Alcatraz, the "rock," was intended to house the most "desperate criminals" (such as "Machine Gun" Kelly and Al Capone) and the bureau's most troublesome prisoners. By the early 1960s, the federal prison authorities, particularly Attorney General Robert Kennedy, considered Alcatraz, which housed only 275 prisoners, an expensive failure and closed it in 1963. Its prisoners were dispersed among the other federal prisons, mostly Atlanta and Leavenworth, the two most secure prisons next to Alcatraz.[14]

In the late 1960s, the BOP constructed a new small prison in Marion, Illinois, as an experiment in behavior modification. The prison was built with a range of housing sections with varying degrees of security. The prison planners intended to house 350 prisoners who were supposed to work their way through the levels, increasing their privileges by demonstrating good conduct. In 1973, however, the BOP returned to the policy of concentrating troublesome prisoners in one place and began transferring them to Marion's "control unit." The BOP administrators continued to send more troublesome prisoners to Marion and reclassified it in 1979 as their only Level VI (highest security) penitentiary, designated for prisoners who, according to Ward and Breed,

1. Threatened or injured other inmates or staff.
2. Possessed deadly weapons or dangerous drugs.
3. Disrupted "the orderly operation of a prison."

discusses the problems with the Marion pris. sys. (supermax): lots of violence

124   The Warehouse Prison

4.   Escaped or attempted to escape in those instances in which the escape involved injury, threat to life, or use of deadly weapons.[15]

After Marion was completely converted to a prison for problem inmates, difficulties similar to those in California's lockup units occurred. Through the 1970s, tensions, hostilities, violence, and disruptions increased. In the early 1980s, the unrest reached new heights. From February 1980 to June 1983, there were 54 serious prisoner-on-prisoner assaults, 8 prisoners killed, and 28 serious assaults on staff.

The turmoil escalated further in the summer and autumn of 1983. In July, two prisoners took two officers hostage in the disciplinary segregation unit, one of whom was stabbed. In the following week, two inmates attacked two officers who were escorting prisoners from the dining hall to their cells. Prisoner-on-prisoner violence increased in this period, and most of the time, the prison was placed on complete lockdown status. On September 5, 1983, a prisoner assaulted an officer with a mop wringer and a chair. On October 10, an officer was assaulted when he tried to break up an attack by prisoners on another prisoner. On October 22, when three officers were moving a prisoner housed in the control unit, the escorted prisoner stopped to talk to another prisoner in a cell, then turned to face the officers, his handcuffs unlocked and a knife in his hands. He succeeded in murdering one officer. That evening, another prisoner was being escorted by three officers from one section of the prison to the recreation cage. With a key in his possession, he was able to unlock his handcuffs. He also possessed a knife. He succeeded in stabbing all three officers, one fatally. The turmoil in the prison continued for another month. Prisoners started fires, threw trash out of their cells, and continued to assault other prisoners and staff. Repeated searches produced weapons, handcuff keys, lock picks, hacksaw blades, heroin, and drug paraphernalia.[16]

The BOP finally instituted new, severe control procedures. David Ward and Allen Breed, who conducted a study of Marion for the U.S. House of Representatives, described the clampdown:

> New custodial procedures were implemented. All correctional officers were issued riot batons and instructed to carry them at all times. A special operations squad, known as "The A Team," arrived from Leavenworth and groups of Marion officers began to receive training in techniques of conducting forced cell moves and controlling resistant inmates. These officers were outfitted with

helmets, riot control equipment and special uniforms. A new directive ordered that before any inmate left his cell he was to place his hands behind his back near the food tray slot in the cell door so that handcuffs could be placed on his wrists and leg irons on his ankles. No inmate was to be moved from his cell for any reason without a supervisor and three officers acting as an escort. Digital rectal searches were ordered for all inmates entering and leaving the Control Unit along with strip searches of inmates before and after visits with the attorneys.[17]

As was the case in California, strategies to control troublesome prisoners greatly increased control problems. Because Marion had not been designed to hold the most troublesome prisoners, many of its features, such as open cell fronts, presented problems to the staff in their attempts to maintain complete control over recalcitrant prisoners. Many states then built new supermax prisons that were designed specifically to hold recalcitrants. These prisons were built to hold prisoners in small, secure, self-contained units. Ward and Breed, in commenting on the inadequacy of Marion's design, described the new type of maximum security prison:

> New generation prisons are generally comprised of six to eight physically separated units within a secure perimeter. Each unit of some 40–50 inmates, all in individual cells, contains dining and laundry areas, counseling offices, indoor game rooms, a wire enclosed outdoor recreation yard and a work area. The physical design of inmate rooms calls for only one or two levels on the outdoor side(s) of the unit to facilitate, from secure control "bubbles," easy and continuous staff surveillance of all areas in which inmates interact with each other and with staff.[18]

In addition, the cells in new supermax prisons usually have solid doors with a shatterproof glass window and an opening through which prisoners can receive their meals or be handcuffed without opening the door. While held in the supermaxs' small, secure units, prisoners can receive all essential services, such as food and medical services. This avoids the problems administrators encountered when they "locked down" an older prison, which greatly disrupted the delivery of essential services to prisoners. In addition, supermax prisoners held in their cells cannot throw things or assault guards, as is the case in the older prisons.

California has become the leader in the construction of super-max prisons. Other supermaxes have been constructed in Illinois, Nevada, New Mexico, Texas, and Minnesota, with many more planned for other states and cities with large jails (including Los Angeles, New York, and Philadelphia). The buildings in the new California maximum-security facilities have highly secure, "180-degree buildings." Three—Pelican Bay, Corcoran, and Tehacapi—have SHUs for prisoners "whose conduct endangers the safety of others or the security of the institution."[19] The SHUs have "pods" or "sections" that house fewer than 40 prisoners and cluster around a central control center from which heavily armed guards look down into the units 24 hours a day. The cells have fully sealed front doors to restrict the throwing of objects by inmates at staff.

The Pelican Bay facility, which was built in an extremely re-mote area in Northern California, is the most isolated, fearsome, and restrictive of the three supermaxes with SHU units. Built in 1990 at a cost of $278 million, it was designed to hold 2,080 maxi-mum-security prisoners, but soon became overcrowded with a population of 3,250. Within the prison itself, the SHU has the ca-pacity to hold 1,056 prisoners, housed in pods clustered around a control center. Each pod has two tiers of 10 cells.

Former California Governor George Deukmejian, when he ded-icated the new prison on June 14, 1990, stated, "California now pos-sesses a state-of-the-art prison that will serve as a model for the rest of the nation. . . . Pelican Bay symbolizes our philosophy that the best way to reduce crime is to put convicted criminals behind bars."[20] This prison has the most complete isolation of any prison since the early Pennsylvania penitentiaries. Not only does it impose severe isolation on prisoners, particularly in the SHU; the prison itself is extremely isolated from the urban population centers from which most prisoners come. Sixty percent of the prisoners housed at Pelican Bay are from the Los Angeles area, which is 900 miles away with no available air transportation. The prospect for regular visits from prisoners' families is extremely remote.

California is not the only state constructing supermax-type prisons. Oklahoma's new "high-max" unit is described in this way:

> Inmates housed in the "high-max" security unit will live 23 hours a
> day in their cells, with the other hour spent in a small concrete

recreation area with 20-foot walls. The space is topped by a metal grate. Theoretically, an inmate could move into the new cellhouse and never again set foot outdoors. The unit's first residents will be the 114 men on death row. The cellhouse also contains a new execution chamber.[21]

Oklahoma prison staff, representing a cross section of the penitentiary's employees, worked with architects to develop plans for the new unit. As designed, guards in the control room of each unit can eavesdrop on or talk to inmates in any cell at the touch of a button. The monitoring device was intended to reduce the number of attacks on prisoners, nip conspiracies in the bud, and protect officers. A corridor behind each cell run allows staff to work on or shut off water and power to each individual cell.

The *New York Times* described New York's new supermax in this way:

> The New York prison Southport Correctional Facility has the same mission: to take the worst prisoners. They will include those who have dealt drugs behind bars, attacked guards, even murdered inmates. At Southport, they are being kept isolated, shackled at the waist and wrists when allowed out of their 6 by 10 foot cells and made to spend their daily recreation hour in newly built cages.[22]

Doing Time in a Supermax

Talks about the set up of California supermaxes. Very strict

The physical layout of the new supermax prisons promotes control. Most of the prisoners in the California supermaxes are housed in 180-degree buildings. These building are divided into three sections by two walls radiating from the middle of one side to the far corners, as shown in Figure 5.1.

Two tiers of cells with solid metal doors, each with a small glassed window, are built along three walls. The elevated control room is located where the diagonal walls meet. From that point, protected by thick bulletproof glass, guards can observe every inch of the three separate dayrooms and each cell front. These guards electronically control the passage in and out of the building and the cells.

According to the official weekday routine, the mainline prisoners are released for breakfast at the "satellite" kitchens in each

Figure 5.1
Layout of a California Supermax Prison Building

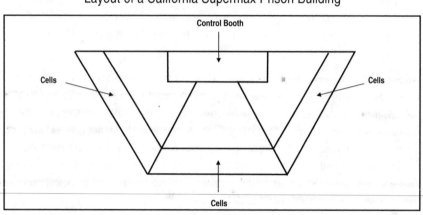

building at about 7:30 A.M., return to their cells for count, and then proceed to their assignments at 8:30. Most prisoners are assigned to work, school, vocational training, or prison industries. They return to their cells for lunch and count at noon, return to work at 12:45 P.M., return to their cells for afternoon count at 5:30, eat dinner in the satellite kitchen at 6:00, return to their cells at 6:45, and, every third night, are released to the dayroom for one hour and 45 minutes. There they play cards or board games at the few tables in the dayrooms, mingle with the other prisoners in their section, or make phone calls. Following this one hour and 45 minute period, all prisoners are locked in their cells for the rest of the night. Prisoners who are not assigned during the day and have the appropriate classification can be released to the yard for three and one-half hours in the morning and in the afternoon. On weekends, all appropriately classified prisoners may spend the day on the yard.

Social Organization

The point system that determines custody level assigns points for time left to serve. Consequently, all lifers start their sentence in a Level IV prison, and supermax prisons have a high percentage of lifers. Most nonlifers in the supermaxes are prisoners who prison administrators believe have a high potential for violence or who have actually been involved in considerable violence in the lower-custody prisons. This means that there is a high proportion of state-raised prisoners and gangbangers who were involved in the mix in other prisons where they got into trouble that resulted in their transfer to the supermax prisons.

The three prisoner-adaptive modes that prevail in the mainline in the supermax prisons are the same as those in the warehouse prisons—withdrawal, doing time, and being in the mix. In the supermax, a greater proportion withdraw. The institutional regimen is conducive to withdrawal. Prisoners are confined to their cells much more and mingle with fewer prisoners when they are out of their cells for meals, work assignments, or dayroom release than in the lower-level prisons. Consequently, they can more easily execute a routine of withdrawal.

Supermax prison regimens also invite doing time. Though the routine is more regimented and restrictive, there is some latitude for going about one's business undisturbed. A lifer who spent the first five years of his term at New Folsom, during which he was "just doing his time," described his daily routine:

0400–0800	I [work] as a cook in the kitchen preparing the food then cleaning the ovens or grill.
0800–0830	I leave work and go back to my cell and get ready for yard.
0830–1200	I would go to the yard and run some laps around the dirt track, when finished I would go to the small yard in the back and put in some work in the garden until they took the garden away from us. I replaced working the garden with playing basketball.
1200–1245	I would be locked in my cell for lunch.
1245–1600	Mon. Wed. Fri. I would stay in my cell and draw or do a different form of art work.
1600–1730	I wait in my cell for a shower.
1730–1800	Locked up for count and reading a book.
1800–1830	I continue to read a book.
1830–1845	I go in to the satellite dining hall for dinner.
1845–2000	I continue to read a book.
2000–2145	Every third night we would be given day room to play cards and use the phone, in which I would participate. Otherwise I would just watch TV.
2145–2300	I would call it a day and go to sleep.[23]

Participating in the mix is more problematic. There are few places and times to hang out, and there is much more surveillance. Still, many Level IV prisoners have a strong urge get into the mix. Some lifers, when they first begin their sentences, react by withdrawing. But many feel the pressure of a long sentence and search for something engrossing to do. Many get into the mix.

Public life in the maxiprisons is dominated by gangbangers, state-raised individuals, and the more criminally oriented outlaws and thugs. Consequently, there are relatively frequent violent outbursts between prisoner factions. The rates of assault and battery in these prisons are three to four times those of the lower custody prisons. Assaults on staff are two to five times more likely. The assaults, stabbings, and melees result in frequent lockdowns, during which all prisoners in a prison building or section are kept in their cells for days or sometimes weeks. Instead of détente, the mood in supermax prisons is one of high tension tinged with a constant anticipation of violence.

> But this place is crazy and I don't think its going to get better, most motherfuckers are doing all day [life], so they don't much give a fuck. Its like the wild west. Everyone hates everyone else.[24]

> Things are up to par here. The usual weekly fistfight or stabbing to screw off our yard. But even that is taken as a given here. If a whole week goes by people really get on their toes [smile]. I think we were on yard ½ hour when two blacks got to boxing. Two incidents last week. So when I go to the yard I get my exercise in quick and hope if the shit jumps off it's after I get my routine in.[25]

> On the yard, you always have someone to cover your back while exercising, when you get water or take a piss. Just the routine here. Hey, if not anything else, I'll be aware of my surroundings. I always have, but more so here.[26]

Among male prisoners in the mix, there is more open racial hostility, voluntary segregation, and active gang and clique participation than in the lower-custody-level prisons. Though most of the hard-core members and leaders of the older gangs—the Mexican Mafia, Nuestra Familia, Aryan Brotherhood, and Black Guerrilla Family—have died or are locked down in the SHUs, many of their affiliates or closet members still circulate on the mainline. Also, some new hostile factions are very active. Recently, Nazi skinheads, who are young descendants of the older Aryan Brotherhood, have engaged in racial violence, and the Norteños and Sureños continue to fight in the supermax prisons.

> Of the possible yard times, I've had 5. Lost one because some blacks were fighting. Back to regular program the next day. Then two whiteboys got into it ½ hour into yard. It looked like one had some type of weapon. Next day, back to regular program. Then day before yesterday a whiteboy got either stabbed or sliced coming in from yard. Everyone slammed today and word is regular program except for the whiteboys. The Mexicans just got off lockup after two months. There was a big fight between southern Mexicans and Bulldogs. See, all this shit is new to me. Bulldogs are from Fresno but they kick it with southerners and don't get along with Norteños (as it's said in Spanish) and they're from Fresno. What's wrong with this picture? All this blue rag, red rag shit started up after I came into the system. There was only the Mafia, Aryan Brotherhood, Nuestra Familia, Black Gorilla Family and it wasn't about where you lived they were from all over and really no set pattern.

> All the guys from the prison gangs are in SHU and won't see a mainline or they got hit with RICO and in the Feds. Or they are dead or dropped out.[27]

On the other hand, prisoners who have served time in Level IV and Level III prisons report that there is greater tolerance for minor rule infractions in the supermaxes:

> They leave you alone in New Folsom [a supermax]. It is like they don't sweat the small stuff. They're just glad your not stabbing somebody. If you don't get way out of line and cause a lot of trouble, they give you a pass. We were making wine every day and the cops just turned their heads.[28]

> What impresses me is how people are respectful here on this yard. It don't mean relax though. The cops are civil and respectful and that impresses the hell out of me.[29]

Another prisoner commented on rule enforcement at New Folsom:

> They don't play stupid games or put you in the hole for stupid shit. If you go to the hole it's for a reason. We're under the gun a lot more, and locked down more often then not, but I'd much rather be here.[30]

Life in SHU

The SHU at Pelican Bay is one of the most punitive prison environments in the United States. It is entirely automated and designed so that inmates have virtually no face-to-face contact with guards or other prisoners. For 22.5 hours a day, prisoners are confined to their windowless cells, built of solid concrete and stainless steel so that they won't have access to materials they could fashion into weapons. They do not work in prison industries, have access to recreation, or mingle with other prisoners. They are not allowed to smoke because matches are considered a security risk. SHU prisoners eat all meals in their cells and leave only for brief showers and 90 minutes of daily exercise. They shower and exercise alone in miniature yards of barren patches of cement enclosed by 20-foot-high cement walls covered with metal screens. The doors to their cells are opened and closed electronically by a guard in a control booth. There are no bars in the facility; the cell doors are made of perforated sheets of stainless steel with slots for food trays. Nor are there guards with keys on their belts walking the tiers. Instead, the guards are locked away in glass-enclosed control booths and communicate with prisoners through a speaker system. The SHU has its own infirmary, its own law library (where prisoners are kept in secure rooms and slipped law books through slots), and its own room for parole hearings. Prisoners can spend years without stepping outside the unit.

At Corcoran and Tehachapi, two California supermax prisons, each SHU building has a 1,577-square-foot, pie-shaped exercise yard surrounded by high cement walls capped by razor wire. Prisoners are individually escorted to the yards, strip-searched on entering and leaving the yard, and allowed to remain on the yard with a maximum of 15 prisoners for up to 4 hours. They are supposed to have 10 hours of yard time a week, but frequently this time is shortened or denied completely for a variety of reasons, such as lockdowns.

SHU Prisoners

California prisoners are assigned to SHU by an Institution Classification Committee (ICC) for the following reasons, according to the state code:

1. The inmate has requested segregation for their own protection and the need can be substantiated by appropriate staff.

2. The inmate is newly arrived at the institution and more information is needed to determine whether the inmate may be incompatible with any element of the general population. No inmate shall be involuntarily segregated for this reason for more than ten days.

3. The inmate has been found guilty of a disciplinary offense sufficiently serious to warrant confinement for a fixed term in segregation, and the term is fixed in conformance with the SHU Term Assessment Chart.

4. The inmate's continued presence in [the] general population would severely endanger lives of inmates or staff, the security of the institution or the integrity of an investigation into suspected criminal activity.[31]

The prisoner types confined in SHUs are, for the most part, hard-core gang leaders, dangerous crazies, young fuck-ups, "monsters," high-profile criminals, and unfortunate "bystanders." Hard-core gang leaders are most commonly individuals who were major figures in the original gangs—the EME, La Nuestra Familia, the Aryan Brotherhood, and the Black Guerrilla Family. These persons were identified as leaders of these gangs or have been charged with major rule infractions and crimes, frequently assaults and homicides. Some of them have stoically adhered to their gang identities and have endured years of lockup in SHUs.

Dangerous crazies are prisoners who repeatedly exhibit erratic and sometimes violent behavior. They may or may not fit into conventional psychotic categories, but other prisoners and prison staff recognize them as crazy and unpredictable. After a few violent acts, usually assaults on other prisoners or staff, they are assigned to SHUs.

Young fuck-ups are prisoners who follow a course that is opposite from settling down. They energetically and carelessly get into the mix and into conflicts, "jackpots," or trouble in prison. They are usually youngsters, many state raised, who are trying desperately to maintain "rep." They get involved in many of the deviant activities that are occurring in the prisoner society, such as gambling, drug use and dealing, and gang activities. The more reckless, rapacious, and violent of them acquire numerous disciplinary actions (beefs) and are sentenced or eventually classified permanently to SHU.

Monsters are persons held for long periods in lockup, during which they are subjected to extreme racial prejudice, harassment by the guards, and threats and attacks from other prisoners. They are converted into extremely violent, relatively fearless individuals, who conduct themselves as if they do not care whether they live or die. They frequently attack staff as well as other prisoners. Examples of this extreme form of recalcitrance abound. George Jackson, held many years in lockup, wrote:

> This monster—the monster they've engendered in me—will return to torment its maker, from the grave, the pit, the profoundest pit. Hurl me into the next existence, the descent into hell won't turn me. I'll crawl back to dog his trail forever. They won't defeat my revenge, never, never. I'm part of a righteous people who anger slowly, but rage undammed. We'll gather at this door in such a number that the rumbling of our feet will make the earth tremble. I'm going to charge them for this 28 years without gratification. I'm going to charge them like a maddened, wounded, rogue male elephant— ears flared, trunk raised, trumpet blaring. I'll do my dance on his chest, and the only thing he'll ever see in my eyes is a dagger to pierce his cruel heart. This is one nigger who is positively displeased. I'll never forgive, I'll never forget, and if I'm guilty of anything at all it's of not leaning on them enough. War without terms.[32]

Jackson, after he had succeeded in overpowering guards who had escorted him back to lockup in San Quentin and in releasing other prisoners in the unit, was shot and killed while running toward San Quentin's front gate. Some of the prisoners he released proceeded to murder two other prisoners and two guards in the lockup unit.

The two prisoners who each murdered a guard while being escorted by three guards at Marion in 1983 were fellow Aryan Brotherhood members who had been held in lockup for many years. They murdered the guards even though they understood that they would suffer severe, immediate, and long-term consequences. They were beyond caring about consequences or even their own lives.

In New York, Willie Bosket, who has served most of his life in prison and has been held in lockup for years, told the court that had just sentenced him to an additional 25 years to life for stabbing a prison guard:

The sentence this court can impose on me means nothing. I laugh at you, I laugh at this court, I laugh at Mr. Prosecutor, I laugh at this entire damn system. I'll haunt this damn system. I am what the system created but never expected.[33]

High-profile criminals are individuals such as Charles Manson and Sirhan Sirhan, who themselves are or whose crimes are so notorious that the prison administrators believe that it would be too risky to let them out on the mainline. It may not be that these individuals would commit violent acts, but they would invite acts against themselves from other prisoners who were trying to earn rep or who resented them. This would bring too much media attention and criticism for the administration's failure to protect these individuals.

Finally, many of the persons in SHU are there because they have been inaccurately identified as troublemakers and have been blamed for acts they did not commit. Many of these unfortunate victims are persons who grew up in neighborhoods or served time in juvenile prisons with other prisoners who became involved in the prison gangs. In the adult prison, though they are not core gang members, they have kept up their friendships with gang members and have been seen by prison staff associating with their gang member friends. These staff, particularly correctional officers, write memos in which they identify these prisoners as gang members.

> Tony Trujillo told that while at Soledad Prison he was informed that he had been identified "by a number of reliable informants" as a "high ranking gang member," a "shot caller" and "recruiter." He declared his innocence and offered to take a polygraph test, but was sent to Pelican Bay SHU anyway. During his SHU incarceration his classification as a gang member was reviewed at least six times. He filed inmate-appeals and finally sued the CDC. After three years in the SHU he was released and told "You were right all along."[34]

Other unfortunate victims or bystanders are individuals who are suspected but not guilty of having committed serious crimes in prison, such as homicide or drug smuggling. Once these bystanders have acquired a "jacket" or label as a gang member or a dangerous prisoner, they are closely watched, even harassed, and accumulate many disciplinary actions. They often end up in SHU.

I was in my cell and this guy I knew was standing in front of my cell talking to me. He was a dude who was always into something, drugs and shit. The cops saw him there talking to me and he got nervous and when they came over, he tossed a little bundle he had under my bed. They swooped in and busted both of us and I got sent to SHU for three months for something I didn't have anything to do with. He told them that it was his but they didn't give a shit. They busted me too.[35]

SHU Routine

Life in SHU is dramatically curtailed. Prisoners spend at least 22.5 hours a day in their cells. They are supposed to be released individually for at least 90 minutes a day to the small exercise area attached to their pod or section. However, many interruptions, for example, any unusually disruptive behavior in the pod or section, interfere with this normal schedule. SHU prisoners are occasionally shackled and escorted from cells for restricted visits, interviews with lawyers or appropriate staff personnel, and scheduled periods in the adjoining law library, which has a limited collection of law texts.

In their cells, prisoners in SHU bullshit with their cell partner, watch TV, read, write letters, do push-ups, fidget, pace, and sleep. Those in SHU for short sentences, 30 days to a few months, pass through this isolation and reduced activity without extreme discomfort and emotional damage. But for those who spend long periods in SHUs, sometimes years, the experience is excruciating and deleterious. The most pressing problem is to keep from "breaking down."

You watch TV, and you read. But most of all you write, write letters. If you have someone to write to, you can keep yourself together by writing them. You need something like this or you go nuts.[36]

Louie Lopez described his daily life in SHU at Pelican Bay when he testified in federal court:

It's like a living nightmare . . . like being put in a space capsule and shot into space. . . . I forget half way through my conversation what I was going to say. . . It's hard even to write letters. . . . It's like I'm falling and can't stop.[37]

Anne Sadler eloquently described the "SHU Syndrome":

> The "SHU Syndrome" identified by psychiatric experts during the
> trial is a common complaint of prisoners. They describe being de-
> pressed and overwhelmed by malaise and indifference. A certain
> mental dullness ensues that makes it hard to think or carry on a
> conversation. Many report irritability and anger, with frequent ep-
> isodes of yelling or cursing, even over trivial matters. Emotions
> can change quickly. Happiness, anger, or anxiety quickly crowd
> upon each other. There is also a lot of fear. The men worry about
> even minor changes in daily routines, like how the food is placed
> on trays or what time the mail comes or why a cell door on the tier
> below just opened. The fear extends to thoughts of the possible
> poisoning of the food or air by the guards. It is very hard for
> cellmates to get along for months and months. They spend a lot of
> energy just avoiding each other in the 8-by-10-foot cells where they
> spend at least 22.5 hours a day together.[38]

As suggested in Sadler's description, a major problem is coping
with one's cell partner. Most SHU cells house two persons. Though
the cells are larger than those in 180 and 270 Level IV and Level III
buildings and the bunks are not stacked, cell partners are in their
cells together at least 22.5 hours a day, day after day, month after
month:

> It got so everything he did irritated me. When he stood up and
> went to the door and peered out through the holes it irritated me.
> When he talked it irritated me, when he slept it irritated me. We
> were partners. I loved the guy, but I got so I couldn't stand being
> around him.[39]

Most SHU prisoners settle in, fight the monotony, do their time,
and struggle to keep themselves together without descending into
profound depression or psychosis. Others, though, stay active in deviant and disruptive behavior. A few of the committed gang members
attempt to pursue their gang activities. The ex-warden at Corcoran,
Bernie Aispuro, stated in a Declaration to the Federal Court:

> Prison gangs use the [SHU exercise yards] for such gang activities
> as the maintenance of internal discipline and cohesiveness; the re-
> cruitment of new members; the training in particular gang activi-
> ties such as modes of assault, modes of smuggling, weapons

manufacturing, and modes of passing messages; "schooling" in gang lore and discipline; passing the word with respect to past and future gang activities, the status of members and leaders of the gang, and other organizational information; and the planning of particular gang criminal activities.[40]

Prisoners with gang ties continue their disputes with members of other gangs (mostly through verbal attacks and threats shouted from their cells). A few powerful gang leaders, through their occasional and limited contacts with mainline prisoners and visitors, order prisoners on the mainline, released prisoners, or outside associates to carry out actions, particularly punitive sanctions against, or even assassinations of, their enemies and ex-gang members. As the leaders of the older gangs—the EME, Familia, Aryan Brotherhood, Black Guerrilla Family, Crips, and Bloods—age and the gangs become more and more disorganized, these attempts are less and less successful.

Some prisoners, particularly crazies and the extremely recalcitrant monsters, engage in an ongoing war with the correctional officers who oversee them in SHU. This war mostly consists of verbal assaults, insults, and threats, but occasionally there are attempts at physical attacks. A team of investigators who interviewed 39 SHU prisoners at Pelican Bay in 1994 described the disruption caused by crazies in SHU:

> Prisoners with psychiatric problems are placed in otherwise quiet pods in order to disturb the calm. These upset and often delusional prisoners scream and yell all the time. They bang their cups on the cell doors, verbally abuse staff and prisoners alike and even throw their excrement at anyone who walks outside their cells. A mentally ill prisoner is often left in such a state for weeks at a time, making life in the SHU pod a nightmare for everyone. Other prisoners become irritable and fights are more common when such a "psychiatric fuse" is placed in a living unit.[41]

In retaliation, some correctional officers have organized and executed extreme, often fatal, physical punishment against SHU prisoners they define as scum, animals, assholes, or troublemakers. Several guards at Pelican identified prisoners who were convicted of child molestation (Chesters), and passed this information to selected prisoners, who then harassed and attacked the Chesters:

FBI agents and state authorities have been investigating stories that a group of rogue Pelican Bay guards browsed confidential prison files looking for convicted child molesters. The guards allegedly shared the names of molesters, derisively called "Chesters" in prison slang. Guards allegedly encouraged predatory inmates known as "shot callers" to harass, attack or intimidate child molesters.[42]

At Corcoran Prison, groups of guards were accused of intentionally releasing prisoners who they knew would fight each other into the small exercise yard together. When the fight ensued, the guards purportedly watched as the gun-tower guard shot the prisoners. Between 1989 and 1995, there were 48 fatal and serious shootings at Corcoran. In the Corcoran State Prison hearings, California State Senator John Vasconcellos closed with the following:

> California correctional officers, on at least a few occasions, have shot and killed an inmate who was locked in a cell, in a fist fight with this cellmate, with no weapons in sight, no indication either inmate was in the act of gravely injuring or killing the other. No other state has done that.

> During the same five years (1989–94) California—with 100,000 inmates—has shot and killed more than 30 inmates, the other forty-nine states plus the Federal Bureau of Prisons—700,000 inmates—have killed a total of six. Of those six, five were killed trying to escape; of our 30, none was killed trying to escape.[43]

The Consequences of Lockup

It appears that the expanded use of lockup in segregation units like SHUs has, on balance, made prisons easier to manage. However, lockup certainly has had a negative effect on the prisoners who have experienced long periods of isolation in the various lockup units.

The Self-Fulfilling Prophecy

When individuals are treated as though they have certain characteristics, whether they actually have them or not, they are likely to develop such characteristics or have them magnified because of the treatment. This phenomenon frequently occurs when prisoners are classified as recalcitrant and placed in lockup units. Many persons who were minor troublemakers, or who were mistakenly believed to be intensely or intimately involved in prohibited activities (such as gang activities), have been placed in the lockup units where they have actually fulfilled the prophecy—they have become serious troublemakers or gang members.

Several processes accomplish this transformation. In the first place, many prisoners are frustrated, angered, and imbued with a sense of injustice when they believe they have been unfairly placed in lockup. As previously mentioned, the process of classifying prisoners to lockup is often based on hearsay. Administrators have always felt a great need to cultivate and rely on information supplied by informers. They have regularly accepted anonymous information ("notes dropped") and have often coerced prisoners into supplying information on other prisoners. For example, administrators usually require a prisoner who is seeking protection or is trying to drop out of a gang to name those who threatened him or were involved in prohibited activities, such as gang activities.

Administrators also have offered significant incentives, such as transfers, letters to the parole board, and placement in protective custody, to informants in exchange for information. Though some of the information supplied by informers is reliable, much is not.[44] The new forms of disruption that prison administrations have been trying to control through the use of informants erupted simultaneously with the loss of cohesion among prisoners and a weakening of the convict code, which dictated, above all, not to snitch. A new ethic based on the principle of everyone for himself, or "dog eat dog," has emerged. Informing for self-gain is consistent with this new ethic and has become much more commonplace. Prisoners even approve of falsely accusing others for self-gain. For example, a prisoner who was transferred from Soledad to San Quentin's SHU claimed to have been the subject of false accusations by an informer:

> I had this good gig, disc jockey on the prison radio, and this black dude wanted my job. So he told them that I was active in the AB [Aryan Brotherhood]. I wasn't. I got a lot of friends who were AB. But I've never been AB. I played a lot of Western music, and lot of

people didn't like that and didn't like me. The rat who snitched me out of the job didn't like my music. But really he wanted to replace me. So he told the man I was an active AB.[45]

The ICC also bases its decisions to assign prisoners to SHU on staff observations, some of which are of questionable validity. The following is an excerpt from the file of a prisoner who was assigned to lockup because of gang affiliations: "I observed inmate A talking to inmates B, C, and D on many occasions. They seem to have been involved in gang type activities together."[46] The highly discretionary and arbitrary nature of the gang designation is revealed in the following California correctional officer's description of the process:

> There's three, four, five different ways that they can be designated as a gang member. They're either northern or southern Mexicans just by birth. If they're from south of Bakersfield, they're going to be southern unit. If they're from north of Bakersfield, they're going to be Nostra [Nuestra] Familia. And that's just something that doesn't change. Now after that, you get associations. If, for example, we're talking about Nostra Familia, and that's the northern gang, and there's an inmate you know associates, has been observed by staff who's seen writings in his letters, if you can use two of the five or six different methods of validation, then you can call him an associate. Letter writing, another inmate telling you, admission of the inmate himself, staff observation, there's several ways to observe and two of the five or six different ways, I believe, will validate him as an associate. Then to be validated member, then I think it's four out of five or six, you have to be observed by staff, have another inmate tell you, through incriminating himself, he can tell you. Now, you may never ever take any of these vows or do any of their footwork or anything, but just because you hang with people from where you come, you associate with them. Once you've been validated as an associate, or validated as a member, then they can give you [an] indeterminate SHU term.[47]

Once in the lockup units, the prisoners experience the extraordinary deprivations inherent in lockup status and frequently witness or are subjected to additional abuse perpetrated by lockup guards who express their extreme racism and general hostility toward lockup prisoners. This harassment further enrages many prisoners:

One day when I got back from the visiting room, inmate M told me that the police had attacked W, a black inmate, while being handcuffed and taken to isolation. We protested according to their ways, and we threw some liquid on officer D, since he was the cause of W getting attacked. They came back and threw tear gas into our cells until we almost died—seriously—I had to wave a towel since I was choking from the gas. They told me that they wouldn't open the door until I got undressed, backed up to the door and stuck my arms out. I did just that. They handcuffed me and dragged me to the other side naked.[48]

Throughout the 1970s and into the early 1980s, the policy in many state prisons, such as Illinois, Texas, and California, was to locate suspected gang members in sections designated for a particular gang. This practice forced prisoners with no affiliation, or a weak one, closer to the gang for two reasons. First, a prisoner placed in a specific gang unit will be viewed as a definite member of that gang and, as a result, is subjected to the threats and attacks of other rival gangs. Second, if a prisoner is accepted by the other gang members, the dynamics of being held in close, exclusive interaction with them strengthens the bonds among them. Consequently, a prisoner with a weak or no gang affiliation is often converted to full membership to that gang by the lockup decision.

Psychological Impairment

Since the introduction of the first penitentiaries, in which prisoners were placed in complete solitary confinement, observers have concluded that isolation from others and extreme reduction of activities produces considerable psychological damage. Charles Dickens, who visited Eastern Penitentiary, the first solitary prison, wrote,

> I am persuaded that those who devised this system [solitary confinement] . . . do not know what it is that they are doing. . . . I hold that this slow and daily tampering with the mysteries of the brain, to be immeasurably worse than any torture of the body.

> My firm conviction is that, independent of the mental anguish it occasions—an anguish so acute and so tremendous, that all imagination of it must fall far short of the reality—it wears the mind into a morbid state, which renders it unfit for the rough contact and

busy action of the world. It is my fixed opinion that those who have undergone this punishment, must pass into society again morally unhealthy and diseased.[49]

Regrettably, only a few systematic studies of the effects of confinement in lockup situations have been conducted. In one, Richard McCleery found that prisoners held in lockup settings for long periods were very prone to developing paranoid delusion belief systems. Terry A. Kupers, a psychiatrist with considerable experience with prisons, provided expert testimony in a suit involving California lockup units:

> Certainly, patients I see in the community who have spent any length of time in Security Housing, Management Control or Adjustment Center units at San Quentin have continued to display irrational fears of violence against themselves, and have demonstrated little ability to control their own rage. I know from many psychotherapies I have conducted and histories I have taken, that even when a patient entered prison angry, the largest part of the fear and rage was bred by the prison experience itself.[50]

> Some of these men [prisoners held in lockup for long periods] suffer mental "breakdowns," be they schizophrenic, depressive, hysterical or other. A much larger number suffer less visible but very deep psychological scars. They do not "break down," but they remain anxious, angry, depressed, insecure or confused, and then likely cover over these feelings with superficial bravado. They might later commit suicide, or merely fail to adjust when released, and become another statistic of recidivism.[51]

Kupers summarized the psychiatric literature on the effects of lockup in the following statement to the court: "There is general agreement today in the scientific community that the stress of life in segregation is the larger cause of high incidence rates of mental disorders amongst prisoners."[52]

A Pelican Bay SHU prisoner puts it well:

> If you have not been informed of this new SHU program here in Pelican Bay, well, I think hell is a better place than this as it is built to break people. Since I have been here [one month] a man has gone literally nutty in the mind. What can you expect when you're isolated from all human contact? You sleep, eat, go to a yard by

yourself, go to classification just to be told that you'll stay in the hole until you parole, die, or debrief, rat![53]

The Northern California Federal District Court stated in its 1995 decision in a lawsuit brought by a Pelican Bay prisoner against the California Department of Corrections:

> Based on studies undertaken in this case, and the entirety of the record bearing on this claim, the court finds that many, if not most, inmates in the SHU experience some degree of psychological trauma in reaction to their extreme social isolation and the severely restricted environmental stimulation in the SHU.[54]

Social Impairment

All prisoners confront extreme difficulties in adjusting to outside life and achieving basic viability. One of the reasons for this is that they have become profoundly habituated to the prison routine, which is quite different from outside patterns, and have been imbued with various forms and layers of the prisoner perspective. Prisoners who have been held in lockup encounter greater difficulties because the routine in lockup is more rigid and abnormal. In addition, many or most lockup prisoners have been influenced by the more extreme and deviant viewpoints (for instance, that of the "outlaw") that prevail in lockup and suffer extreme anxiety and paranoia about living in a world of conspiracies, threats, and actual violence.

Most prisoners held in lockup are eventually released to the outside, often directly from lockup. A SHU prisoner made this point:

> OK. I've been in jail now eight years. Let's say I was going home tomorrow, do you mean to tell me I sit here for eight years confined in a cell resentful of things, chained every minute of my time inside my cell. And they say I am just too dangerous for anything but tomorrow they will parole me to the streets. Is there logic there? There is no logic there. The guy is paroled from these units, straight from the cells, straight to the situation, straight to the streets. How in the hell are they suppose to function out there? Is it possible? It is not anywhere possible. There is no decompression time, there is no re-orientation time or nothing. When I am paroled I will be paroled to

the streets, the outside to where you're at, you know what I mean. But in the meantime every time I see you, I will be sitting like this.[55]

We should be concerned that the prison systems are spewing out such damaged human material. Most will disappear into our social trash heap, politely labeled the homeless or the underclass. A few will violently lash out, perhaps murdering or raping someone, and then be taken back to the dungeon.

Endnotes

1. In the same period, California built six new Level IV—the highest security level—prisons and generally increased the level of security in most of the prisons.
2. Clemmer, *Prison Community*, 71.
3. See Irwin and Austin, *It's About Time*, 89.
4. By 1995, approximately 5 percent of the nation's state prison population was assigned to some form of segregation. See Criminal Justice Institute, *The Corrections Yearbook, 1995, Adult Corrections* (South Salem, NY: Criminal Justice Institute, 1995).
5. See Irwin and Austin, *It's About Time*, 91.
6. From a letter sent to the Prison Law Collective in San Francisco and distributed by them in 1975 in a document titled "Descriptions of O Wing Soledad."
7. George Jackson, *Soledad Brother* (New York: Bantam, 1970), 23.
8. Ruling of Alfonso Zirpoli, Federal District Judge, Northern California District, in *Johnny L. Spain et al. v. Raymond K. Procunier et al.*, 18 December 1975, p. 5.
9. Prisoner interview, San Quentin, 1979.
10. See Min S. Yee, *The Melancholy History of Soledad Prison* (New York: Harper and Row, 1973) for a complete description of the events and the court decision.
11. Terry Kupers, M.D., Declaration for U.S. District Court for Northern California, *Wright v. Enomoto*, 30 June 1980, pp. 5, 7, and 9.
12. California Department of Corrections (CDC), *Violence in California Prisons: Report of the Task Force on Violence, Special Housing, and Gang Management*, November 1986, p. 5.
13. Robert Slater, "Psychiatric Intervention in an Atmosphere of Terror," *American Journal of Forensic Psychiatry* 7, no. 1 (1986): 8–9.
14. See David A. Ward and Allen F. Breed, *The United States Penitentiary, Marion, Illinois: A Report to the Judiciary Committee, United States House of Representatives*, October 1984, for a complete description of this transition.

15. Ibid., 3.

16. Ibid., 7–9, describes these events.

17. Ibid., 11–12.

18. Ibid., 32.

19. California Department of Corrections (CDC), *Operations Manual,* State of California, updated through 1 May 2000, p. 581.

20. *Los Angeles Times,* 1 May 1990, p. A1.

21. *Sunday Oklahoma,* 24 February 1991, p. B16.

22. *New York Times,* 20 April 1989.

23. Schedule written by a Solano prisoner, spring 2001.

24. Letter from a prisoner in Pelican Bay, February 2000.

25. Letter from a prisoner in Pelican Bay, August 1999.

26. Letter from a prisoner in Pelican Bay, August 1999.

27. Letter from a prisoner in Pelican Bay, August 2000.

28. Prisoner interview, Solano, March 2002.

29. Letter from a prisoner in Pelican Bay, August 2000.

30. Letter from a prisoner at New Folsom, fall 1999.

31. *Operations Manual,* p. 581.

32. Jackson, *Soledad Brother,* 164–165.

33. *New York Times,* 20 April 1989.

34. From prisoners' statements made in 1993 in San Francisco federal court, *Madrid v. Gomez,* as reported in *Pelican Bay Prison Express,* no. 3, December 1993, p. 3.

35. Prisoner interview, Solano, March 2002.

36. Prisoner interview, Solano, April 2002.

37. Testimony in San Francisco federal court, *Madrid v. Gomez,* as reported in *Pelican Bay Prison Express,* no. 3, December 1993, p. 1.

38. Anne Sadler, "The Same, Only Worse," *Pelican Bay Prison Express* 2, no. 4 (May 1994): 1–2.

39. Prisoner interview, Solano, April 2002.

40. In Tony et al., *Melendez Longoria v. Robert G. Borg, et al.;* U.S. District Court, Eastern District of California, 3 December 1993.

41. Sadler, "The Same, Only Worse," 3.

42. Pamela A. MacLean, "Inmate Denounces Guard Who Shot Him," *Daily Journal,* 26 January 2000, p. 1.

43. "Closing Statement," *Corcoran State Prison Hearings,* chaired by John Vasconcellos, California State Senate, 22 October 1998, p. 3.

44. I asked a former director of the California Department of Corrections, who had worked for several years overseeing the classification process, how reliable he thought information from informers to be. He responded, "About 30 percent."

45. Prisoner interview, San Quentin, March 1983.

46. From San Quentin prisoners' files, read in March 1983.

47. Robert Schultz, "Life in SHU: An Ethnographic Study of Pelican Bay State Prison" (master's thesis, Humboldt State University, April 1991), 104.

48. From a letter written to the Soledad Defense Committee in 1971 and circulated in a document labeled "Descriptions of O Wing Soledad," p. 3.

49. Dickens, *American Notes*, 156.

50. Terry A. Kupers, "Authoritarianism and the Belief System of Incorrigibles," in Donald R. Cressey, ed., *The Prison* (New York: Holt, Rinehart, and Winston, 1961).

51. Declaration to the U.S. District Court for the Northern District of California, *Wright v. Enomoto*, 23 July 1980, pp. 5, 15.

52. Declaration to the U.S. District Court for the Northern District of California, *Wright v. Enomoto*, July 23, 1980, p. 4. Kupers specifically cited the following articles in reaching his conclusions: W. Bromber et al., "The Relation of Psychosis, Mental Defect, and Personality Types to Crime," *Journal of Criminal Law and Criminology* 28 (1973): 70–89; S. B. Guze et al., "Criminality and Psychiatric Disorders," *Archives of General Psychiatry* 20 (1969): 583–591; J. Kloech, "Schizophrenia and Delinquency," *The Mentally Abnormal Offender* (1968): 1928; D. Wiersnian, "Crime and Schizophrenics," *Excerpta Criminologica* (1966): 169–181.

53. Letter from a Pelican Bay prisoner sent to Prisoners' Rights Union, Sacramento, California, 1990.

54. *Madrid v. Gomez*, (9 F. Supp. 1149, N.D. California, 1995), p. 215.

55. Schultz, "Life in SHU," 153. ✦

Chapter 6

Harm

The *official* purposes of imprisonment do not include harming prisoners. However, as Todd Clear, a student of imprisonment, pointed out, imprisonment invariably does harm: "Professionals in the field of corrections are loath to admit that they are bureaucrats whose jobs it is to implement judicially decreed harms."[1] Robert Johnson, on the other hand, believes that the harm is unintended:

> There is much value in Clear's book, but it is, in my view, misleading to say that we as a society seek to harm or damage offenders when we punish them. Pain and suffering need not produce damage and, indeed, can be a source of moral education.... Moreover, the general thrust of modern prison practice is to minimize pain and suffering and, in my view, to avoid inflicting damage on offenders. Pain has become, in other words, a necessary evil we aim to minimize, not a policy of choice.[2]

It is not clear to me who "we as a society" are or whether or not people who have been or are involved in structuring penal practices have intended to harm prisoners. The fact remains that imprisonment does considerable harm to prisoners in obvious and subtle ways and makes it more difficult for them to achieve viability, satisfaction, and respect when they are released from prison. Some of this harm is directly related to the intended "pains" that are inherent in imprisonment. Much of the harm, however, stems from other features of imprisonment in which it was not intended. We will examine some of the main sources of harm in the warehouse prison, particularly as it occurs in Solano State Prison.

Health and Disease

The modern prison, including warehouse prisons such as Solano, is a good place to maintain general health because of the consistent routine, adequate diet, and absence or great restriction of many common deleterious activities, such as drug and alcohol use and cigarette smoking. Moreover, many male prisoners exercise regularly; some of them follow a strict workout routine.

However, the prison is a terrible place in which to cope with a serious ailment. The main reason for this is that the prison system does not have adequate staff or resources to deal with major health problems, such as heart disease, AIDS, hepatitis C, or tuberculosis (TB). Because so many prisoners have a history of intravenous (IV) drug use, HIV and hepatitis C infections are rampant in prison. Further, prisoner sexual practices and tattooing spread HIV and hepatitis C, and the crowded living in these institutions promotes the spread of TB.

State governments are unwilling to allocate funds to combat these prison epidemics because the clientele are convicts whose special personal needs rank at the bottom of the state's priorities. Julia Lusky, in an article on prison plagues (hepatitis B and C, TB, and HIV/AIDS and other sexually transmitted diseases), noted that

> the high level of disease among prisoners when they enter the correctional system presents the authorities with two clear options: intervene to treat those who are ill and to arrange for treatment to continue when the person leaves prison—or let the infections fester and spread.[3]

The inadequate prison medical delivery system is one in which prisoners have difficulty or find it impossible to obtain adequate medical treatment. When a medical condition presents, prisoners must first get past a screening process to see a doctor. At Solano, as at most prisons, prisoners must first see a Medical Technical Assistant (MTA), a correctional officer with a small amount of special training in medical issues who acts as a screening agent. Most MTAs share the general prison staff's cynicism regarding prisoner motivations and honesty and automatically deflect most prisoners' requests for medical attention. As one prisoner I interviewed put it: "Man, you can't get by those motherfucking MTAs. They think everyone is trying to bullshit them and you have to be fallen down, half dead, before you can get by them."[4]

If prisoners with a serious medical problem succeed in obtaining an appointment with one of the prison's physicians, the chances are still great that they will not receive adequate medical treatment. A Pelican Bay prisoner confided, "I kept complaining about my hernia and the best they would do is give me a hernia belt that I never got."[5]

There are several reasons for this, all related to the fact that prisoners' health is a low priority in the state administration's list of concerns, and therefore insufficient funding is allocated. First of all, many prison physicians are not as highly trained, current in their medical knowledge, or dedicated to their practice as physicians practicing on the outside. Prison doctors are frequently older, retired military doctors who are not highly motivated, highly trained, or current with medical advances. Moreover, these physicians are more likely to be general practitioners than specialists. If a specialist is required, access to one is limited.

In addition to dealing with issues of medical treatment quality, availability, and costs in the face of escalating health problems in prison (i.e., HIV, TB, and hepatitis C), the Department of Corrections has greatly restricted some treatments offered prisoners. In 2001, they stopped treating many prisoners infected with hepatitis C with the drugs interferon and ribarvirin because of the tremendous costs.[6]

Anthony Crane, a prisoner at Solano, wrote about the mishaps that beset one prisoner when he sought medical treatment for his injured penis:

> Probably the medical care not afforded inmates is the most discussed irritation amongst prisoners. Actually, given the number of people in California prisons, the institution in general, and the medical department specifically, when it is able, does its best to administer needed medical assistance to inmates. Hiring and retaining qualified personnel [are] at the root of the problem of poor medical assistance, as in the case of Mr. Fields.

> Mr. Fields is an elderly man who has been locked away for the better part of fourteen years. Although the remnants of his youthful spirit still shine through his age-altered exterior, he unfortunately is the victim of numerous ailments characteristic of people of his not so golden years of sixty.

It all began when the authorities transferred him from a northern prison to the southern facility of Chino. Mr. Fields usually takes his showers at night, but uncomfortable from his long journey, he decided [to] take one upon his arrival that morning. Unfamiliar with the facility's showers, he turned the water on, and got in to wet himself, before stepping out to lather. With a face full of soap, he stepped back in, but the temperature of the water had changed to scalding hot. Mr. Fields claims it nearly burnt the head of his penis off. As the story unfolds, he implored the building officer to call for medical assistance.

Mr. Fields' supplications fell upon deaf ears, until he wrote a request to the medical department to be seen. Seven days later, upon the viewing of an obvious burn, the physician diagnosed him as having a venereal disease, and promptly prescribed penicillin shots. One to be administered then, and two more within the next two weeks to follow.

"Well, what the heck," Mr. Fields said. "At least the penicillin [will] clear up the infection."

Everything was coming along fine until the last injection. Mr. Fields dropped his trousers and leaned across the table to receive his last shot, while the nurse babbled about it being her first day on the job. Extremely irritated, he thought it better to just get the shot and get it over with. Well, as fate would have it, she broke the needle off in his behind. She panicked and ran off, leaving Mr. Fields groaning in pain, while she tried to find help. For the next hour, two other medical technicians tried to remove the needle, but it was too deeply embedded into his buttocks.

Mr. Fields limped around the yard for the next month pending a scheduled surgery to remove the needle from his sciatic nerve. The only conversation anyone could get out of him was the amount of excruciating pain he was suffering from the needle embedded in him.

Finally, he was taken to the medical clinic for an X-ray before surgery. Somehow an X-ray of the prostate of another inmate was mistakenly introduced into his file. Unbeknownst to Mr. Fields, he was scheduled for prostate surgery, but in the meantime prostate medication was prescribed for him until the surgery.

Poor Mr. Fields just couldn't seem to win. The medication caused him chest pains and shortness of breath, and he swelled up like a balloon. He complained of the swelling and that he was having an adverse reaction to the medication, and was told by another medical technician that all he needed was to lose some weight.

Well three weeks ago Mr. Fields was chained and taken to the institutional hospital. When I saw him again he was walking around on crutches mumbling to himself. After greeting him, he explained that he was under anesthesia before they discovered he didn't have a prostate problem. Looking down at this hospital slipper, I asked him why his big toe was bandaged. He chuckled and said although they didn't operate on his prostate while he was under anesthesia, they'd elected to operate on his in-grown toenail, and circumcised him. I couldn't figure for the life of me why they'd circumcised him. Maybe it was because of the burn. During the remainder of the conversation he said that the medication the physician had prescribed for pain, made his stool as hard as a rock. Now when he grunted, his penis and his big toe ached.

We laughed, me more so because of the humor involved; him, to keep from crying. I asked him if he should notify the doctor about the problems he was having with his medication. He just sat there for a minute before taking a deep breath and turning to me. "No. Besides," he said, "next time they might castrate me."

Mr. Fields' medical fiasco is one of the many stories until now untold about prison health care. There are many more, but unfortunately [the patients] took their respective stories with them to their graves.[7]

It is probably true that many, perhaps most, prisoners with serious medical problems would not have received better medical care if they had not been sent to prison. Most of them were poor and living chaotic lives on the outside with conditions related to medical neglect. However, in prison they have no other means to acquire medical help, so when they are denied treatment, they feel trapped and hopeless.

Psychological Damage

Imprisonment can offer individuals a psychologically beneficial "respite." I argued, in *Prisons in Turmoil*, that most prisoners were caught in somewhat destructive social webs or were being swept along out of control, careening and ricocheting through the days. Imprisonment affords these persons a respite from their involvements, during which they can extricate themselves from destructive dynamics, sort through their values and beliefs, pull themselves together, and make new plans and preparations for a new effort at life. The longer the respite lasts, the more likely it becomes that prisoners drift into special prison-nurtured belief systems and lose subtle skills required to function in the outside world.[8]

In addition to the well-recognized consequences of imprisonment labeled "prisonization," long imprisonment, particularly in the new warehouses, assaults and disorganizes the personality in other insidious and subtle ways, including loss of agency, assaults on self, and damage to sexual orientation.

Loss of Agency

Agency is "the capacity, condition, or state of acting or exerting power."[9] Prisoners steadily lose their capacity to exert power and control their destiny as they serve time in prison. Prison life is completely routinized and restricted. The following is an example of the way a prisoner's day is laid out for him or her:

Weekday	
6:00 A.M.	Breakfast
6:30–7:00 A.M.	Stand in front of education building and wait for work
7:00–10:30 A.M.	Work
10:30–11:00 A.M.	Break time on the yard
11:00–11:30 A.M.	Lunch in the cell
11:30 A.M.–2:00 P.M.	More work
2:00–3:30 P.M.	Recreation (yard or dayroom)
3:30–6:30 P.M.	Lockup
6:30–7:00 P.M.	Dinner
7:00–8:00 P.M.	Lockup
8:00–8:45 P.M.	Night yard or dayroom
8:45–9:30 P.M.	Dayroom or lockup
9:30 P.M.	Lockup until breakfast

Weekend

6:30–7:00 A.M.	Breakfast
7:00–8:30 A.M.	Lockup
8:30 A.M.–noon	Yard or dayroom
Noon–1:30 P.M.	Lockup
1:30–3:30 P.M.	Yard or dayroom
Rest of day	Same as weekday[10]

This type of routine is followed week after week, month after month, year after year, with occasional deviations. A Solano lifer wrote about his world, the prison:

> In my world, I can't choose what I want to eat, when I want to sleep, or when I want to do anything. Everything I do is planned each and every day, from the time I get up to the time I go to sleep.

> In my world, everyday is the same, Saturdays are like Mondays, and Tuesdays are like Sundays, there is no difference.

> In my world, my life is lived on a basis of commands. Decisions are made, not by me, but by those who are in control.

> In my world, I have less than five minutes to consume a meal or be punished if I cannot! I cannot have an extra orange, apple, or banana should I choose. I can't go to the store and buy fruit, it is done for me, their choice not mine!

> In my world, there are no lakes, no oceans, no parks, places to go to except walk in a circle, but it will always be the same circle, never changing.

> In my world, boredom is the killer, nothing to do, no place to go, nothing but exist each day, day after day, after day, after day, every day is the same in my world, for you see my world is the world of prison.[11]

A prisoner may go to the library and wait his turn to use its limited facilities, to sick call, or to an occasional visit. By and large, however, most prisoners follow repetitive and restricted courses that dull their senses and corrode their abilities:

> The innocuous taste of my world, devoid of any emotional nourishment, is gradually overpowering. Bleak and colorless walls, insipid disgusting meals, and phlegmatic, timeworn daily routines, staked upon overcrowding; unadulterated trivia by unwarranted

and irrational guardian harassment all collaborate to numb my faculties. In tiny surreptitious doses, anesthesia is dripped into my heart—a formerly complacent heart that is slowly beginning to resemble my dreadful surroundings.[12]

Moreover, prisoners are trapped in a maze of rules. *Title 15*, the manual given to each prisoner that contains the rules governing all facets of institutional activity, is 189 pages long. Many "acceptable" practices are spelled out in fine detail. For example, the following describes required grooming style:

3062. Inmate Grooming Standards

(A) An inmate's hair shall be clean, neatly styled, and groomed, as specified in these regulations, when he/she is away from the immediate area of his/her quarters.

(B) An inmate's hair shall have no lettering, numbering, or designs of any kind cut, shaved, dyed, painted, or in any way placed in the hair or on the scalp of the inmate.

(C) An inmate shall not alter the appearance of his/her hair by changing its natural color.

(D) An inmate shall not possess a wig or hairpiece unless deemed medically necessary by the Chief Medical Officer and authorized, in writing, by the appropriate Institution's Division Regional Administrator.

(E) A male inmate's hair shall not be longer than three inches and shall not extend over the eyebrows or below the top of the shirt collar while standing upright. Hair shall be cut around the ears, and sideburns shall be neatly trimmed, and shall not extend below the mid-point of the ear. The width of the sideburns shall not exceed one and one-half inches and shall not include flared ends.

(F) A female inmate's hair may be any length but shall not extend over the eyebrows or below the bottom of the shirt collar while standing upright. If hair is long, it shall be worn up in a neat, plain style, which does not draw undue attention to the inmate.

(G) A female inmate may possess and use hair holding devices (such as, but not limited to, barrettes, pins, clips, and bands). If used, hair holding devices shall be unadorned, transparent, or similar in color to the hair. Beads or similar ornaments are not authorized for use in the hair.

(H) An inmate's face shall be clean shaven at all times, except as follows:
   (1) Mustaches are permitted for male inmates and shall not extend below the top of the upper lip, and shall extend to the corner of the mouth but not more than one-half inch beyond the corner of the mouth.
   (2) An exemption from shaving shall only be authorized by the appropriate Institution's Division Regional Administrator and only when an exemption is deemed medically necessary by a physician. Such exemption must not exceed ninety days. If the condition persists, another exemption request shall be submitted. Facial hair permitted by such an exemption, shall not exceed ¼ inch in length.[13]

Years of following repetitive, restricted routines and of being regulated by an extensive and somewhat rigidly enforced body of rules steadily erode the skills prisoners will need to cope with life in the outside world with its relatively rapid pace, lack of structure, and vast number of choices.

Assaults on the Self

The ongoing human enterprise of maintaining oneself as a functional entity requires a balance of social interaction and privacy. Prisoners, many of whom arrived at the prison with deeply damaged or dysfunctional psyches, could greatly benefit by regular contacts with sympathetic and "wise" others for emotional sustenance and empathy and for assistance in understanding of their surroundings.[14] In prisons like Solano, however, they are regularly jammed together with other prisoners who are more threatening than supportive and more immature or ignorant than wise. Moreover, they are closely supervised by unsympathetic, even hostile, staff, who are also mostly unwise. This is not the type of human interaction that helps individuals construct a more viable orientation for the future.

Prisoners have a great need for privacy for reflection, a time during which to arrange and integrate the confusing multitude of feelings and ideas that steadily impinge on their consciousness. These insights must be sorted out if one is to have a sufficiently cohesive concept of oneself—a requirement for getting by in the world. Prisoners require privacy to plan reasonable, productive, and rewarding courses of action and projects, and to perform many personal tasks, such as toilet functions, that humiliate many if not most people when performed in public.

Some forms of imprisonment afford too much privacy and not enough interaction with others, at least with helpful, insightful, and sympathetic others. In other forms, such as the dormitory sections of warehouse prisons, there is an almost total lack of privacy. More than half of prisoners in Solano, all Level II prisoners, are jammed together in dorms, dayrooms, and the yard, where they live 24 hours a day in a crowd with *no* privacy. Level III prisoners are housed in small double cells, which offer more privacy. However, for about 14 hours every day, they are squeezed into an 8-by-12-foot area with their "cellie," whom they may or may not like or get along with, and in the presence of whom they must defecate, urinate, belch, fart, and masturbate. All in all, a prison like Solano may be one of the worst places to keep or to get oneself "together."

Damage to Sexual Orientation

The involuntary celibacy of imprisonment is not only painful but also has a more or less permanent impact on prisoners' psychological orientations.[15] Robert Johnson identified two problems of living in the prison monosexual milieu:

> One is the pressure toward homosexual satisfaction of one's sexual needs, which provokes anxiety in many prisoners. The other is the tendency for traditionally male personality traits such as toughness to become exaggerated in the absence of the moderating effect of persons of the opposite sex (women in men's prisons, men in women's prisons), thus distorting in psychologically painful ways the image of manliness (in the men's prison) and womanliness (in women's prison).[16]

Most prisoners (particularly male prisoners) are uncomfortable with or made anxious by prison homosexual patterns, not so much because they feel "pressure toward homosexual satisfaction of one's sexual needs," but because they are regularly confronted with and disturbed by the complex and unique prison homosexual activities. In addition to recognized prison homosexuals—the punks and queens—many heterosexually oriented prisoners, particularly those who have grown up in prisons (such as state-raised prisoners) or have spent many years in prison, engage in sex with other prisoners. Edward Bunker, in his novel, *Animal Factory,* presents an insightful ethnography of prison life in the 1970s:

> It was a jocular credo that after one year behind walls it was permissible to kiss a kid or a queen. After five years it was okay to jerk them off to "get 'em hot." After ten years, "making tortillas" or "flip-flopping" was acceptable, and after twenty years anything was fine. So the banter said. It was not a true reflection of the ethos, which condemned anything that didn't ignore male physiology. It did, however, reflect a general cynicism about roles played in the privacy of a cell.[17]

As I suggested earlier and as Bunker hinted at, most male prisoners do not engage in homosexual behavior, but they are nervous about it. Always present are prison sexual predators in search of new victims they can seduce or rape. Additionally, prisoners, in humor or to intimidate, regularly impute homosexuality to others. The following exchange, a typical example of the "dozens" carried on constantly by convicts in the Big House, demonstrates the style of homosexual imputation engaged in by most prisoners:

> Two convicts approach a third, who is known by one of them. One introduces the third to his companion, "Tony, this is Charlie," and he adds in an afterthought, "He's my kid" [punk or prison homosexual]. Charlie quickly retorts, "I got your kid hanging, you punk."[18]

Consequently, all prisoners are on alert on the issue of homosexuality, about which there is constant tension. The result is that many prisoners experience considerable discomfort regarding their sexual identity and develop an inordinate distaste for homosexual practices and a dislike of homosexuals.

Another lasting effect of involuntary celibacy is a distortion in prisoners' sexual tastes and desires. I wrote about the impact of living in the monosexual prison world:

> Being a convict was making voyeurs out of us. Pictures of women became powerful stimulants. One day I was walking down the tier and glanced down at a newspaper lying on the floor. I spied a picture of a women's face that grabbed my attention. I stopped, picked up the discarded newspaper and stared at the face. There

[handwritten margin note: "On this section he kind of contradicts himself"]

was something about her, the smile, the eyes or something. She was overwhelmingly beautiful to me. But then the ache set in, deep in my gut. The possibility of being close, getting to know, romancing a woman like this was completely absent, not that my chances would have been that much greater if I was on the outside. But on the outside, there would be some small chance and this small chance would change the subjective experience considerably.[19]

Because of these prison-induced distortions—exaggerated "machismo," homophobia, and distorted sexual preferences—released prisoners have special problems adapting to outside social arrangements and relating to conventional members of the opposite sex.

Anger, Frustration, and the Sense of Injustice

Though rehabilitation has not been a stated purpose of imprisonment since the onslaught of penal conservatism, the public continues to express its desire that prisoners come back into society prepared to live an "honest" life and *not* to be a threat to public safety. I commented in the last chapter on the weakness of current prison rehabilitation programs. But beyond not being educationally or vocationally prepared for life on the outside, prisoners are ill-prepared to achieve the goal of rehabilitation, because the prison experience incites their anger, resentment, and sense of injustice toward the conventional society. As I argued in my earlier study of the career of the felon,

> Adult criminals have felt some sense of injustice for various reasons for many years. This feeling stemmed, first, from their perception of the inequality in the social circumstances in which they were born, grew up, and competed as adults. Second, they perceived inequality and unfairness because of corruption and class bias in the way they were handled by law enforcement agencies and the courts.[20]

In the 1970s, California prisoners' anger and sense of injustice were focused on the indeterminate sentence system. Today, this anger and sense of injustice are aroused because inmates are being forced to live by arbitrarily enforced, restrictive, and "chickenshit" rules; by their pervasive degradation by staff; and by their economic exploitation.

Chickenshit Rules

In the new warehouse facilities, prisoners are governed by a vast and pervasive set of rules. These rules frustrate and anger prisoners because of the extensive and arbitrary manner in which they are enforced. First, it is difficult to know all the rules, much less comply with them. Beyond that, many of these rules intrude into prisoners' ordinary practices and significantly interfere with their attempts to carry on their already excessively reduced life routines. These rules are seen as "chickenshit." Dannie Martin, a prisoner in federal prison at Lompoc during its shift to a new, more regulated regimen, commented on the new rules:

> As the saying goes, it's the little things that make a house a home. To those who face the mind-killing boredom of long prison sentences, small changes take on large significance in this our home-away-from-home. . . .
>
> He [a new warden] also managed to curtail most of the small liberties enjoyed by the convict population. Before his arrival, we had been permitted to wear our own clothes. Now we were to wear strictly tucked-in and buttoned-up government issue. And our recreational opportunities and food went from bad to worse. . . .
>
> No sooner did the warden close the yard than we lost our chairs, and that hurt. For as long as most of us can remember, we've had our own chairs in the TV rooms as well as in our cells. There's little enough in here for a man to call his own, and over the years these chairs have been modified and customized in an amazing degree—legs bent to suit the occupant, arm rests glued on, pads knitted for comfort. And the final personal touch is always the printing of a name on the back.[21]

A lifer interviewed at Solano revealed his anger at the succession of restrictive rules passed by the administration over the last few years: "I don't know what it would take to get us to stand up to them. They took away our family visits. They took away our weights. They made us shave our beards and cut our hair. Next they'll tell us to bend over, so they can fuck us in the ass."[22]

Many, perhaps most, prisoners find it impossible to obey all the new rules, and thus they put themselves in regular jeopardy of receiving "beefs" (disciplinary actions). For example, if prisoners followed the rules governing smoking, they would not be able to smoke for 10 to 12 hours at a stretch.

Many rules also require subjective interpretation. For example, there is a rule prohibiting disrespect toward employees (as well as other prisoners). After the introduction of female guards into the prison, the problem of male prisoners making sexual gestures, comments, and approaches to these guards arose. Some female guards were particularly sensitive to actions they interpret as sexual harassment This led to an infraction the prisoners refer to as "reckless eyeballing," which is a highly subjective interpretation of disrespect.

More important, the rules are enforced with considerable inconsistency and arbitrariness. One of the best examples of this is the appeals procedure, which is elaborately spelled out in six pages of the CDC *Operations Manual*. The description of the procedure begins as follows: "Any inmate or parolee under the department's jurisdiction may appeal any departmental decision, action, condition, or policy which they can demonstrate as having an adverse effect upon their welfare."[23] The regulations go on to describe how appeals are to be submitted, the time limits in which prisoners should submit them and administrators should rule on them, the grounds for rejection or denial of appeals, restrictions and punishments for "abuse" of the appeal procedure, and, most important, "exceptions to the regular appeal process."

The appeal process has the appearance of a legitimate, due process system; however, in reality it usually fails to conform to basic standards of due process and renders arbitrary and biased decisions. The main reason for this is that the process remains internal to the institution. If an appeal is denied and the prisoner pursues it, it passes up the through the levels of the prison bureaucracy. First, an appeal must be reviewed informally by the staff involved directly in the issue. If the appeal is not resolved to a prisoner's satisfaction at this level, it is passed up to an "appeals coordinator." If resolution is not achieved there, the appeal is passed on to the "institution head or their designee." Last, it is reviewed by a "designated representative of the director." There is no eventual appeal to an outside, impartial decision maker, such as an ombudsman, which many organizations, including some prison systems, have employed.

Any appeal process that does not eventually shift to an impartial adjudicator is invariably subject to systematic abuse. The overseeing staff, bosses, administrators, or chiefs, who make the final decisions, always have considerable incentive for ruling in favor of "their side." This is particularly true in the prison bureaucracy in which the appellants are convicts, individuals deemed less than trustworthy, and in which the decision makers strongly believe there is a need to maintain solidarity in their ranks. A lifer, who has worked for years as a clerk handling the appeals paperwork, commented on the processes:

> I can't remember when a convict outright won an appeal. First of all, it takes months to get through the process. [The officials] just stall everyone. Then the most they ever get is to be found guilty but no punishment. That means the administration *knew* the convict was right but they wouldn't rule against the cops.[24]

In sum, to get by in prison, prisoners must skip around the complex obstacles of excessive rules inconsistently and arbitrarily enforced by "cops," who more or less despise and distrust them. Over the years, coping in this way instills a sense of powerlessness as well as frustration and anger.

Degradation

Degradation ceremonies, which are part of the processes of arrest, incarceration, adjudication, and eventual imprisonment of felons, have been thoroughly examined by students of criminal justice. The degradation begins the moment a prisoner enters the jail: "Prisoners receive much more than the treatment required to introduce them to the jail and hold them there. They are impersonally and systematically degraded by every step in the criminal justice process, from arrest through detention to court appearance."[25] Other degradation ceremonies, such as regular strip searches and humiliating confrontations with staff, extend throughout a prisoner's sentence. However, the most persistent and insidious degradation is the "hostility and contempt directed at them by police officers, deputies, and other criminal justice functionaries."[26]

In Chapter 3, I examined the sources of these negative attitudes toward prisoners and the prisoners' countervailing contempt and hate for guards. I want to emphasize that treating prisoners with contempt and hostility, and persistently and systematically casting them as unworthy, harms them in complicated and somewhat unexpected ways. Many are psychologically scarred. More reject their rejectors, turn away from conventional society, and embrace an outsider, usually criminal, viewpoint. Pete Earley related the following statements made by a state-raised "habitual criminal":

> As the years go by and you get older, you realize more and more that your life is considered a failure by society's standards. . . . You are a jailbird. You don't have any money, no house, no job, no status. In society's eyes you're a worthless piece of shit. Now, you can buy into what society says and decide you really are a piece of shit or you can say, "Fuck society, I'll live by my own rules." That's what I did. I decided to live by my own standards and rules. They aren't society's but they are mine and that's what I've done. In your society, I may not be anybody, but in here, I am.[27]

This degradation further angers prisoners and leaves them ill equipped for assuming conventional life on the outside.

Economic Exploitation

Most prisoners I interviewed believe that the California prison system operates as a big business and the profit motive guides important decisions.

> It's all just business. I've watched it. Whenever there are a few empty beds around here, you wait. You'll see a bunch of guys getting violated. They got to keep the place full. They get paid by the convict. You watch it. They fill the place up by bringing guys back in, then they go to legislature and get more money to build a new prison.[28]

Though the prisoners' view of how the system works is somewhat distorted, it is based in reality. Prison systems are big businesses, and many groups, such as guards' unions, architects, construction companies, prison hardware manufacturers, and prison professionals, have an economic interest in expanding prison populations. Prisoners understand this and have developed a profoundly cynical view of the operation, which they see as corrupt and unjustly exploitative and oppressive.

There are some profit-making practices in the prison operation that directly affect prisoners and are seen as particularly corrupt and exploitative of them and their families. The most blatant of these is the telephone policy. In California prisons, pay telephones are located in all housing units and are readily available to prisoners. Prisoners may only make collect calls from these phones, which are installed and maintained by a private company, which charges an extra fee of $7 per call. This fee is paid by the person (usually a family member) receiving the call. This fee is split by the private company and the CDC. The CDC's share goes into the state's general fund. In the year 2000, California earned $36 million from this source.

Prisoners feel that this is gross exploitation of them, their friends, and their families, who are usually poorer people and less able to pay this fee. Several prisoners told me that they believe that the CDC unscrupulously delays their mail to encourage phone use. At present, a letter may take as long 21 days to be delivered to a prisoner.

Moreover, prisoners must pay an added 10 percent fee for every item they purchase through the canteen or any other source. This fee goes into the Inmate Welfare Fund along with any other money prisoners possess. This fund totaled $10.1 million in 1998, at which time some California prisoners sued the state to receive the interest from this money. The state informed the courts that the money held in the Inmate Welfare Fund had not been deposited in interest-earning accounts. Litigation continues on this issue, and prisoners in other states have filed similar suits. Regardless of the outcome of these cases, California prisoners feel the state has cheated them or has earned money on their money. As California prisoners' attorney Herman Franck views it, the state is stealing from the prisoners, and though each convict is losing only a few dollars, when you consider the vast number of prisoners, "150,000 small thefts becomes one big, fat theft."[29] In addition to aggravating prisoners' sense of injustice, these practices corrode the administrators' claims of moral superiority and reduce prisoners' sense of moral inferiority and responsibility.

Prisonization

Donald Clemmer, in his classic study, *The Prison Community*, recognized that prisoners take on, "in greater or less degree," the "folkways, mores, customs, and general culture of the penitentiary."[30] Prisonization occurs on several levels. The first is the "taken for granted" set of deeply imbedded interpretations and responses that prisoners acquire through living in the unique, routinized prison world in spite of any conscious effort to avoid acquiring them. Months or years of getting up at a certain time to certain signals, going about the day in a routine fashion, responding to certain commands, being among people who speak a certain way, and doing things repetitively inures prisoners to a deeply embedded set of unconscious habits and automatic responses. An example of an unthinking act performed by a parolee in the first week after his release reveals the operation of this effect of prisonization:

> I was coming out of a theater and I came to this guy standing at the front entrance with a uniform. He was an usher or something. All the sudden I was standing there with my hands up above my head waiting for the guy to frisk me, like they do every time you pass through some gate in prison.[31]

The next level of prisonization consists of the special values, beliefs, and habits most prisoners carry or practice and impart to others. In previous eras, there tended to be a single, overreaching convict code. This code has fragmented and weakened considerably due to the growing heterogeneity and conflict among prisoners. However, there still is a pervasive set of prison attitudes, beliefs, mannerisms, and speech habits that most prisoners acquire. These include attitudes toward authorities (represented by guards and other prison staff), stool pigeons, sexual deviants (particularly child molesters), and other races. Regrettably, many persons who had no racial prejudices prior to incarceration acquire them in prison, where they have to cope with racial hostilities and threats of racial violence.

Prisonization also includes acquiring a special vocabulary (with words such as *car*, which are indigenous to the prison), a set of prison mannerisms, and grooming styles (prison tattooing being the most manifest example). These characteristics will also obtrude into actions and relationships that prisoners attempt to take or form on the outside.

Many prisoners become deeply involved in some of the prison's criminal subcultures, such as those of various drug users, "gangstas," or "outlaws," and acquire a full-blown deviant identity. Finally, there is the identity of the "old con":

> The final level of the perspective of the convict is that of the "old con." This is a degree of identification reached after serving a great deal of time, so much time that all outside-based identities have dissipated and the only meaningful world is that of the prison. The old con has become totally immersed in the prison world. . . .
>
> The old con tends to carve out a narrow but orderly existence in the prison. He has learned to secure many luxuries and learned to be satisfied with the prison forms of pleasure—e.g., homosexual activities, cards, dominoes, handball, hobbies, and reading. He usually obtains jobs which afford him considerable privileges and leisure time.[32]

With the growing number of lifers serving very long sentences, this level of prisonization is becoming increasingly prevalent. At the extreme end of the spectrum are "LWOPs" (Life Without Possibility of Parole)—prisoners who will never be released. Ernest Patrick, a lifer, wrote:

> The lifers who have no hope of pardon or parole to look forward to, have to face the hardship of doing time. If they have no hope for release, they must start to think of the alternatives to doing time, such as suicide or escape. Given these deadly choices, maybe they can find it in themselves to cope with the rest of their life in prison.[33]

When I asked a group of lifers how they did their time, one said, "I'm not doing time, this is my life."[34]

Conclusions

Many aspects of imprisonment hamper prisoners' preparation for life after prison. They are coerced into repetitive, excessively reduced routines and trapped in an ongoing state of extreme control formed by an extensive body of rules inconsistently, arbitrarily, and prejudicially enforced by guards and other administrators. This situation is extremely frustrating and painful, because prisoners view the overseers who exercise complete control over them as benign, disinterested incompetents at best, or as arbitrary and insidious enforcers at worst.

For prisoners serving short sentences (less than two years), this routine of imprisonment is relatively less deleterious than imprisonment in former times or in more punitive states than California. Some of these short-termers, particularly young state-raised convicts, gangbangers, and thugs, are a volatile and disruptive force; they get into trouble, escalate their legal problems and their prison "classification," and thereby worsen their imprisonment situation. However, most short-termers float through their sentences with little damage to their persons or impact on prison society.

However, 60 percent of Solano's population are serving sentences of more than 5 years, and 27 percent are serving more than 15 years. For long-termers, the new situation of doing time, enduring years of suspension, being deprived of material conditions, living in crowded conditions without privacy, with reduced options, arbitrary control, disrespect, and economic exploitation is excruciatingly frustrating and aggravating. Anger, frustration, and a burning sense of injustice, coupled with the crippling processing inherent in imprisonment, significantly reduce the likelihood of prisoners who may pursue a viable, relatively conventional, non-criminal life after release. The difficulties and the failures they experience will be examined in Chapter 7.

Endnotes

1. Todd R. Clear, *Harm in American Penology: Offenders, Victims, and Their Communities* (Albany: State University of New York Press, 1994), 5.
2. Johnson, *Hard Time*, 61.
3. Julia Lusky, "The Plagues of Prison," *New Letter of the Western Prison Project*, Summer/Fall 2002, p. 8.
4. Prisoner interview, Solano, spring 2000.
5. Prisoner letter, Pelican Bay, October 1999.
6. Two prisoners in my research "focus" group are infected with hepatitis C, are symptomatic, and are being denied treatment. I have consulted with the Prison Law Project, which is suing the Center for Disease Control (CDC) over inadequate medical treatment for prisoners and have been informed that they were not able to force the department to change its policy on hepatitis C because it was supported by the National Institute of Mental Health (NIMH) physicians.
7. Anthony Crane, "Prison Story," manuscript written in 2001 at Solano State Prison.
8. Irwin, *Prisons in Turmoil*, 240.

9. *Webster's Third New International Dictionary* (Springfield, MA: G. & C. Merriam, 1971).

10. Schedule of one lifer at Solano.

11. Richard E. Karr, "In My World" (prisoner poem, spring 2002).

12. Donald D. Hairgrove, "A Single Unheard Voice," in Johnson and Toch, eds., *Crime and Punishment*, 147.

13. California Department of Corrections, *California Code of Regulations: Title 15*, (Sacramento: CDC, 2000, 36–37).

14. Hans Toch listed such regular contacts as one of the essential "needs" of prisoners (*Living in Prison*, 17).

15. Gresham Sykes, in his seminal study of the prison, *The Society of Captives*, listed this as one of the major pains of imprisonment.

16. Johnson, *Hard Time*, 66.

17. Bunker, *Animal Factory*, 86.

18. Irwin, *Prisons in Turmoil*, 7.

19. Irwin, "Rouge," 275.

20. Irwin, *Felon*, 51.

21. Dannie Martin, "The Gulag Mentality," *San Francisco Chronicle*, Sunday Punch section, 19 June 1989, p. 5.

22. Prisoner interview, Solano, spring 2001.

23. *Operations Manual* (California Department of Corrections), 530.

24. Prisoner interview, Solano, April 2001.

25. John Irwin, *The Jail* (Berkeley: University of California Press, 1985), 67.

26. The depth and pervasiveness of these negative attitudes were regularly brought home to me when I was being cleared by the gate officer upon entering Solano. If it was a guard that had not cleared me before, upon inspecting my ID card, which designated me as a "researcher," he or she would frequently, out of curiosity, ask, "What are you researching?" When I responded, "Prisoners," he or she would then inquire, "How do you study them?" When I responded that I interviewed them, he or she would frequently and sincerely respond, "Do you believe what they say?"

27. Earley, *The Hot House*, 77.

28. Prisoner interview, Solano, March 2001.

29. "Inmates Go to Court to Earn Interest on Prison Accounts," *Wall Street Journal: California*, 17 November 1999, p. 1.

30. Clemmer, *Prison Community*, 299.

31. Prisoner interview, San Francisco, 1967.

32. Irwin, *Felon*, 84.

33. Ernest Patrick, "Meaning of 'Life' in Prison," in Johnson and Toch, eds., *Crime and Punishment*, 143.

34. Prisoner interview, Solano, fall 2001. ✦

Chapter 7

Reentry

Due to the excessive expansion of prison populations over recent decades, prisoners are literally pouring out of the prisons. In 1996, for instance, 475,000 state and federal prisoners were released from prison. In 2002 the number exceeded 600,000. This number has grown so large that the issue of prisoner "reentry" has finally caught the attention of federal bureaucrats and criminal justice experts, triggering a burst of interest and activity. However, as is frequently the case, the actions and programs developed in response to the newly recognized problem are based on misconceptions. Further, the measures recommended or implemented ignore the real problems of prisoner reentry. Because public safety dominates most officials' and experts' thinking, the real problems of men and women leaving prison to return to the free world are obscured.[1] Jeff Glasser, in a *U.S. News & World Report* story, wrote:

> Sobered by the statistics, criminal justice professionals are wrestling with ways to manage the felon influx. The Clinton administration has proposed a $145 million package to provide drug treatment, court supervision, and job training to returning offenders. Attorney General Janet Reno calls inmates' aftercare a "public safety" issue. "They're going to victimize [the community] again" in the absence of new programs. She tells *U.S. News*, "Why don't we stop it with a carrot-and-stick approach?" Skeptical police groups say the money would be better spent hiring more people to keep an eye on the lawbreakers. "What they need to do is put 50,000 to 60,000 additional parole and probation officers on the streets so we can monitor these people," says James Fotis, director of the Law Enforcement Alliance of America.[2]

The emphasis on public safety sidesteps the most important problem: the overwhelming difficulties ex-prisoners face attempting to establish basic economic and social viability on the outside. The secondary problem, achieving a minimally satisfying outside existence, is likewise ignored.

The emphasis on public safety is partially based on the misconception of the intentions of prisoners released from prison. Many academic experts and criminal justice practitioners believe that a high percentage, perhaps the majority, of released prisoners intend to continue their criminal careers. My experience and research has convinced me that before their release, *most* prisoners desire to live in a somewhat conventional manner.[3] They want to get a job to support themselves and their families, find a place to live, develop a satisfying sexual and emotional relationship, and live some version of a "good life." They understand that to succeed in achieving these goals they must avoid the activities and relationships that resulted in their imprisonment. To obtain a sense of prisoners' general intentions before release, I asked 86 prisoners who were attending prerelease classes at Solano State Prison to anonymously choose between the following two postrelease paths:

1. There is a job waiting for me upon release that allows me to live a relatively secure, conventional, and comfortable ($15.00 or more per hour) lifestyle.
2. I will get back into the fast life, thugging or some other form of criminal activity, rather than settling down.

It is true that some prisoners do intend to return to their former criminal activities. As one prisoner put it, "I like what I was doing on the streets. I like running around in nice cars, the women, drugs. I'm going right back to it when I get out."[4] However, the vast majority, 70 out of the 86, chose option number 1, which was to go to a job and stay away from crime.

The truth is that most released prisoners do not go to a job and stay clean. This is not because they planned to return to crime; rather, it is because they are stigmatized, prisonized, ill-prepared social cripples, and their experiences on the outside disorganize, discourage, and eventually derail them. In the first place, most are not able to find jobs that allow them to live a relatively secure conventional and comfortable lifestyle. If they get a job, it is usually one that pays minimum wage—not enough to support them.

Furthermore, it is very likely that they will not be able to find a decent place to live and will, therefore, be forced to live on skid row, sleep in shelters, or remain homeless, surrounded by other ex-convicts who are also losing their battle to "make it" on the outside. These released prisoners are also burdened with parole regulations that hinder more than help them in their efforts to return to society. I have divided the problems released prisoners face into several separate categories which I present in roughly the order in which they typically beset a released prisoner.

The Initial Impact of Reentry

Prisoners' problems of reentry begin with the disorganization they experience moving from the prison setting, to which they have become deeply acculturated (prisonized), to the radically different outside society. In an earlier study of parole, I interviewed and observed a sample of released prisoners in their first days on the outside. I described the disorganization many experienced:

> The ex-convict moves from a state of incarceration where the pace is slow and routinized, the events are monotonous but familiar, into a chaotic and foreign outside world. The cars, buses, people, buildings, roads, stores, lights, noises, and animals are things he hasn't experienced at firsthand for quite some time. The most ordinary transactions of the civilian have dropped from his repertoire of automatic maneuvers. Getting on a streetcar, ordering something at a hot dog stand, entering a theater are strange. Talking to people whose accent, style of speech, gestures, and vocabulary are slightly different is difficult. The entire stimulus world—the sights, sounds and smells—is strange.
>
> Because of this strangeness, the initial confrontation with the "streets" is apt to be painful and certainly is accompanied by some disappointment, anxiety, and depression.[5]

These experiences often derail ex-prisoners, who then impulsively take actions that greatly disrupt their progress outside:

> The convict's attempts to settle down and to get his feet on the ground are, however, often thwarted by a barrage of disorganizing events which occur in the first days or weeks on the outside. In

spite of his optimism, preparedness, and awareness of the experiences in store for him, the disorganizing impact on the personality of moving from one meaning world into another, the desperation that emerges when he is faced with untold demands for which he is ill prepared, and the extreme loneliness that he is likely to feel often prevent him from ever achieving equilibrium or direction on the outside. Often a sincere plan to "make it" in a relatively conventional style is never actualized because of the reentry impact. Many parolees careen and ricochet through the first weeks and finally in desperation jump parole, commit acts which will return them to prison, or retreat into their former deviant world. Many others, though they do not have their plans destroyed and do not immediately fail on parole because of the experiences which accompany their return to the outside community, have their plans, their perspectives, and their view of self altered.[6]

The extent to which prisoners experience disorganization from the reentry shock varies according to the amount of time they served in prison, the number of times they have been released in the past, and the settings into which they are released. Many lower-class, nonwhite prisoners return to neighborhoods in which a high percentage of the inhabitants, particularly the young males, have been in prison, and therefore the language, the meanings, the accents, and the gestures of others in the setting are somewhat similar to those in prison.[7]

Getting By

To become viable citizens, parolees must first secure a place to live and some means of support—typically, a job. To accomplish these, more fundamental matters must be addressed. Working clothes, a driver's license or other form of photo identification, tools, and occasionally medication for chronic medial conditions must be acquired.[8] Most prisoners step into the outside world with a small bundle of stuff under their arm, a little bit of money, perhaps their $200 "gate" money, and that is all. An ex-prisoner I interviewed had been out several weeks and still hadn't been able to look for a job because he had no official identification.

I got out after 16 years and I didn't have any paper proving who I was, no birth certificate, nothing. I went to several DMVs [

Department of Motor Vehicles] to try to get an identification card, but they told me that I need some proof of who I was. I finally got my parole officer to write a letter on their paper with their letterhead stating who I was. I took this to three different DMVs until finally one gave me an ID.[9]

Finding a Place to Live

It is extremely difficult for parolees to secure housing on release. According to Joan Petersilia, who studied prisoners returning to the outside society, "Parole officials say that finding housing for parolees is by far their biggest challenge, even more difficult and important than finding a job."[10] A *few* released prisoners move in with their spouses, parents, or other relatives. However, many parolees' relatives live in government-subsidized, low-cost housing projects that exclude parolees. Consequently, most released persons have to locate a place to live on their own. They face several major obstacles in accomplishing this goal, the most obvious of which is the cost of housing.

Again, as throughout this book, I will use California as an examplar.[11] California parolees are required by law and parole rules to return to the jurisdiction in which they lived before imprisonment. Most of them were living in big cities—Los Angeles, San Francisco, Oakland, San Diego, Long Beach, and Sacramento. The rents in these cities have risen dramatically in the last two decades. With the exception of the most run down skid row areas, rents are too expensive for parolees living on the income they can hope to make, minimum or near minimum wage. In addition, many private, low-cost housing units exclude ex-convicts.[12]

Parole agents have contacts with some apartment managers and owners of cheap housing. With few exceptions, these units are located in run-down, skid row areas where there is a concentration of other parolees and ex-convicts, many of them living on the edge, perhaps using drugs or alcohol and engaging in many illegal acts and parole rule violations. The agents can place parolees in residential programs, such as Sober Living, which has units in many locations in the big cities, but most of these are for special category prisoners, such as drug and alcohol abusers, and they impose strict living rules. Most parolees who cannot live with their relatives initially must live in skid row areas where they are in regular contact with other parolees, many of whom they knew in prison, where there is considerable danger of being robbed, assaulted, or harassed by police.[13]

> On his release from Chino state prison in July, broke and with no home to go to, Demetrious Williams got on a bus and headed for downtown Los Angeles. The career burglar had previously lived in the Crenshaw area and the Inland Empire, but he had only $200 "gate" money and needed a quick place to shower and sleep. There seemed few alternatives but skid row, where more than 60 social agencies crowded a 50-block expanse.
>
> Months later, out of work and with few prospects, he is still downtown at a homeless agency on a forbidding stretch of skid row, trying to dodge drug dealers and crime that could land him back in prison.
>
> "If you don't have family very close or friends, you have nowhere to stay but the streets," said Williams, whose thick eye-brows and mustache are flecked with gray. "In prison, I heard about the services word-of-mouth." A lot of people know about skid row.[14]

Amanda Ripley, writing in *Time* magazine, reported that "30% to 50% of big-city parolees are homeless."[15]

Finding Work

Parolees also face tremendous difficulty in securing a job, any job. Most employers are unwilling to hire ex-prisoners. In a survey of four cities—Atlanta, Boston, Detroit, and Los Angeles—Harry Holtzer discovered that more than 60 percent of 3,000 employers would "probably not" or "definitely not" hire an ex-prisoner.[16] When ex-prisoners fill out a job application, there is invariably a question asking them if they have ever been arrested. If they indicate no and a future check reveals that they have, they are usually fired. If they indicate they have, there is little chance of being hired. Joan Petersilia commented,

> Whether or not the felon is legally eligible for the job or not, research suggests that most employers will ask about the applicant's criminal record and once it is revealed, the applicant's chances of being hired are significantly reduced.[17]

Over many years of conducting research on released prisoners, I have found only a few instances in which parolees succeeded in getting around this obstacle. Those few usually indicated on the form that they had not been arrested and then, when discovered, made a plea to stay employed.[18]

Job availability for ex-convicts has gotten much worse since 1975. According to Joan Petersilia,

> At the end of the 1960s, when the country had more employment opportunities for blue-collar workers than it does now, there was some movement to reduce the employment barriers and studies revealed a full-time employment rate of around 50% for parolees.[19]

During the 1960s, when I first studied the reentry problem, there was a very different attitude toward ex-convicts. Many businesses were willing to address the special employment problems ex-convicts faced and began hiring them. Since then, the negative image of the criminal that emerged in the general society has resulted in the loss of many employment opportunities. Many cities and counties have barred ex-convicts from most or all city jobs. The state government of California bars parolees from employment in law, real estate, medicine, nursing, physical therapy, and education.[20]

Presently, some companies, such as Save-On Drugs, Target, and Kmart, do hire ex-convicts. These companies pay minimum or slightly better than minimum wage, and most of them employ parolees on a less than full-time basis. This way, they avoid having to give parolees medical and other benefits. Many retail companies, warehouses, car washes, and fast food operations also hire ex-cons, all at minimum or close to minimum wage and for less than full time.

Trade unions will admit ex-convicts as apprentices, but they must secure a job in the field first and then join the union and follow the union's apprenticeship program. Often this operates as a Catch-22, because many employers will not hire a parolee. Also, in many trades, even regular union members have trouble getting hired. The construction field offers the best opportunities, but the pay is less than in other trades. Ex-prisoners who had considerable trade training in prison have a decided advantage in getting a job in a particular trade. A few prison vocational training programs are taught by instructors with union ties, and they can, therefore, get some prisoners into the unions. However, my interviews and the data available from the California Department of Corrections (CDC) suggest that very few ex-prisoners secure trade union jobs.

Job Placement Program

The CDC has job counselors with offices at the various district parole offices, and these counselors hold job workshops and work individually with parolees who seek their services. The state and federal governments fund several job placement offices, such as One Stop and Work Place. Private organizations, particularly churches, are establishing job placement programs for ex-prisoners. In fact, former Governor of California Gray Davis distributed $7.4 million to churches to support job placement for ex-prisoners.

It is my observation that these programs do three things. First, they refer ex-prisoners to minimum-wage, usually less than full time jobs at various retail businesses, car washes, warehouses, and janitorial services. Second, they conduct regular workshops where there is some job referral and, more important, a great deal of motivational support. The message the program staff deliver, frequently with considerable enthusiasm and eloquence, is "You can make it if you don't give up." Third, and perhaps most important, these programs created many jobs *in* the programs. Most of the program staff themselves, often the directors, are ex-convicts. These persons are making a better salary than most employed ex-prisoners and are performing work they enjoy and believe is valuable. In effect, they have careers. This type of career is very popular among prisoners and ex-prisoners. When I have asked prisoners what they would like to do in the future, many say they want a job counseling other people, usually young people. They argue that their experience gives them special skills for this.

Parolee Unemployment

In spite of these job placement efforts and in spite of the fact that until the recent recession there has been a low rate of unemployment in the general society, over 70 percent of California parolees remain unemployed.[21]

Parolees are excluded from most good-paying jobs, but with some effort and a little luck they can find a low-paying job of the types I've described. As one agent put it, "If they want to work, they can work. They don't want to work. I've sent them out on jobs, good jobs—$13 an hour. They work a few days then get high and don't make it to work."[22] The agent was exaggerating when he claimed that he was able to secure for parolees jobs earning $13 an hour, but it is true that most parolees can secure minimum-wage jobs. Still, 70 percent are unemployed.

There are several reasons for this. Some ex-prisoners, particularly those having more experience with deviant and criminal behavior patterns and having been more profoundly prisonized, cannot "get it together" enough to hold a job, any job. Their lack of civilian skills, their lack of minimal resources, and their prisoner speech patterns, mannerisms, and habits ill suit them for conventional employment routines and settings. They have great difficulty interacting with other employees and customers. They often resent authority, have a short fuse, blow up with little provocation, and have trouble taking orders. Or they have difficulty getting to work or getting to work on time. The progress of the following ex-prisoner reveals several of these problems.

John, a 50-year-old white man, was discharged from federal prison after serving 17 years. Through contacts with a person who worked in a job placement position for ex-prisoners, he obtained a job at a restaurant and bike rental business on the beach in Santa Monica. Though he was very different than the other employees, he initially got along well and after a week on the job was promoted to a position with more responsibility. He said he was enjoying the work. However, after several weeks he went to the owner of the business and indicated that he felt out of place because he had never worked around "squares" before. He had been in prison most of his life. Then he failed to show up for work one day. He phoned the owner and told him that he had trouble getting to work on the bus. He had to take three buses from the San Fernando Valley to get to Santa Monica—a two hour trip. In an interview later, he told me that he had gotten on the first bus on his route and told the driver to tell him when they came to his stop. The driver failed to do this and he ended up going way out of his way. By the time he got back on track he thought it was too late. This set him back. Also at the time he was in conflict with the relatives with whom he was living. This and his growing discomfort with his relationships with his fellow workers resulted in his starting to drink. His relatives moved him out of their house to a small run-down trailer where he was surrounded by other persons who were living on the edge and drinking all day. He tried to come back to work another time, but then gave it up. When we interviewed him several weeks later, he was not working, was drinking and his health had visibly deteriorated.[23]

Some ex-prisoners are mentally or physically incapable of holding a job. In the last few decades, the prison has received many persons who, before the 1970s, would have been handled by the mental health system. As Joan Petersilia points out,

> Persons with mental illness are increasingly criminalized and processed through the corrections system instead of the mental health system. In 1955, the number of mental health patients in state hospitals had reached a high of 559,000. New antipsychotic drugs were developed in the 1950s, and by prescribing them to people with mental illness, many could remain in the community rather than being placed in mental hospitals. . . .

> In recent years, a growing number of seriously mentally ill people [have] been sent to prison. Ultimately, most of them will be released to the community.[24]

Mentally incapacitated prisoners are ushered through the prison system, in which they usually receive special medication and are housed in special units. When they are released, the parole agency becomes the substitute for the mental health system, and it must develop a program for them that will allow them to survive outside. This means the parole agency places these parolees in private or public institutions or acquires welfare assistance, such as government assistance for them so they can live at home or in cheap housing. However, these persons remain unemployed. The following describes a parolee who, accompanied by his mother, was waiting to see his agent at the Long Beach Parole Office.

> Carl, a 33-year-old parolee who is physically and mentally "challenged," was released on parole in 1999. He has been returned to prison twice for parole violations: once for absconding and once for possession of a controlled substance. He is on medication and is not able to work. His mother is keeping him in a motel. She is trying

to obtain SSI assistance for him. While I interviewed him and his mother, he nervously paced the room. He was agitated and angry.[25]

While it is true that the majority of released prisoners could hold jobs, they often give up after failure to locate a job or after working on a low-paying job and quitting or getting fired. There are several reasons for this. First, minimum-wage jobs do not meet their minimum standards for a "good life" on the outside. When planning their future, many prisoners feel that in prison they have been deprived of most ordinary life satisfactions, and they look forward to making up for this after their release. They desire a life on the outside that has (1) at least adequate financial compensation, (2) no "slave" traits, that is, menial, subservient, poorly paid work, and (3) pleasureful experiences. The latter includes the pleasures entailed in socializing with friends, sexual fulfillment, recreation, and perhaps some excitement.[26] The minimum-pay jobs available to them do not meet these standards. Moreover, they learn, after working in a minimum-wage job for a short time, that the pay will not allow them to afford a decent apartment, buy clothes, feed themselves well, or buy a reliable automobile, and it is certainly not enough to support a family or a spouse. They also soon learn that, in spite of what the parole agents or placement counselors tell them, these minimum-pay jobs rarely lead to others that pay adequate salaries.

The second reason parolees are unmotivated to seek employment is that they rely on others for support and then become adjusted to a dependent existence. They are taken in by family members or a sexual partner. Some become attached to programs, particularly church programs, that supply them with minimum support. Others obtain county assistance, such as SSI, or receive pay from the county for caring for a dependent relative.[27] Still others earn some money through the underground economy that flourishes in any poor urban setting or through occasional involvement in petty illegal activities, such as trading stolen property or drug trafficking.

Dealing With Parole

Most prisoners are released on parole supervision, and this presents other obstacles for ex-prisoners attempting to live on the outside. Data from several states suggest that prisoners who are discharged from prison, that is, have no parole supervision, return to prison at a lower rate. A study of recidivism in three states—Kentucky, Texas, and Pennsylvania—revealed that persons discharged directly from prison with no parole returned to prison less than half as often as those released on parole (Table 7.1).[28]

Table 7.1: Reincarceration Rates for Three States

Release Type	Kentucky	Texas	Pennsylvania
Parole Supervision	53%	26%	50%
Discharged	18%	11%	19%

For reasons other than differential criminal involvement, parolees are reincarcerated more frequently than prisoners who are released with no parole supervision. First, the activities of parolees are under close scrutiny by a peace officer with special authority, particularly the authority to search the parolee's person or place of residence at any time without a search warrant. Most parolees follow a typical working-class or lower-class life routine and frequently engage in the commission of petty crimes, such as marijuana use. These infractions are much more likely to be discovered when committed by parolees than nonparolees.

A second reason is that parole imposes a set of "conditions" or special rules to which parolees have considerable difficulty conforming. California parolees may not travel more than 50 miles from their residence without their agent's permission. They must comply with all parole agent instructions and inform them in advance of any change of residence. There is a strict prohibition on possession of a firearm. There is also a prohibition on possessing a knife with a blade longer than two inches (except kitchen knives, which must be kept in one's residence) and "any instrument or device which a reasonable person would believe to be capable of being used as a weapon."[29] In her study of persons released from prison, Joan Petersilia included the following list of "common" parole conditions:

- Responding to the parole agent within 24 hours of release.
- Not carry weapons.

- Reporting changes of address and employment.
- Not traveling more than 50 miles from home or not leaving [t]he county for more than 48 hours without prior approval from the parole agent.
- Obeying all parole agent instructions.
- Seeking and maintaining employment or participating in education/work training.
- Not committing crimes.
- Submitting to search by the police and parole officers.[30]

Particular categories of parolees, such as sex offenders and substance abusers, must meet "special conditions." Sex offenders are required to register with local police, to refrain from entering child safety zones, and to participate in sex offender therapy. Drug abusers are usually required to submit to regular urinalysis and to participate in substance abuse programs.

Most parolees do not obey all the rules, and most parole agents do not expect them to. The agents try to reach an explicit or implicit understanding with the parolee that he or she must strictly obey some rules, such as keeping in contact with the agent (not absconding), not using drugs, and keeping his or her behavior within tolerable limits, particularly staying out of jail. In general, this works. However, there is a catch in this arrangement. Often the agent is aware of and tolerates minor parole rule violations. When the parolee goes too far, such as tests dirty several times for drug use or fails to report to the agent for a period of time, the agent initiates parole violation procedures. Then the agent not only charges the parolee with the more serious infraction but also includes all the little previously tolerated infractions. Parolees frequently feel betrayed when this occurs.

A high percentage of parolees are vulnerable to violation. Most are unemployed. They occasionally use drugs or drink too much. They may fail to make contact with their agent. They leave their county and drive without a driver's license or insurance. Or they commit a host of other parole rule violations or petty crimes. A parole agent may search a parolee's residence without a warrant at any time. Some agents do this more frequently than others, and they usually do it more often in the parolee's early stages of parole or when the agent suspects that the parolee is committing crimes or is in violation of the conditions of parole, such as drinking, using drugs, or not reporting to the agent. When agents search a parolee's residence, they frequently find evidence of a parole violation. As one parole violator reported, "Man, when he came in and looked around, he found an empty beer bottle, and violated me."[31]

A third reason that parole is an impediment to parolees is that they are forced to engage in activities that interfere with normal workday routines. In the early stages of their parole, many parolees have to report to the agent once a week, most at least once a month. These contacts must be made during the day. They must travel to the agency, usually by public transportation, and sometimes wait an hour or two to meet their agent. In addition, special category parolees (such as sex offenders) or those who are defined as having an alcohol or drug abuse problem are required to participate in special programs that involve daily meetings over several weeks. If a parolee tests dirty in one of the regular urine tests, he or she is often required to participate in a substance abuse program (SAP) that meets all day, five days a week, for several weeks.

One ex-prisoner, whom James Austin and I interviewed in our 1994 study, revealed the difficulties and the determination required to deal with parole and make a successful adjustment on the outside.

> I had about $1,200 when I got out that I had saved when I was out on OR [release on own recognizance program]. I knew from my crime and record I was gonna get time, so I worked and saved my money.

> I first got a hotel room in downtown Burlingame, the only flea bag hotel there, and went to an AA meeting that night. The next day I went to see my parole officer, and he started right off reading all my arrests, saying you did this and that. But I finally struck a deal with him that if I didn't drink or drive a car without a license he would keep off my back. But if I did, he would violate me and charge me with everything he could. He lived up to the bargain for a year and then I got another parole agent.

> By then I was already in San Francisco State. I had signed up with the Rebound Project [a program that helps ex-prisoners enter San Francisco State University] while I was in CMC [a state prison near

San Luis Obispo]. I had a small apartment in San Carlos for $400 a month. I was busing it to school three days a week. Two hours there, two hours back. I got a job at Walgreen's. I was selling liquor at night to guys who were just like me. But I was attending AA and had made up my mind that I was gonna change my life. And I never took a drink. Then I worked for awhile selling cars. Then selling TVs at Mathew's in Daly City. I bought an old beat-up Buick that had a pretty good motor and got two years out of it. About 25 thousand miles.

The next parole agent was a real tough guy. First thing he told me was, "It's obvious you've been pulling some scam for a year." So he put me back on maximum custody. The other agent, even though he put on the tough-guy act, left me alone. This guy had me coming in once a week, had me pissing in the bottle, and he would show up at my house at six in the morning trying to catch me at something. But I had decided that if they were going to send me back, they were gonna have to fabricate something. I wasn't doing nothing. I didn't even have kitchen knives in my house. I made the decision, also, that I was gonna stay out of their face. I learned that in prison. If you stayed out of people's face and stayed away from places where shit started, you wouldn't have any trouble. I never went in the day room or to the iron pile [the weight workout area]. That's where guys got stuck [knifed]. So I did the same on the outside. I had to learn to keep out of people's faces outside, too. One time some guy in the library got in my face and I got back in his. I didn't have the little stamp on my ID card that you had to have to check out reference books and he wouldn't give me a book. They hadn't sent me the stamp yet. So we got into it. But I try now to keep out of everyone's face. Sometimes some of these PC [politically correct] students get on my nerves. The little assholes don't know shit, and they're telling me what's politically correct. But I still stay out of their face.

Then I got another agent. They didn't tell me and I went to the office and the old agent said he had sent me a letter telling me that I had been transferred to a new agent. He didn't send me no letter. It's lucky I had gone to see the old agent when I did, because I was supposed to report to the new agent the next day and I wouldn't have ever known it and they could have violated me. This guy was like the first one. By that time I had finished two years of college and had no arrests. So he left me alone. Now I am gonna graduate with a 3.7.

But I had a lot of good luck, too. A lot of times I got behind in my rent, but I had good landlords. Really nice guys and they let me slide. They could have kicked me out and where would I have been? The parole agency wasn't gonna help me. They're too busy trying to bust guys.[32]

Styles of Parole Supervision

As officially defined, the parole agent position has conflicting, dual purposes. One is policing parolees. In California, as in many states, parole agents are "peace officers" with the power of arrest and the right to carry firearms. The other purpose is that of a helping agent—a social worker. In the past, particularly during the height of the rehabilitative era and its correctional rhetoric, there was some effort on the part of criminal justice experts and planners to justify this mix with a paternalistic theory, that is, the parole agent operates like a parent who mixes discipline and support. The following description from the CDC's *Parole Agent Manual* in use in the late 1960s is an example of this type of mixture:

> Parole supervision is an integral part of the correctional process. It is by this means that the true purpose of parole is satisfied. Every effort is made to protect society from further transgressions on the part of the offender; while at the same time attempts are made to assist the parolee in becoming a self-sustaining, law-abiding, and contributing member of society.[33]

Earlier studies of parole supervision, using these two variables—assistance and control—formed the typology of parole agents shown in Figure 7.1.[34]

Today, California parole officers lean more toward policing. Joan Petersilia noted, "An ethnographic study of parole officers in California concludes that while rehabilitation remains in parole's rhetoric, as a practical matter, parole services are almost entirely focused on control-oriented activities."[35] In my recent research of the Long Beach Parole Office, I discovered examples of both extremes. One agent, who was in charge of "second strikers"—individuals with two convictions who would receive a sentence of 25 years to life if they receive another—stated emphatically that he strictly enforced the

Figure 7.1 Typology of Parole Agents

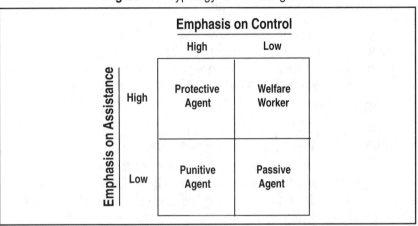

rules. When I asked him about his approach to dirty urine tests, he stated that he violates parolees when they test dirty, even for marijuana. He continued, "Marijuana is an illegal drug, and I'm not going to make an exception for it."[36] While I interviewed him, the agent received a phone call from a parolee who had been released that day and was stuck in downtown Los Angeles and was not going to be able to get the parole office that day. The agent sternly informed him that he was required to report that day and that he was subject to a violation if he did not. He then hung up on the parolee.

Other agents see themselves as helping agents and do their best to assist parolees in locating jobs and finding residences, to supply parolees with whatever resources the agency has to offer, and to keep them out of trouble. One agent, a young recent college graduate I interviewed, said that was how he operated; he tried his best to not send parolees back to prison. "My job is to keep them out of jail. I try to treat them like I would want to be treated."[37] However, he indicated, he has limited resources.

Most agents fall somewhere in between these two extremes. Often they vary their approach according to their perceptions of the individual parolees. They try to help parolees whom they believe are trying; those who are not, they police:

> If I see they are trying to do something for themselves, I'll work with them. They have to show me something. If I know that they

are going to do right, I'll send them out on a good job. I'll ask them if they have any skills. I can tell if they want to work or not.[38]

Parole supervision, like prison work, has become more bureaucratized, and there is much more pressure on agents to fulfill formal tasks, such as keeping records, making reports, and meeting deadlines. Julie Preggar, a UCLA graduate student studying parole in Los Angeles, noted:

> Agents may not have given up on the idea of rehabilitation and treatment, but they are not evaluated on that basis. At most, their formal responsibility is limited to acting as a referral service and a link to the network of services available in the larger community. On a day-to-day basis, agents in the Second Striker unit are not evaluated on their return-to-custody rates. Instead, they are judged by whether or not they have met all of the minimum supervision specifications in a given month.[39]

At the time of my late-1960s study, *The Felon*, parolees had to prevent their agents from discovering many of their acts and practices, as in the case of "shacking up" with a woman or "smoking a little dope." They hid these actions through deception or distance:

> The "successful" parolee (that is, the parolee who at least temporarily appears to be successful to the agent and agency), presents a performance which falls within the agent's tolerance limits. Those activities which are outside these limits are kept from the agent by deceiving him or by maintaining distance. For instance, if the parolee decides to live with a woman and believes that the agent will not tolerate this, he deceives the agent by renting a room which he does not actually use and placing some clothes and personal belongings there. Or he may just depend on distance, and he lives with a girl and does not tell the agent.[40]

Today, however, it is enough that parolees make a token performance—that is, report to the agent, appear to look for a job, stay off drugs, do not get caught more than 50 miles away from the parole agency, and stay out of jail. However, today parolees' circumstances are more overwhelming than in the 1960s. Housing and jobs are much harder to find. Consequently, parolees are in much greater need of assistance and much more likely to be in violation of the conditions of parole or to drift into crime and face arrest.

Because of the greatly increased drug use, mental problems, and material difficulties parolees experience, the agency is put in the position of acting as a social welfare agency. However, because of a serious lack of funds, it is unable to effectively provide welfare services. Rather than directly provide services, agents more often direct parolees to job placement programs, mental health agencies, and schools. However, as Joan Petersilia observed, few services for parolees exist:

> In California, for example, there are few services for parolees. There are only 200 shelter beds in the state for more than 10,000 homeless parolees, 4 mental health clinics for 18,000 psychiatric cases, 750 beds in treatment programs for 85,000 drug and alcohol abusers.[41]

The parole agency has limited financial resources to give direct help to parolees. Each "unit" within a parole district office receives an inadequate amount of discretionary money to distribute to parolees in need of assistance—to pay rent, for transportation, to buy tools, or for food. In 2001, the unit I observed received $46,000. This unit supervises about 700 parolees at a time. One-third of the discretionary funds had to be spent on parolees convicted of sex crimes, a special category for which the law requires that the agency supply housing in addition to close supervision. That left about $50 for each of the other parolees. In reality, agents have to refuse most parolees' requests for financial assistance. Julie Preggar recorded the following comments made by Los Angeles parole agents:

> Agent 1: When we first started, we did have a little bit more money than we have now. And being able to house somebody or pay for a drug program until maybe their General Relief started just made things a lot easier. Or sometimes just helping them out maybe with clothing for interviews or work tools, tuition, books. You know, I've got a request on a guy right now that wants some books and I've gotta figure out how much that's gonna be and I'd like to give it to him. Because he's doing really well. But I don't know if I can.

> Agent 2: So I had somebody coming in that I would have loved to have given a bag of bus tokens, a food voucher. These people were like living in a motel room and he was doing day labor just to pay the rent to have five people in a motel room. And he's like, "Could you give me a food voucher? Can you give me a bus token?

Anything, anything would help. Even if it's just $20, whatever." So I came back to the office, big sign on the door that we're all outta money. And I'm thinking oh my god. This is a family that really just needed whatever. Just I felt really, really awful about that because I know what's happening. The 290s [sex offenders] are eating up all the money. And they come in between the first and fifth of the month and the money's gone.[42]

Patterns of Adjustment After Prison

Failure

Most released prisoners return to prison. Since 1990, in California, recidivism (return-to-prison) rates have reached as high as 80 percent. Most of these ex-prisoners were returned to prison for parole violations. In 1999, 67 percent of California prison admissions were parole violators.[43] Today, however, there is more effort to keep parolees on the streets, and only between 50 and 60 percent return to prison in the first two years after release.[44] Nationwide, the rate is even lower. A study conducted by the Bureau of Justice Statistics of the rearrest and return to prison rates in 15 states indicated that 51 percent of the prisoners released in these states in 1994 returned to prison within three years.[45]

Some parolees return to prison because they are convicted of a new felony. Others are arrested for a crime but are returned to prison in violation of their parole without a conviction for a new crime. Many are returned for violation of conditions of parole only. The relative numbers of these different forms of recidivism vary over time and from state to state. The general historical trend has been that the percentage returned for violation of parole has steadily increased, especially since 1980. Nationwide, the percentage increased from 17 percent in 1980 to 35 percent in 1999. In California, which has the highest recidivist rate in the country, the percentage climbed to 66 percent in 1999.[46]

The most common parole violation is drug use, usually discovered through a dirty urine test. Of 47 parole violators whom I interviewed, 25 had been returned to prison for drug abuse. Two were returned for not reporting to their agent (absconding) and five, for a new felony conviction. This was not a representative sample of California's parole violators, but the results do reflect, very generally, that drug abuse is the major reason for parole violation. Drug abuse is discovered mainly through the regular urine testing to which parolees who have drug use indicated in their "jacket" (official records kept on them) must submit. New felony convictions were 25 percent of my small sample, but they are usually 50 percent in larger studies.

Parole agents exercise great discretion when deciding to report a violation for drug use and failure to report. The policy "coming down" from the central office, probably initiated by the California governor, greatly influences agents' caution in this discretion. Don Macallair, executive director of the Center on Juvenile and Criminal Justice, recently made the point that the extraordinary failure rate of parole in California

> has little to do with the nature of California's inmates and everything to do with the nature of the "system." Parole revocation is a function of politically driven decision-making and institutional self-interest. The state's parole board is comprised of nine gubernatorial appointees who have little background in parole practice or reform. Instead, they pursue a one-dimensional approach that routinely returns offenders to prison for the slightest infraction.[47]

Parole violators whom I interviewed gave the following reasons for their violations:

- The guy found an empty beer bottle and he violated me.
- I failed to report and then he caught me with drug paraphernalia.
- My wife was pissed at me and called the cops on me for something I didn't do.
- I had one dirty test and he violated me.
- My parents had a gun in the house and I got violated for having access to a gun even though I didn't live there.[48]

When measured by this one indicator, recidivism, the plight of released prisoners is bleak. Recidivism, however, is a simplistic measure that reveals little about the success or failure of prisoners after their release. Most parolees *eventually* stay out of prison, but the majority of them would not consider their life a success. Nor would any informed observer. This is because many parolees, I suspect a majority, eventually end up living an isolated, impecunious, dependent life on the margins of society. However, some parolees who are "doing all right" on their own terms—that is, holding down a job, paying their rent, and getting by—are sent back to prison for some petty crime or minor parole violation.

Even if we greatly lowered the rate of imprisonment for violation of parole conditions, the actual success of released prisoners, as I define it, would be very low. Proceeding from my knowledge of the viewpoints of released prisoners, I have identified four postprison lifestyles: doing good, dependency, drifting on the edge, and dereliction.

Doing Good

A few released prisoners "make it," and "do good." That is, they get a good job and put together a noncriminal, stable, more or less rewarding life on the outside. Usually those who succeed in making it do so because they have several advantages. They have a job or a trade to which they can return. They have a family who can support them while they are looking for work or have connections that help them get a job. They have unusual determination, intelligence, and the skills required to penetrate conventional institutions, such as middle-class verbal skills and knowing how to dress and comport themselves to fit into conventional settings. In other words, they can pass as conventional people and thus infiltrate the conventional world.

Doing good involves attending school or having a good job, one with adequate pay, security, and job satisfaction. It might also entail other dimensions of stability and satisfaction: a suitable residence, rewarding friendships, and perhaps marriage and a home. These are very difficult for ex-convicts to achieve because of their debilitating prison experiences and their ex-convict stigma. But a few do succeed.

> After serving two years for drugs, Carol, a 40-year-old white woman, has tenaciously followed a path of self-improvement. Soon after release, she went to work telemarketing at minimum wage and located a small two-room apartment in Hollywood that she could barely afford. After displaying considerable stability in her initial work setting, she obtained a job as a placement counselor for The Work Place, a federally funded, state-managed placement program. She also enrolled in college and worked toward

finishing her BA. Her grade point average is 3.95. In progressing to where she is today, she overcame many obstacles. She was fired from her first job placement position by the California Department of Corrections, which had control of the program, because she was an ex-convict. (It is ironic that the CDC, which was managing a program for finding work for ex-convicts, fired someone because they were an ex-convict.) She was rehired by the same program to work in the California Youth Authority. (She indicated that this incident was a serious blow to her sense of self-worth.) She went on to a job in a program that arranges mentors for ex-prisoners. She is continuing her college work, has moved to a larger apartment in the Los Feliz neighborhood, a respectable Los Angeles residential neighborhood, and has purchased a used BMW in good condition. She is off parole and is now planning to attend graduate school at Pepperdine University when she receives her BA. It appears that she is well on the road to a successful, rewarding post-prison life.

Kevin, a 39-year-old black man, served 21 years in prison since he was a juvenile. He served nine years straight in the last sentence. When he had three years served on that last sentence and was in Pelican Bay in the SHU unit for being involved in "gang banging," they passed the three strikes law and he realized that he was going to serve his life in prison if he continued doing the things he was doing. He decided that he was going to reverse his life and "do exactly the opposite of what I had been doing." "I got a GED book and started reading. I became a sponge for everything. I read Napoleon Hill and he teaches you determination, to never give up. I began studying the Bible. I started right there and when I got out six years later, I was ready. Now I've been out three-and-a-half years, no problems with my agent, no violations. In the first 18 months I had a lot of obstacles. But I had learned two things: you have to work hard and you have to make the right decisions. When I got out I had no place to stay. My mother was in Las Vegas. The agent put me in the Posada Motel, right in the middle of skid row in Pasadena. But I was determined. I did just the opposite of what I had done before. I stayed away from the guys using dope. I moved in with my uncle for 15 days but he caught me using weed and kicked me out. I went back to the motel, but this time I got a little better room. It was about twice as big as my cell, but it had everything I needed—a little refrigerator, a hot plate—and I stayed there for eighteen months. I got a job telemarketing for $6 an hour, then I started working for a friend who had a little construction business and he finally got me into the cement mason union as an apprentice. Now I'm making $14 an hour. I've moved and have a little apartment in a nice neighborhood. And I got my daughter living with me. I never lost contact with her while I was in prison. I wrote her every week, at least. Now I got her living with me and she is getting A's and B's in school. When I got out she was living with her grandmother and getting D's and F's. I told her I'd give her $20 for every A and $10 for every B she got. And I would fine her $10 for a D and $20 for an F. Now she is doing good and wants to go to college. I stopped smoking cigarettes because of her. Now I been walking with the Lord since June."[49]

Dependency

Most parolees fall into a life of dependency. Typically, they make some efforts to find and hold a job, yet fail at both. They find some dependent method of surviving: living with a relative, wife, husband, girlfriend, or significant other; receiving government support, such as SSI or General Assistance (GA); or attaching to some support program, such as Sober Living or various church support groups. Some of them make money by "scuffling" or in underground or petty illegal economic activities. A parolee I interviewed in an earlier study spelled out the nature of scuffling:

> Then I got out and started scuffling to get by. I was cleaning the streets. A friend had a pickup and we'd go around and pick up anything. An old stove or refrigerator, sitting on the sidewalk. We picked up this old dirty Persian rug and we cleaned it up and sold it to some hippie. We were living from day to day.[50]

Loïc Wacquant described hustling for survival in the new ghetto:

> The mainstay of subsistence, however, is furnished by the odd jobs and marginal trades that have flourished in the past decade in the inner city. Some ghetto residents will babysit the children of neighbors, run errands for them, cut hair or grass, repair electrical appliances, shovel snow in the winter, collect pop cans for small sums of money, or "pick up junk outa the alley" for resale to those even less fortunate than they. Others yet become occasional street peddlers

or vendors, sell their blood, or go to day labor places in the hope of obtaining any kind of stopgap employment. . . .

One may also find irregular employ at an illegal "after-hours" club, operate a "gypsy cab," become a "jack-leg" mechanic or one of those "insurance artists" who try (especially when weather conditions are bad) to provoke auto or bus accidents in which they deliberately get injured with a view toward attempting to collect monetary damages.[51]

Following are three examples of dependent living:

Johnell, a 31-year-old black male parolee, served 38 months for receiving stolen property. When he was released he went to work on a union job as a laborer, but was laid off after nine months. He could get another job if he paid his union dues. Now he is unemployed and living with his mother. But he is not suppose to live there because it is public housing and they "don't like no parolees living there." He was about to get off parole and he "caught a DUI" (driving a vehicle under the influence) and they put him in the "star program"—a drug and alcohol abuse program conducted at the parole office. Now he has nine or ten more months of parole. He says he is trying to stay away from his old friends and find a job. He went back to the union three months ago, but wasn't able to get back in. "I'm just trying to find some work and stay out of the system. I want to get a good job, take advantage of things, have a good life, but I can't do it broke."

Boony, a 24-year-old Cambodian, served four years for house burglary. He has been out eight months. He lives with his family. He was violated twice—once for "being around guys with drugs" and once for being late for the star program. He was put in the county jail but not sent back to prison. Now he says he is having a hard time finding a job. He went to a job agency and they sent him to a warehouse job. He says he "is not inclined to work at that kind of job." He went "to a lot of places and filled out applications." "I was at that point, I couldn't get a job and I wasn't gonna get a job." Now most of the time he stays home. He lives with his family. He has had four agents. The one he has now strikes him as a person who, as long as you don't cause him any extra work, will leave you alone—but he leans toward a social worker.

Fredo, a 25-year-old black man, served 28 months for possession of a firearm and another 11 months for violation of parole. He had been out eight months when interviewed. He is living with his mother and father and is not employed. He recently tested dirty for PCB [an animal tranquilizer used illegally as a recreational drug]. He said he told the agent before the test that he was dirty. They put him in the star program for 20 days. They placed him in a dishwasher job paying $180 a week. He says, "I gave it up. I got too comfortable on the streets." He now is "just hangin' in. I'm not the kind of guy that gets depressed. I'm hanging out, that's all I know, that's what I was brought up doing." He says he would like to get into school. "I been trying to do this for years. I'd like to talk to youngsters, to tell kids. I got a lot to tell them."[52]

After a few failures obtaining or keeping a job and some success at surviving in a dependent manner, many parolees appear to lose their spirit and their aspirations to achieve some form of the good life. They become content with "hanging out" or "laying around."

Drifting on the Edge

Many parolees cross back and forth, outside and inside the law and the parole rules. For a while, they may hold menial jobs or live with their families, on welfare, in programs for ex-prisoners. Then they drift back into crime. They begin using drugs, lose their jobs, stop reporting, and are arrested or violated by their parole agent. They go back to prison for a short stay, then begin the process over again. A parolee I interviewed in 1985 illustrated this pattern:

> When I got out I moved in with my cousin in the Haight [the San Francisco Haight-Ashbury district]. I wanted to stay away from the crime element, the prey-type of environment. I met this guy at a club who said he thought I would be a good bouncer because I was big, so I worked at this place at Turk and Eddy [in the Tenderloin district] for 10 months. I lost that job because I was staying up too late and I started using some drugs. So then I started selling a little dope. I'd take $100 and buy some crack and make $300. But I was using and the agent sent me back to San Quentin for a 90-day violation. . . .
>
> Now I'm out, no job, and I don't want to go back; I'm not going back. My aspiration is to be a public relations man, but I haven't had any luck in finding anything like that.[53]

Dereliction

Many parolees fail to achieve minimum stability, even in dependent situations. They gravitate to the world of the homeless street people who live from day to day, drinking, hanging out, and surviving by making the rounds of soup kitchens and homeless shelters. A study of homeless persons in New York, conducted in the early 1990s, revealed that 80 percent of the homeless had been in jail, prison, or a mental hospital.[54] It is my belief that a long-term follow-up study of released prisoners would find that a relatively high percentage, perhaps more than 25 percent, end up on skid row. A Los Angeles police captain, who had participated in a "sweep" of L.A.'s skid row on November 20, 2002, remarked, "The area has the highest concentration of parolees in the state, almost 2,000."[55] In one of my earlier studies, a 43-year-old homeless black man described his descent into dereliction:

> I been violated three times. Twice for absconding, once for a dirty drug test. I've been to the county jail four times. I was in a substance abuse program for a little while. One time I had a little job for awhile as a janitor in a machine shop. They fired me. Said I had a drinking problem. Now I'm living on the street. I just got out of an alcohol program. I stay at the shelters when I can. You sign up and they have a lottery. I'm getting welfare and am waiting for a room through the Tenderloin Housing. As soon as I get a room, I can clean up and keep my clothes clean and get a little job. Been staying away from Safeway, stealing booze. I'm determined to stay out this time. I've been to the shelter on 5th and Bryant, a multiple service center for the homeless. They're gonna develop a job around my skills, fix my resume.[56]

Dannie Martin, who served several sentences in state and federal prisons, and who published a novel and a series of stories about prisons in the *San Francisco Chronicle*, wrote about a fellow ex-con he ran into on the streets of San Francisco in the early 1990s:

> I looked him over for a long moment before I realized it was Jesse. A far scruffier Jesse than the neat, well-groomed convict I had known in prison. His hair was long and his arms were dirty from digging in garbage cans. His mustache was shaggy and his Levis looked as if they had never been washed, but he stood there smiling. . . .

"I came out here with the $50 they gave me trying to build a new life," he told me, "but found out there's no free admission. I'd need to make $1,000 a month just to live in some dingy hotel. I couldn't get a good enough job to even do that so here I am." . . .

"I remember those dreams and schemes we had behind the wall about how sweet it was out here," he told me over sandwiches at the Beano Café on Valencia. "I never even considered the possibility I'd wind up like this. I'd gotten so used to free meals and all my needs being met that it was a real culture shock coming out here to the free world." . . .

"They'd rather hire someone from another country than an ex-con," he said. "I guess it's because of the different way they think you're going to carry yourself. I know I became sort of institutionalized, and everyone out here is expected to have that 911 mentality. I've found it very hard to adjust my values to this world." . . .

"About the time I was getting desperate enough to rob something, I ran into a guy on the street with a shopping cart who told me I could do pretty good recycling cans and bottles. He taught me the ropes and I've been on the street ever since. It's hard, but like I said, it's a damn sight better than being in prison."[57]

'Laying Low'

Today, two factors overwhelm most ex-convicts and compel them to "lay low." The first is that they are not able to get a job that pays them enough to live at a level anywhere near the good life they aspired to or even a minimally, economically viable level. Of the many reasons for this, the most important is that they are excluded from most good jobs. Moreover, they lack the basic skills required to get a good job. They were ill-prepared before going to prison, and the prison experience further damaged their capabilities. Finally, they reject the jobs that are available to them—the minimum-wage jobs that involve work they detest and find undignified according to the standards they acquired in their preprison deviant lives or in prison.

After getting by unemployed and dependent for a period of time, ex-convicts tone down their life aspirations and become reconciled to an impecunious life on the edge. Most of them, like

Jessie (whom Dannie Martin talked about in the previous section), because of their fear of being rearrested and going back to prison, perhaps with a "third strike" and a sentence of 25 years to life, try hard to stay away from criminal involvement. What they do is "lay low." This pattern of giving up and not looking for work is not unique to ex-prisoners. Increasingly, unsuccessful former participants in the work force are withdrawing. David Leonhardt, in an article in the *New York Times*, wrote:

> But even the strong economy of the late 90s failed to reverse the gradual overall increase in the number of men dropping out of the labor force. It also could not halt the long-term rise in the duration of unemployment for those people who kept looking for work and therefore appeared in the official statistics.
>
> Many of these workers have now been out of the job market for long enough that they may never come back. If they do, they are almost certain to make much less than they once did.[58]

The second factor compelling ex-cons to lay low is that they want to avoid going back to prison. They are tired of doing time. They know that if they go back with another felony they will serve a very long sentence. They are older and do not think that they can endure the deprivation, tension, danger, and aggravation that imprisonment in the contemporary prison involves.

As I discussed earlier, many ex-convicts get by and, at least for a period of time, become more or less comfortable in their dependency. They have aged and, therefore, have less energy and drive. Also, the dependent life may have caused their health to deteriorate, further reducing their energy and drive.

Laying low entails, most of all, avoiding "thugging," that is, consciously engaging in those criminal patterns that previously got them into prison or engaging in any serious new criminal pursuits, such as robberies, burglaries, or drug dealing. Laying low means avoiding use of the more expensive and addictive drugs, such as heroin, crack, cocaine, and "meth." It also means not getting tangled up in the petty criminal activities that many ex-prisoners engage in, such as shoplifting and petty drug dealing, which can result in a felony conviction—particularly in the case of an ex-convict—and a return to prison, perhaps with a third strike and a sentence of 25 years to life.

Laying low also entails staying away from former associates and hangouts, where serious and petty crime regularly occurs. It means staying at home, in one's room, confining personal interaction to a few people—family, girlfriends, boyfriends, wives, husbands, children, and very close friends. D.R., a 51-year-old Chicano I interviewed in the early 1990s, was laying low:

> I used drugs, speed, the first day. It scared the hell out of me. I've been clean ever since, since July, nine months. It's the first time I've been clean when I was out since I first went to the joint in the '60s. I feel kinda weird I'm gonna stay clean and get off this parole. It's hard to do, but I'm not goin' back.

> I tried to get work, but there is this thing. You have to say you were in prison. If you don't it's a violation. Who's gonna hire a 51-year-old that's been in prison most of his life?

> I'm getting GA. My room's $270. That leaves me 70 bucks. Not much. I'm trying to get SSI—drugs and having been in the system all these years. They tell me that you go once and they deny you. You go again and they deny you. Then the third time they give it to you.

> I eat in restaurants once in a while. But usually I buy food at the food bank. A friend of mine has a hot plate. Sometimes I eat at Glide or that gay church on Gough. I go there on Christmas, New Year, and Easter. I go up to the firehouse on Third St. where they collect toys for kids. They give out soup in the afternoon. My sister sent me some clothes and every month I buy something like these jeans.

> Most of the time I stay alone. I stay away from the TL [Tenderloin district where there is a lot of drug dealing, prostitution, and crime]. I watch TV a lot. I go to the library and walk around a lot. I like to go to the Golden Gate Park and the wharf. Last month I went back to Arkansas and visited my sister. The parole agent let me go. When I got back, he said he won a bet on me. The supervisor said I would never come back.

> I go to the shelters sometimes to talk to people. I try to tell the youngsters how it is. Maybe I can help them a little. So they can stay away from the shit I got into.[59]

As this older ex-convict's adjustment reveals, laying low segues into dereliction. But many cannot maintain a stable, dependent existence and slip into homeless street life. They start using alcohol or drugs, fail to keep up their rent payments, loose their GA or SSI, go to jail, and return to the streets. Sometimes, they reestablish a stable dependent adjustment. More often, they bounce back and forth between street life and the jail. Many face early death from alcoholism, poor nutrition, hepatitis C (rampant among drug-using convicts and ex-convicts), and numerous other ailments associated with street life. Chuck Terry, in his study of "The Fellas," a cohort of drug addicts whom he followed after their release from prison, tells of one "fella" who was nearing the end of the course—death:

> At this time, Brains is perhaps the worst "casualty" of all the fellas. After almost 3 years clean he began taking prescription drugs to get high. Before long, the pill taking was supplemented by heroin injections. His relapse was especially painful to me because I had a close, personal relationship with him the entire time he was clean. He always had a positive outlook, regularly went out of his way to help people, knew a great deal about music which is one of our shared interests, and was just great to be around. Not long after he started using drugs again he called me on the phone to ask for money. I could barely understand him because his words were too slurred. Within the next year he had spent several months in jail for being under the influence of narcotics. Since then he has contacted me by mail on several occasions claiming he was homeless, in bad health, and in desperate need of money. Kickstand told me just the other day that he believes Brains has had several unnecessary surgeries on one of his shoulders for the single purpose of obtaining prescription drugs. Whether that is true or not is basically irrelevant. Suffice it to say that the man is really struggling. Someone from Hope House recently told me they saw him showing up "on the line" (the "line" of homeless people who show up there for free food and shelter) now and then and that he looks like a walking corpse. Hopefully he will get to the point where he again seeks recovery. If he doesn't, I'm afraid he may die very soon.[60]

"Laying low" and that which follows—dereliction and early death—appear to be the final accomplishment of the contemporary methods of imprisonment and parole. Thus, troublesome, threatening, sometimes truly dangerous, lower-class members—the new surplus population—have been ultimately disposed of in the least expensive and bothersome fashion imaginable.

Endnotes

1. For example, Jeremy Travis, former director of the National Institute of Justice and current fellow of the Urban Institute, which has received federal and private foundation money to study the reentry problem, wrote in the pamphlet *From Prison to Home:* "The release of prisoners back into the community poses two fundamentally interrelated challenges: First, how to protect the safety of the public, and second, how to foster an individual's transition from life in prison to life as a productive citizen" (Washington, DC: Urban Institute, June 2001, p. 6).

2. Jeff Glasser, "Ex-cons on the Street," *U.S. News and World Report,* 1 May 2000, p. 18.

3. In my years of close contact with prisoners and ex-prisoners while a prisoner, as an organizer of prisoner support groups, and as a reseacher of prisoners, which includes research of persons leaving California prisons in the late 1960s (*Felon*) and James Austin's and my interviews of persons entering prisons in three states in the early 1990s (*It's About Time*), I have been consistently reassured that *most* persons passing through the prison make up their mind to attempt to live a noncriminal life and stay out of prison.

4. Prisoner interview, Solano, July 2002.

5. Irwin, *Felon,* 113–114.

6. Ibid., 113.

7. Loïc Wacquant recently argued that a "mesh" between the ghetto and the prison has formed, in which, because of the heavy flow back and forth between the ghetto and the prison, the prison is like the ghetto and the ghetto is like the prison. See "Deadly Symbiosis: When Ghetto and Prison Meet and Mesh," *Punishment and Society* 3, no. 1 (2001): 95–134.

8. While conducting research at the Long Beach District Parole Office, I encountered a parolee on the day of his release who had been on psychotropic medication during his incarceration. He was very upset because he had tried without success to get assistance from an agent to locate a clinic where he could get his prescription renewed.

9. Ex-prisoner interview, Los Angeles, May 2002.

10. Joan Petersilia, *When Prisoners Come Home* (New York: Oxford University Press, 2003), 120.

11. I use California as my penal exemplar for two reasons. First, most of my personal and research experience has been with the California prison system. Second, California has had the most prominent state prison system since World War II. It led the country in the swerve toward corrrectional institutions, in turmoil in the 1970s, and now leads in the punitive era and the escalation of prison populations.

12. In July and August 2001, I attempted to locate an affordable residence for a parolee outside the downtown, skid row, or South-Central areas of Los Angeles. I wanted to avoid these areas because of the concentration of crime, violence, and other parolees living there. I contacted rental agencies, housing projects, and apartment complexes. I toured many neighborhoods. Through an ex-convict who was moving to a larger, more expensive apartment, I was able to rent the apartment she was living in. This apartment, just south of Hollywood Boulevard, was very small with two rooms slightly larger than a prison cell. The rent was $550 a month. I was lucky to find it.

13. On November 20 and 21, 2002, a team of Los Angeles police officers and California Department of Corrections parole agents conducted sweeps of the Los Angeles downtown skid row and arrested parolees.

14. Carla Rivera, "Homeless Often Take a One-Way Street to Skid Row," *Los Angeles Times,* 30 November 2002, p. A1.

15. Amanda Ripley, "Outside the Gates," *Time,* 21 January 2002, pp. 58–62.

16. Harry Holtzer, *What Employers Want: Job Prospects for Less-Educated Workers* (New York: Russell Sage, 1996).

17. Petersilia, *When Prisoners Come Home,* 116.

18. Petersilia offers a thorough discussion of the employment problems of parolees because of their criminal records.

19. Petersilia, *When Prisoners Come Home* 89. Petersilia refers to Jonathan Simon, *Poor Discipline: Parole and the Social Control of the Underclass* (Chicago: University of Chicago Press, 1993), for this employment figure.

20. "Challenges of Prisoner Reentry and Parole in California," California Policy Research Center Brief Series, June 2000.

21. In a CDC study of parolees released from 1 July 1996 to 30 June 1997, more than 70 percent were unemployed in each of the four quarters of that year. This remains true.

22. Parolee agent interview, Long Beach Parole Office, July 2002.

23. Ex-prisoner interview, North Hollywood, California, spring 2002.

24. Petersilia, *When Prisoners Come Home,* 36–37.

25. Author's field notes, August 2001.

26. For example, I immediately gravitated to the ocean upon release and discovered surfing and fellow surfers, which I firmly believe satisfied many of my "special" needs as an ex-prisoner.

27. Two young healthy men I interviewed in Long Beach were receiving county pay for caring for relatives, one the mother of his girlfriend (summer 2002).

28. These figures were derived by James Austin in his study in 2002 of postrelease in these states (Institute on Crime, Justice, and Corrections, George Washington University, Washington, DC: in preparation).

29. In the spring of 2002, I interviewed two parolees at Solano State Prison who had been sent back to prison because their agents discovered "artifact" weapons displayed on their walls. One had hung an Indian tomahawk (his wife was Native American). The other had displayed a Central American machete.

30. Petersilia, *When Prisoners Come Home*, 82.

31. Interview with parole violator, Solano, summer 2001.

32. Irwin and Austin, *It's About Time*, 127–129.

33. *Parole-Agent Manual*, (California Department of Corrections, 1965), PA-III-00.

34. Daniel Glaser, *The Effectiveness of a Prison and Parole System* (Indianapolis, IN: Bobbs Merrill, 1964), 431.

35. Petersilia, *When Prisoners Come Home*, 80. The ethnographic study referred to is Mona Lynch, "Waste Managers? New Penology, Crime Fighting, and the Parole Agent Identity," *Law and Society* 32, no. 4 (1999): 839–869.

36. Agent interview, Long Beach Parole Office, June 2002.

37. Agent interview, Long Beach Parole Office, August 2002.

38. Agent interview, Long Beach Parole Office, July 2002.

39. Julie Preggar, "Memo-Parole," memos for a master class, February 2003, University of California, Los Angeles, Department of Sociology, p.10.

40. Irwin, *Felon*, 168.

41. Petersilia, *When Prisoners Come Home*, 81.

42. Preggar, "Memo-Parole," 10.

43. See Jeremy Travis and Sarah Lawrence, "Beyond the Prison Gates: The State of Parole in America (Washington, DC: Urban Institute, 2002), 23.

44. The Research Branch of the California Department of Corrections released its findings after a follow-up study of 60,179 "first releases to parole" in 1998. After two years, 55.17 percent had returned to prison.

45. Bureau of Justice Statistics, 2002.

46. See Petersilia, *When Prisoners Come Home*, 148.

47. Don Macallair, "Reforming California's Failed Parole System," *San Francisco Chronicle*, 21 April 2003, p. B7.

48. Interviews of parole violators, at Solano, October 2002.

49. Parolee interviews, Los Angeles, October 2002.

50. Irwin and Austin, *It's About Time*, 131.

51. Loïc Wacquant, "The New Urban Color Line: The State and Fate of the Ghetto in Post-Fordist America," in Craig J. Calhoun, ed., *Social Theory and the Politics of Identity* (Oxford and Cambridge: Blackwell, 1994), 247.
52. Parole officer interviews, Long Beach Parole Office, July 2002.
53. Irwin and Austin, *It's About Time*, 131–132.
54. Martha Burt, *Over the Edge* (New York: Urban Institute and Russell Sage, 1992).
55. Quoted in Andrew Blankstein and Richard Winton, "130 Arrested in Sweep of Skid Row," *Los Angeles Times*, 21 November 2002, p. B12.
56. Irwin and Austin, *It's About Time*, 156.
57. Dannie Martin, "Home—But Not Free: Prison Is Tough but Getting Out Is Tougher," *San Francisco Chronicle*, Sunday Punch section, 9 August 1992, p. 3. Dannie Martin was sent back to prison for parole violations soon after writing this article.
58. David Leonhardt, "Out of a Job and No Longer Looking," *New York Times*, 29 September 2002, p. D4.
59. Quoted in Irwin and Austin, *It's About Time*, 130–131.
60. Charles M. Terry, *The Fellas: Rocky Roads Toward Addiction, Prisonization, and Reintegration* (Belmont, CA: Wadsworth, 2003), 177. ✦

Chapter 8

Disposal of the New 'Dangerous Class'

In the preceding chapters, I examined the consequences of the war on crime. I argued that states such as California maintain complete control over their dramatically enlarged prison populations in newly designed warehouse prisons backed up by supermax prisons. After failing to prepare prisoners in any significant way for life after prison and, in fact, damaging them profoundly, the penal institutions have herded them into a life on the margins of society, where they lie low and do not cause too much trouble.

In Chapter 1, I argued that the war against crime was mounted by conservative politicians and aided by the media, who used street crime as a diversion and who militated against the new ghetto dwellers, who were perceived as a dangerous class. In this chapter, I more thoroughly examine these developments.

The War on Crime

The conventional wisdom is that the punitive swing and the resultant escalation of prison populations were brought about by the public's reaction to the steady increases in crime after World War II and to its rapid elevation after 1967.[1] As suggested previously, the actual changes in crime rates do not support this idea. Though crime rates did increase between 1967 and 1974, they were fairly level before and after that time period.[2] In the early 1960s, conservative politicians, particularly Senator Barry Goldwater, attempted to stir up the public's fear of crime. The public *was* concerned with crime after the mid-1960s, when crime, along with civil rights and antiwar demonstrations and urban riots, increased. However, it was the formation of the new inner-city ghettos that finally tipped the scale, elevated the public's fear, and ushered in the punitive era. Thousands of jobless, young ghetto dwellers, whose aspirations had been heightened by the promises of the War on Poverty and whose anger and audacity had been excited by the Civil Rights movement and its failures, milled about their neighborhoods,"gangbanged," "thugged," abused drugs, and, worst of all to the respectable middle class, forayed out into the nation's cities. They greatly alarmed the general society and became a target for opportunistic politicians who had been milking the crime and drug issues. The politicians' punitive campaigns against crime and drugs were supported by conservative criminologists, who warned about the growing prevalence of "wicked people" and "criminal predators."[3] These developments motivated state and federal politicians—Republicans and Democrats alike—to pass a steady stream of laws that brought about our unprecedented imprisonment binge. In this chapter, I examine the formation of the new ghetto and reactions toward it that produced this outcome.

The Change in Employment Opportunities

To appreciate the situation of the new ghetto dwellers, let us first consider the job opportunities that existed for lower-class people prior to the radical changes in the political economy that occurred after 1970. My experiences in 1947 make a good starting point. In my senior year, I managed to graduate from San Fernando High School with all Ds. The students of San Fernando High, located in a small incorporated municipality within Los Angeles, were mostly working-class and lower-class whites with a minority of Mexican Americans. I was "hanging out" and drifting toward crime. On three occasions, however, I decided to follow the path traveled by most of the other males with whom I had graduated and get a job. On these occasions, I proceeded to one of the plants located in the San Fernando Valley, submitted an application, and was hired.[4] Most of my fellow high school graduates had gone to work at these plants or at the many construction projects that abounded in the Valley in those years—1947 through the 1950s. At that time, it was relatively easy for a youth, with or without a high school diploma, to get a job. These jobs started off with a salary of $60 to $100 a week, an amount on which a young person could begin adult life, that is, rent an apartment, save a little and buy a car, plan to get married, and look forward to buying one of the tract houses that were sprouting up all over the Valley.

After 1980, however, the best jobs most young working-class or lower-class youths could hope for were minimum or close to minimum wage jobs in the service sector, such as fast food or retail. The income earned in these jobs was insufficient to enable them to embark on a self-sustaining adult life. Moreover, this kind of work did not lead to better positions with adequate salaries and a self-sufficient lifestyle, let alone anything resembling the "good life," the accoutrements of which meanwhile were being persistently advertised in the mass media. Tamar Lewin, in a 1994 *New York Times* article, described the experiences of a young man entering the job market in that year:

> Andrew Flenoy, a twenty-one-year-old living in Kansas City, did better in 1994 than many, holding down a steady job paying a cut above the minimum wage. In fact, he had even enjoyed some recent promotions, rising at a food catering firm from dishwasher to catering manager. Through that sequence of promotions, however, his earnings had increased from $5.50 an hour to only $6.50 an hour—the equivalent of only about $12,000 a year working full-time year-round. Whatever satisfaction he had enjoyed from his promotions had quickly paled. "Now he is tired of the burgundy and black uniform he must wear," a reporter concluded, "and of the sense that he works every day from 6 A.M. to 2 P.M. just to earn enough money so that he can come back and work some more the next day." "My resolution for 1994," Flenoy remarked, "is that if nothing comes along I'll relocate and start from scratch somewhere else."[5]

Since the 1970s, this has been the situation for most young people entering the job market. For inner-city dwellers the situation is *much* worse. William Julius Wilson quotes a 25-year-old Chicago West Side dweller:

> Four years I been out here trying to find a steady job. Going back and forth all these temporary jobs and this 'n that. Then you gotta give money at home, you know you gotta buy your clothes which

cost especially for a big person. Then you're talking about my daughter, then you talking about food in the house too, you know, things like that.[6]

Unless the inner-city youths, through some lucky break, family connections, or Herculean tugs at their bootstraps, land one of the few good jobs—like a union job—among the very few that exist in their social worlds or get a college education, perhaps with some postgraduate training, they are destined to struggle to survive in the inner city, dependent on their families or welfare or on hustling, dealing drugs, or "thugging."

Well, lately like I said I have been trying to make extra money and everything. I have been selling drugs lately on the side after I get off work, an it has been going all right. . . . Like I was saying you can make more money dealing drugs than your job, anybody. Not just me but anybody, for the simple fact that if you have a nice clientele and some nice drugs, some nice 'caine or whatever you are selling then the money is going to come, the people are going to come.[7]

What happened? In 1965—except for the country's initial, small-scale involvements in Vietnam; persistent racial discrimination, which was being brought to our attention by the Civil Rights move-ment; and "pockets of poverty" that Michael Harrington had recently rediscovered—all appeared to be well in the United States.[8] David Halberstam, commenting on Ford Motors' introduction of the Mustang, a symbol of America's auto-industry-driven, successful economy, characterized the prosperity in the land:

It came out in 1964, at what would prove to be the highwater mark of the American century, when the country was rich, the dollar strong, and inflation low. It was almost twenty years since the end of World War II, and it was more than a decade since the end of the Korean War. The Vietnam War was still a guerrilla action involving relatively small numbers of American advisers. The bitter and costly part of that war, which was to take more than fifty-one thousand lives, divide the country, start a runaway inflation, and completely divert the nation's attention, was still ahead. The economy was expanding. Though many of the forces that would afflict American industry were already beginning to form, they were not yet visible, and the domestic economy had never seemed so strong. . . . There was enough for everyone; the country was enjoying unparalleled prosperity, and the pie was bigger than ever. The pie would turn out to have its limits after all, but at [that] halcyon moment, the future seemed unbounded.[9]

And, as Bennett Harrison and Barry Bluestone revealed in their examination of the "U-turn" the U.S. economy subsequently took in the 1970s, in the 1960s the pie was not only growing but also "the shares were becoming more equally distributed among working people and their families."[10]

The Failed War on Poverty

When he came to power (after the assassination of President John Kennedy in 1963 and then his own election in 1964), President Lyndon Johnson set out to complete Franklin D. Roosevelt's New Deal—the array of programs introduced to fight the poverty of the Great Depression of the 1930s. As Marshall Frady put it in his review of Robert Caro's biography of Johnson: "All he wanted was to be the greatest president in the history of the Republic, by abolishing with his Great Society benefactions all poverty, hunger, and racial wrong from the land."[11] Johnson first tackled racial discrimination and, with his extraordinary influence in Congress, succeeded in passing the Civil Rights Act in 1964. Then, he introduced his plan to wage a "War on Poverty." He enlisted the help of some of the country's most progressive political thinkers—Sargent Shriver, President John Kennedy's brother-in-law, who had headed the Peace Corps; Michael Harrington, the prominent socialist who rediscovered poverty in America; Frank Mankiewicz, a Peace Corps official who later became Attorney General Robert Kennedy's press secretary and then Senator George McGovern's presidential campaign manager; and Paul Jacobs, a former Trotskyite who, through his writing and documentary filmmaking, had become a respected, progressive intellectual. These radical thinkers went to work on a grand plan to fight poverty in America. When they were well into their plan, Johnson informed Shriver that the plan would have to be put on hold. Johnson had decided that he must win the Vietnam War first and there was not enough money to fight both wars simultaneously. Harrington described these developments in his book, *The New American Poverty:*

The day before Shriver was to make his first presentation to the President, Frank Mankiewicz, Paul Jacobs, and I decided, rather quixotically, to write a proposal setting forth what should be done rather than what seemed politically expedient. So we developed a fairly radical statement of that consensus about the need for coordination, arguing that there would have be considerable *restructuring of the economy and society* if poverty was to be abolished. To our surprise, Shriver incorporated about 80 percent of our ideas into the outline he took to Johnson. Even more astonishing, Shriver reported that the President said that if it took such measures to win the fight, he would take them.

But our relatively radical version of the task force's consensus never came to pass—and neither did any version of it. The "war on poverty," James Sundquist (a member of the task force) shrewdly remarks, became "the poverty program." LBJ's soaring phrases—an "unconditional" war on poverty—came to describe a very worthwhile, extremely modest, and, with a few exceptions, conventional reality. . . .

The basic reason why Lyndon Johnson's commitment "to eliminate the paradox of poverty in the midst of plenty" failed was the war in Vietnam. . . . I had long imagined a conversation between Sargent Shriver and Lyndon Johnson. When I talked to Shriver in the fall of 1982, he confirmed that it had actually taken place. In 1966, Shriver, obviously assuming that the standard federal pattern was going to prevail, drew up an ambitious, long-range budget for OEO [Office of Economic Opportunity] that would allow it to fulfill its promise. He went to see the President in Texas in the early autumn and was told that because of the expenditures for Vietnam, there was not enough money to fulfill his request.

Why not raise taxes? Shriver asked Johnson. That, he was told, can't be done to the Democrats in Congress on the eve of an election. The President then went on to say that Secretary McNamara had assured him that the war would be over by the end of the year. In 1967 there would be no problems.[12]

What occurred after Johnson's fateful decision is well known. He continued on his "march of folly,"[13] precipitated the massive war protest movement, then declined to run for a second term, having failed in both war efforts—poverty and Vietnam.

Regrettably, Johnson did not publicly announce that he was temporarily abandoning his War on Poverty. He continued with the rhetoric about the war, formed the Office of Economic Opportunity, and obtained some money for a few poverty programs. A small, dedicated army of poverty warriors fought on with meager funds. Some programs were initiated and supported, such as Head Start, Newgate, Job Corps, and Vista. However, these were programs that nibbled at the edges of poverty and did not get close to its core, which was the excessive unemployment or underemployment of the lower classes, particularly the nonwhite lower classes.

Whether Johnson's architects of the War on Poverty would have succeeded in developing a successful plan or Johnson would have followed it to victory is far from clear. However, it is very clear what happened after his abandonment of the War on Poverty, then his failure in Vietnam, and the resulting Republican takeover of the federal government. Nixon and the other conservative government figures used Johnson's feeble poverty programs as evidence that "liberalism," which the Democratic Party had pursued for the preceding decades, had been a total failure. This imputed failure justified the reinstitution of laissez faire capitalism and the perpetual wars on crime and drugs.

The New Poor

After Johnson's failures, President Nixon began a complete conversion in economic and, more particularly, criminal justice policies. The policies of the "welfare state" were rejected and an era of laissez faire capitalism and punitive criminal justice policies began. The result was a dramatic alteration in the situation of the poor, particularly the inner-city poor (who were increasingly nonwhite, mainly black). Several developments shaped the new poverty. The first of these was a series of dramatic changes in American business practices. These changes were precipitated by a decline in profits earned by American businesses.

The Profit Squeeze

At the end of the 1960s, the profits of American corporations stagnated and then began to decline. Economists Bennet Harrison and Barry Bluestone have documented what they label as the "profit squeeze":

> Whether measured as business owners' share of the total national income or by the conventional rate of return on investment, profits peaked in the mid-1960s and continued to fall or stagnate for the next fifteen years. From a peak of nearly 10 percent in 1965, the average net after tax profit rate of domestic nonfinancial corporations plunged to less than 6 percent during the second half of the 1970s,—a decline of more than a third.[14]

They argue that the sudden emergence of international economic competition, to "which U.S. business leaders were initially blind," caused this profit squeeze.[15] They further pointed out that only a few American businesses experimented with new forms of the "organization of work and in labor-management relations, designed to increase productivity and thus allow their firms to cope with higher costs."[16] Most businesses adopted different strategies:

> American corporations were left with a limited number of ways to regain their lost profits. They could get out of the producing end of business altogether and find alternative ways of making a paper profit. They could, in the words of Arnold Weber, Assistant Secretary of Labor under President Nixon, "zap labor." Or they could make a new bid to control government so as to reduce their taxes and the cost of meeting government regulations. In the end, under the banner of "restructuring," they did all three. They abandoned major parts of their basic operations in traditional businesses in favor of what Robert Reich has named "paper entrepreneurialism." They found ways to cut the cost of labor drastically. And they cajoled government—both Democratic and Republican administrations—into coming to their rescue. Along the way, some of America's most fundamental values and institutions were challenged and transformed, notably the nation's long-standing commitment to a rising and more equally shared standard of living.[17]

The Deindustrialization of America

One of the first responses of American business to foreign competition was to move a great portion of their manufacturing "offshore" to take advantage of cheap labor. Harrison and Bluestone pointed out that "domestic employment attributable to manufacturing fell from 27 percent in 1970 to 19 percent in 1986."[18] Due to the North American Free Trade Agreement (NAFTA) and other changes in American business practices and government policies since 1986, the transfer of manufacturing has greatly increased. The result of this shifting of production offshore and the reduction or complete cessation of the manufacturing of many products inside the United States (e.g., steel) was a drastic reduction of higher-paying jobs.

> In studying 92 manufacturing industries that account for 97 percent of total manufacturing employment in the nation, we found that employment in one-third of [these] industries either entered a long-term decline after 1968 or saw previous growth totally arrested. These troubled industries had accounted for more than seven million jobs in 1969.[19]

The Congressional Budget Office calculated that up to 2.1 million workers were "dislocated" in 1982 because of changes in employment opportunities.[20]

Zapping Labor

The second strategy American businesses used to increase their profits was to "zap labor." First, they forced workers, even unionized workers, to accept lower wages. According to Harrison and Bluestone, between 1964 and 1980, wages

> rose more or less continuously, in step with increases in productivity and rises in the cost of living. Then, during the recession of 1981–82, concessions exploded onto the labor scene. In the latter year, the trough of the recession, 44 percent of the unionized work bargaining for new contracts took wage cuts or forewent increases for at least the first year of the new contract.[21]

Businesses established two-tiered wage structures, newly hired workers accepting lower wages than those paid to senior employees.[22] More important for our focus, which is the unemployed and underemployed inner-city workers, businesses established part-time work routines. In this way they avoided paying many benefits or giving regular raises to the part-timers. In addition to the greatly increased use of "temps," they leased out many tasks to smaller companies who did not pay high wages. This shift to "contingent labor" involved millions of workers:

> One estimate, assembled by *Business Week*, is that contingent labor—leased and temporary workers, involuntary part-timers, employees of subcontractors, and home workers—grew from 8 million in 1980 to 18 million by 1985. That number is nearly 17 percent of the total work force.[23]

Finally, they avoided unions:

> [A] growing number of corporate managers have sought, with great success, to cut the cost of labor by pursuing what is referred to in business circles as "union avoidance." Part of this strategy is tied to the outsourcing of parts and service.... The other involves a direct attack on unions in already unionized firms.[24]

David Gordon reviewed these same changes and argued that American business changed to a "stick strategy" in dealing with labor. This strategy involved a relationship of conflict rather than cooperation with labor:

> During the boom years of the 1950s and 1960s, many corporations and most labor unions understood that they would jointly share in the economy's prosperity. As one feature of the compact, real wages steadily rose. Since the mid-70s, many U.S. corporations have abandoned that understanding. They have demanded union give back on both wages and benefits. They have tossed away the presumption that, over time, their employees are entitled to wage or benefit increases. They have grown more and more hostile to - arrangements guaranteeing employment security, turning increasingly to temporary and contingent workers. When they hire replacements, they are inclined to insist on two-tier, or even multi-tier replacements, steadily ratcheting down the earnings that workers with given skill levels could reasonably expect on the job.[25]

These business operational changes that "zapped" labor were aided or greatly promoted by the federal government, even the Democratic administration of President Jimmy Carter:

> By the time Jimmy Carter moved into the White House, the federal government was ready to help, but it did not quite know how. Over the next decade, it learned. With deregulation and corporate tax

cuts, tight money and military spending, Washington tacitly under-wrote—and then increasingly lent active support to—most of the restructuring efforts that took place within American enterprise.[26]

With the election of Ronald Reagan, federal government support for laissez-faire capitalism and zapping labor became explicit and vigorous:

> A combination of old- and new-style conservatives had succeeded in capturing the ideological high ground well beyond the wildest dreams of the theoreticians who had managed Reagan's electoral victories in 1980 and again in 1984. The long-lost World War II expansion of social spending and market regulation—the legacies of the New Deal and its offspring—was arrested, along with any pretense of industrial policy or public planning. *Laissez faire* was back in fashion, having lain dormant since the days of Herbert Hoover.[27]

In the 1990s, unemployment fell dramatically. The new economy produced 2 million new jobs. But most of these were not the high-paying jobs that were lost in the 1970s and '80s. They were jobs in the "service field," which, according to Michael Harrington,

> will pay about half the wage of factory jobs which are disappearing. In 1983, the Bureau of Labor Statistics . . . said, there would be half a million new jobs for both nurse's aids and janitors, 400,000 opening for fast-food workers, [and] 377,000 for general office clerks.[28]

Loïc Wacquant characterized the jobs created between 1970 and 1984 as follows:

> During this period, a polarized labor demand, characterized by a widening gulf between high-wage, credentialed positions and variable-schedule, low-paying jobs, offering few benefits and no security, became a structural feature of the new American service economy. Thus, of the 23 million positions created between 1970 and 1984, a full 22 million were in the service sector, and today upwards of three-fourths of all employment is in the service industries. But nearly a third of all jobs generated in the 1980s were part-time positions and 75 percent of them were filled by people who would prefer to work full-time. Furthermore, many of these service jobs pay between four and six dollars an hour, a far cry from

the hourly rate of $12 to $15 common in unionized, durable-goods manufacturing. Indeed, half of the jobs added between 1970 and 1983 paid less than $8,000 a year.[29]

The economic restructuring of the economy after 1970 resulted in the stagnation of formerly secure and affluent workers' wages and greatly increased instability of their occupational future. What is more important for this analysis is that it meant that the lower classes, particularly the nonwhite, inner-city dwellers, were completely excluded from the American dream of affluence and upward mobility. This exclusion followed their rising expectations inspired by the 1960s radical movements and the government's promises of getting rid of poverty. As Michael Harrington put it,

> The stable black working class and a growing black middle class made real gains in the sixties, and even in the seventies. At the same time, a great mass of poor blacks was denied the chance that had come to all of the traditional (pre-World War I) immigrant groups. That is, at that point at which they arrived in the urban labor market ready to climb up the ladder of social mobility, the bottom rungs were being hacked off the ladder. So many blacks are in danger of disappearing down a hole in the American occupational structure.[30]

As it turned out, they were "disappeared" by the penal organizations into the prisons.

Demise of the Radical 'Movements'

Another factor that impinged on the new poor during the 1970s was the sputtering out of the radical movements that had been so important to the country and to the attitudes of black people in the 1960s. Starting with the Civil Rights movement and then the antiwar, women's, and, finally, the prisoner movements, thousands of blacks and other minorities—usually supported, sometimes led or sometimes egged on by white activists—organized, marched, sat in, demonstrated, and rioted. These "movement" activities gave the activists purpose and many minorities hope. When the movements died out or flamed out in ugly displays of violence, as some of the more radical fragments had,[31] they left poorer members of the minority groups disillusioned, stranded, and despised by the emerging "moral majority," which was blaming "Negroes" and white "communists" for most of society's problems. Michael Harrington, who had been intimately involved in the 1960's movements, commented on the demise of these movements and the resulting disillusionment:

> The black ghettos of 1963–64, when the poverty issue was placed on the agenda, were not in revolt. Between 1965 and 1968, *after* Lyndon Johnson's commitment, they were. One of the unintended consequences of that declaration of social war was to legitimize suffering, to make it honorable rather than shameful and therefore possibly militant. Another result was to excite expectations that, above all after the tragic decision to massively escalate the war in Vietnam, could not be satisfied. Frustrated hope is a potent but not always rational force. It began to pulse in the second half of the sixties.[32]

The New Ghetto

In spite of the Civil Rights movement, which had brought about substantial changes in the legal status and upward mobility of many African Americans and other nonwhites, the poorer members of these groups (who were the majority) remained in decaying inner-city ghettos. They were held there by enduring practices of racial discrimination, ties to their families and communities, and their lack of money to pay for better housing. Also, many of them were trapped in ill-conceived federal housing projects.[33]

The inner cities had taken a dramatic turn for the worse. Many of the ghettos had experienced devastating riots, which had damaged or destroyed many buildings and houses, most of which were not repaired or replaced. The banks and the federal government had "redlined" inner-city neighborhoods, that is, defined them as poor investment risks and refused to lend money for new construction or business start ups in these areas. Many stores, banks, and businesses that provided services for local residents had closed or moved away. In some places, only liquor and mom-and-pop grocery stores and check-cashing businesses remained. As Loïc Wacquant, who studied the Chicago ghetto, put it,

> The once-lively streets—residents remember a time, not so long ago, when crowds were so dense at rush hour that one had to elbow one's way to the train station—now have the appearance of an

empty, bombed-out war zone. The commercial strip has been reduced to a long tunnel of charred stores, vacant lots littered with broken glass and garbage, and dilapidated buildings left to rot in the shadow of the elevated train line. At the corner of Sixty-third and Cottage Grove Avenue, the handful of remaining establishments that struggle to survive are huddled behind wrought-iron bars. The only enterprises that seem to be thriving are liquor stores and currency exchanges, these "banks of the poor" where one can cash checks, pay bills and buy money orders for a fee.[34]

The factories and other businesses that had employed large numbers of urban lower-class and working-class members had shut down or moved far away. Most of the upwardly mobile former members of these communities had moved out to more affluent, respectable neighborhoods.[35] What were left were the poorest, unemployed, uneducated, disorganized, and disaffiliated ghetto dwellers. William Julius Wilson, who studied Chicago's poor neighborhoods, pointed out that because of unemployment, the urban ghetto is more devastated than before:

> A neighborhood in which people are poor but employed is different from a neighborhood in which people are poor and jobless. Many of today's problems in the inner-city ghetto neighborhoods—crime, family dissolution, welfare, low levels of social organization, and so on—are fundamentally a consequence of the disappearance of work.[36]

It is not just severe unemployment that reduces the life chances of inner-city inhabitants but the lack of all forms of "social capital." Borrowing the concept of Pierre Bourdieu,[37] Wacquant elaborated on the problems of black American ghetto dwellers:

> I draw on the concept of social capital developed by Pierre Bourdieu to highlight what I consider to be the major social-organizational cause of the continued degradation of social conditions and life chances in the black American ghetto: the *erosion of "state social capital,"* that is, organizations presumed to provide civic goods and services—physical safety, legal protection, welfare, education, housing, and health care—which have turned into instruments of surveillance, suspicion, and exclusion rather than vehicles of social integration and trust-building. The near-total breakdown of public institutions, combined with and abetting the withdrawal of the

wage-labor economy in the context of extreme and unyielding racial segregation, has accelerated the shrinking of the ghetto's indigenous organizational basis and helped concentrate in it the most dispossessed segments of the urban (sub)proletariat, thereby further depreciating the informal social capital available within it.[38]

Wacquant distinguished the former "communal ghetto" from the new "hyperghetto":

The *communal* ghetto of the immediate post-war era, compact, sharply bounded, and comprising a full complement of black classes bound together by a unified collective consciousness, a near-complete social division of labor, and broad-based communitarian agencies of mobilization and representation, has been replaced by what we may call the *hyperghetto* of the 1980s, whose spatial configuration, institutional and demographic makeup, structural position and function in society are quite novel. . . .

What is distinctive about black ghettoization today is, first, that it has become spatially as well as institutionally differentiated and *decentered,* split, as it were, between a decaying, if expanding, urban core on the one hand, and satellite working-class and middle-class neighborhoods located on the periphery of cities and, increasingly, in segregated suburbs often adjacent to the historic Black Belt. . . . Indeed, in that very period when legal changes were presumed to bring about its amelioration, the inner city has been plagued by accelerating physical degradation, rampant insecurity and violence, and degrees of economic exclusion and social hardship comparable only to those of the worst years of the Great Depression.[39]

Wacquant suggested that the hyperghetto is like the prison in many important ways:

Two examples illustrate well this increasing conformance of the hyperghetto to the carceral model. The first is the *"prisonization of public housing,"* as well as retirement homes, single-room occupancy hotels, homeless shelters, and other establishments for collective living, which have come to look and feel just like houses of detention. "Projects" have been fenced up, their perimeter placed under beefed-up security patrols and authoritarian controls, including identification-card checks, signing in, electronic monitoring, police infiltration, "random searches,

segregation, curfews, and resident counts—all familiar procedures of efficient prison management." Over the past decade, the
Chicago Housing Authority has deployed its own police force
and even sought to institute its own "misdemeanor court" to
try misbehaving tenants on the premises. Residents of the Robert Taylor Homes, at the epicenter of the South Side, have been
subjected to video surveillance and required to bear special ID
cards, as well as pass through metal detectors, undergo
patdown searches, and report all visitors to a housing officer in
the lobby. In 1995, the CHA [Chicago Housing Authority]
launched massive paramilitary sweeps under the code name "Operation Clean Sweep," involving pre-dawn surprise searches of
buildings leading to mass arrests in violation of basic constitu-
tional rights quite similar to the periodic "shakedowns" intended
to rid prison wards of shanks [knives] and other contraband. As
one elderly resident of a District of Columbia project being put
under such quasi-penal supervision observed: "It's as though
the children in here are being prepared for incarceration, so
when they put them in a real lock-down situation, they'll be
used to being hemmed in."[40]

Ghetto Youth

As joblessness increased in the country and fell more heavily
on the inner-city poor, it weighed most heavily on young people in
the ghettos. This spelled trouble for the society, because these
youths were in a different frame of mind than young members of
the lower class in earlier eras. These contemporary, mostly nonwhite, inner-city youth still had to endure considerable police harassment and some police brutality. However, they were not
victims of Jim Crow laws and other forms of blatant discrimination
or the threats of extreme violence, such as the widespread lynch-
ings, which their progenitors faced and which had so greatly influenced the older generations' life strategies. To a great extent, the
Civil Rights movement had psychologically liberated and emboldened the new ghettos dwellers. These youths were assertive,
aggressive, and demanding.

As we should expect, they were not willing to passively endure
their reduced circumstances. After all, they were in their physical

prime. Young people reach their peak of physical abilities and sexual energies between the ages of 14 and 25. In that period, they are struggling in a state of moral and cognitive confusion to be somebody. The ghetto youths of the late 1960s and early 1970s, excluded from conventional paths to fulfill their intense desires and needs, were available for any activity that promised profit, respect, and excitement. Douglas G. Glasgow, who studied the emerging "black underclass" at the time of the Watts riot (1965), described the Los Angeles ghetto youths who were poised to riot:

> The youth of my study had tried many of the ways to adapt to underclass confinement but were nevertheless a unique section of the underclass. They were first and foremost young, strong, and physically healthy Black men, who despite their desire to achieve, to become something, and to find a job were at a very early age of fourteen, fifteen, or sixteen well on the way to permanent underclass status. As young inner-city men, and a part of the Black urban experience of the fifties, they responded to their rejection with explosiveness; they used fire to bring a nation to a standstill, forcing it to examine their condition.[41]

In the 1960s, they joined in the radical movements and remained ready to demonstrate, strike, riot, and loot if a riot started. As the movements died out, the ghetto youths were left to hang out on the streets. There, they concocted myriad enterprises to keep themselves busy, earn some respect, bring some excitement into their otherwise dull lives, and, if they were lucky, earn themselves some money. They formed neighborhood gangs and carried on wars with other gangs. They pimped or pretended to pimp;[42] used and sold drugs; stole from each other, their neighbors, and families; and frequently crept out of their neighborhoods and stole from more affluent white people, particularly those living in neighborhoods contingent to the ghetto.

The Crime Wave and Race

The rate of "index crimes (theft, robbery, assault, rape, and murder), as measured by the Uniform Crime Reports (UCR), peaked in 1973, while the homicide rates peaked in 1972 and 1980. Figure 8.1 shows a chart of the rates of crime measured through UCR, a federal data-gathering system that collects reports of "index" crimes from police in all reporting jurisdictions in the United States and compiles them into an annually published report.

As the graph indicates, crimes rose steadily between 1960 and 1965. However, a close study of the method of gathering these "rates" reveals that, to some extent (perhaps a great extent), the increase in this 15-year period was due to increased reporting by police jurisdictions rather than actual increases in crime. One indication that there was no true increase in crime is the fact that homicides, which are the most reliably reported crimes, appeared *not* to have increased during that period (Figure 8.2).

Figure 8.1
Index Crimes Reported to Police (1960–2001)
Rates per 100,000 Population

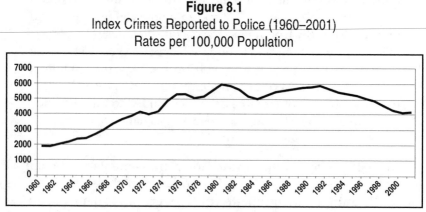

Source: Uniform Crime Reports

Figure 8.2
Homicide Rates (1953–1999)
Rates per 100,000 Population

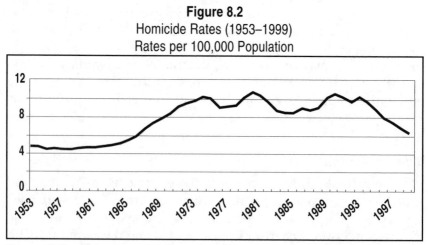

Source: Uniform Crime Reports

However, between 1965 and 1974, crime rates rose significantly. This is reflected in the dramatic increase in the UCR data *and* the doubling of the homicide rate. After 1975, the crime rates remained relatively flat. The UCR shows some minor rises and declines until 1990, and then they start a steady decline. The National Victimization Surveys, which began in 1973, indicate very different trends. Violent crimes—homicide, rape, robbery, aggravated and simple assault—remained steady between 1975 and 1995 and then declined rapidly (Figure 8.3). Property crimes, according to the victimization surveys, declined steadily after 1979 (Figure 8.4).

To understand the rise in crime rates after 1965, demographic patterns must be considered. After 1965, the huge population surge, the people born from 1945 through 1955, the "baby boomers," began to enter into the life stage in which they were most likely to be involved in crime. Most "street crime," that is, the crime that draws the severest public negative reaction, is committed by males between the ages of 15 and 25. Consequently, a great

Figure 8.3
Violent Crime Rates (1973–2002)

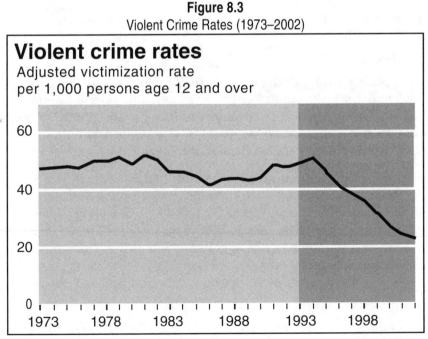

Violent crime rates
Adjusted victimization rate
per 1,000 persons age 12 and over

Source: Bureau of Justice Statistics, National Victimization Survey, retrieved 2003: *http://www.ojp.usdoj.gov/bjs/glance/viort.htm*, rev. 9 September 2001

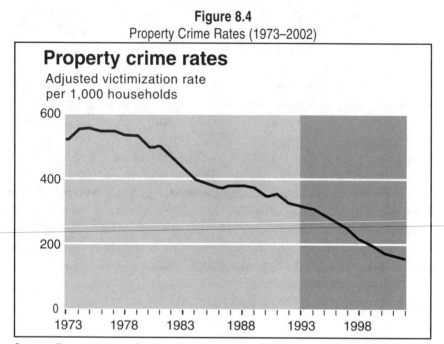

Figure 8.4
Property Crime Rates (1973–2002)

Property crime rates
Adjusted victimization rate
per 1,000 households

Source: Bureau of Justice Statistics, http://*www.ojp.usdoj.gov/bjs/glance/house2.htm*, rev.
9 September 2001

deal, perhaps most, of the increase in crime that occurred between
1965 and 1975 was committed by members of a population bulge
passing through the high crime-committing years. Ghetto youths
contributed disproportionate to these elevated rates. William Julius Wilson offered good examples of this contribution:

> In examining the figures on homicide in Chicago, it is important to
> recognize that the rates vary significantly according to the eco-
> nomic status of the community, with the highest rates of violent
> crime associated with communities of the underclass. More than
> half of 1983 murders and aggravated assaults in Chicago oc-
> curred in seven of the city's twenty-four police districts, the areas
> with a heavy concentration of low-income black and Latino
> residents.
>
> The most violent area is the overwhelmingly black Wentworth Av-
> enue police district on the South Side of Chicago. Indeed, in 1983,
> 81 murders (11 percent of the city total) and 1,691 aggravated assaults

(13 percent of the city total) occurred in this four-square mile district which contains only 3.4 percent of the city's total population.[43]

Conservatives Respond to the New Poor

While the new, poorer, more isolated and disorganized ghettos were forming and the radical movements were flaming out, conservative politicians, backed by the Christian right and the emerging "moral majority," were denouncing the liberal ideas on crime and its control that had influenced criminal justice policies for three decades. The new right, led by Senator Barry Goldwater, argued that liberal government programs had promoted crime rather than reduced it. As Goldwater put it,

> If it is entirely proper for the government to take away from some to give to others, then won't some be led to believe that they can rightfully take from anyone who has more than they? No wonder law and order has broken down, mob violence has engulfed great American cities, and our wives feel unsafe in the streets.[44]

Lyndon B. Johnson, when he ran for president against Goldwater in 1963, espoused very liberal ideas on the causes of crime:

> There is something mightily wrong when a candidate for the highest office bemoans violence in the streets but votes against the war on poverty, votes against the Civil Rights Act, and votes against major educational bills that come before him as a legislator.[45]

He later changed his tune when public opinion, influenced by Goldwater and other conservative right-wing politicians, shifted toward a more conservative view of crime control. In 1965, he stated to Congress that "the present wave of violence and the staggering property losses inflicted upon the nation by crime must be arrested. ... I hope that 1965 will be regarded as the year when this country began in earnest a thorough and effective war against crime."[46] He then initiated the Law Enforcement Assistance Act (1965) and the Safe Streets Bills (1967).

Johnson's acquiescence to the conservatives was too late, however. He was stamped with the stigma of liberalism, and Richard Nixon represented the emerging popular view. Nixon insisted that the real causes of crime were not poverty or unemployment but "insufficient curbs on the appetites or impulses that naturally impel individuals towards criminal activities." He concluded that the "solution to the crime problem is not the quadrupling of funds for any governmental war on poverty but more convictions."[47]

The conservatives won the day. According to Katherine Beckett, in, *Making Crime Pay,*

> As a result of the prominence in the election campaign, the crime issue received an unprecedented level of political and media attention in 1968. And the conservative initiative bore fruit: by 1969, 81% of those polled believed that law and order had broken down, and the majority blamed "Negroes who start riots" and "communists" for this state of affairs.[48]

It was at this point in time that ex-liberal Senator Patrick Daniel Moynihan shifted toward a conservative position on crime: "Among a large and growing lower class, self-reliance, self-discipline and industry are waning: . . . families are more and more matrifocal and atomized; crime and disorder are sharply on the rise."[49] He suggested that the government practiced "benign neglect" of the ghetto. And neglected they were. Segregation of non-whites in inner-city neighborhoods continued, and conditions in the ghettos worsened.

The law-and-order movement that began in Johnson's presidency was stepped up in Nixon's. Though the federal government was not directly involved in the control of most crime, which was the purview of local governments, Nixon did greatly increase aid to the states and local communities for increased crime-control activities. Federal funds allocated to state and local governments through the Law Enforcement Assistance Administration (LEAA), established by Johnson, increased from $300 million in 1968 to $1.25 billion in 1974. Nixon next declared a war on drugs, which he vigorously promoted until he was disgraced and forced to resign by the Watergate scandal.

After Nixon's resignation and the election of President Jimmy Carter, the nation's attention shifted from crime and drug abuse to the OPEC oil embargo, the economy's stagflation, and the Iranian hostage crisis. Crime was on the back burner. However, it was simmering in several locations in our society. The new right, or "the moral majority," led by Christian evangelists, such as Jerry Falwell and Pat Robertson, was taking shape, and a central issue for them was the "moral decline" in America. This emerging conservative constituency believed that rioting Negroes and communists were tearing the country apart. The country was ripe for exploitation on the crime issue.

Rediscovery of the 'Criminal Type'

After 1975, many academics and other experts who had been the architects and major supporters of the nonpunitive, rehabilitative penal approaches drifted to the right. They moved right because of shifting government policies, particularly the change in the types of research that government agencies would fund, the loss of support in the general society for their liberal ideas, *and* their own shift in sympathies. They too, after all, were members of the newly affluent middle class and shared a diffuse sense of being victims. The send-off in the shift was James Q. Wilson's widely read and enthusiastically accepted book, *Thinking About Crime* (1975), in which Wilson, a Harvard professor, went against the historical tide in criminology. He argued that America's crime problem was caused by the unraveling of the country's social fabric and the resulting development of an increasing number of persons with bad characters, many of whom become "habitual criminals," who commit most of the serious crimes and should be incapacitated. "Wicked people exist. Nothing avails except to set them apart from innocent people."[50]

The dominant academic perspective on crime swung over to the law-and-order position. Wilson's suggestion that "wicked" people commit most of the serious crime was an idea that was right down the conservative government's alley and one it was willing to grant big bucks to prove right. A series of studies appeared that purported to demonstrate that a special *type* of criminal committed most serious crimes. Sarnoff Mednick, W. F. Gabrielli, and B. Hutchings reported their findings of a study of Danish twins raised apart.[51] They suggested that there was a genetic link in criminal behavior. Peter Greenwood of the Rand Corporation published a study that identified a category of robbers and burglars who were "high-rate" offenders and who had committed most of the crime of the cohort they studied.[52] A large cadre of the leading criminologists entered the search for the "criminal type," "career criminal," and "high rate offender."[53] Then James Q. Wilson, with a fellow Harvard social scientist, Richard Herrnstein, published *Crime and Human Nature,* in which they claimed to have carefully reviewed all the important studies on crime causation and concluded that the evidence suggests that genes and early childhood experiences, rather than social and economic disadvantage or teenage peer culture, cause most crime.[54]

These criminologists, many of whom occupied the most prestigious positions in leading universities and on government bodies, succeeded in supplying the government with a body of polished, academically sophisticated theories to support the government's new war on crime. These ideas focused attention on individuals who, because of bad genes or bad families, were deeply committed to criminal behavior.

Reagan and the Crime Issue

President Ronald Reagan, both in his campaign for president and during his term in office (1981–1989), raised crime and drug use to the top of his agenda and began a new war against both. In defining the crime and drug problems, he (and President George H. W. Bush after him) put primary blame on the welfare state and the leniency of the courts. As Katherine Beckett pointed out,

> Like conservatives before them, the Reagan and Bush administrations went to great lengths to reject the notion that street crime and other social problems have socioeconomic causes. Reagan's first major address on crime, for example, consisted of a sweeping philosophical attack on "the social thinkers of the fifties and sixties who discussed crime only in the context of disadvantaged childhoods and poverty-stricken neighborhoods."[55] This theme appeared again and again in Reagan's speeches on crime.[56]

Beckett has collected many statements by Reagan on the causes of crime and drug abuse:

> Here in the richest nation in the world, where more crime is committed than in any other nation, we are told that the answer to this problem is to reduce our poverty. This isn't the answer.... Government's function is to protect society from the criminal, not the other way around.[57]

Choosing a career in crime is not the result of poverty or of an unhappy childhood or of a misunderstood adolescence; it is the result of a conscious, willful choice made by some who consider themselves above the law, who seek to exploit the hard work and, sometimes, the very lives of their fellow citizens.[58]

The crime epidemic threat has spread throughout our country, and it's no uncontrollable disease, much less an irreversible tide. Nor is it some inevitable sociological phenomenon. . . . It is, instead, and in large measure, a cumulative result of too much emphasis on the protection of the rights of the accused and too little concern for our government's responsibility to protect the lives, homes and rights of our law-abiding citizens. . . . The criminal element now calculates that crime really does pay.[59]

It is important to recognize that in his conservative interpretation of the crime and drug problems and his escalation of criminal justice efforts to control them, President Reagan was not being driven by public opinion but was attempting to manipulate it. The "new right" shared his views and supported the escalation, but the majority of the public did not at first. Katherine Beckett, in her study of the relationship between public opinion and the escalation of penal measures, argued that Reagan did not "harness a preexisting momentum for a crackdown on drugs."[60] The following paragraph and Figure 8.5 support Beckett's perspective:

[P]ublic opinion polls indicate that public concern about drugs did not increase prior to the Reagan administration's declaration of war in 1982. For example, as of 1981, only 3% of the American public believed that cutting the drug supply was the most important thing that could be done to reduce crime, while 22% felt that reducing unemployment would be more effective. Furthermore, the percentage of poll respondents identifying drug abuse as the nation's most important problem had dropped from 20% in 1973 to 2% in 1974 and hovered between 0% and 2% until 1982. In sum, there is no evidence of an upsurge in concern about drugs prior to Reagan's declaration of war. The erroneous identification of public opinion as the primary impetus for the government's campaigns against crime and drugs obscures the political nature of these efforts.[61]

President George H. W. Bush followed Reagan's policies of focusing on street crime, particularly black street crime, in advancing

Figure 8.5

Public Attitudes Toward the Most Important Problem Facing the Nation,
(1981–1995)

Percentage of Public Agreeing

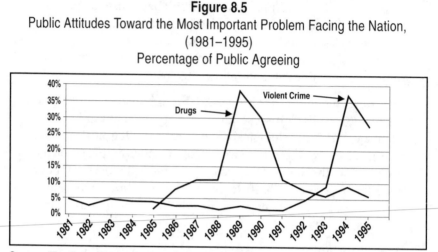

Source: *The Gallup Report, 1981–1995* (Princeton, NJ: Gallup Poll, 1996) as reported in the *Source Book of Criminal Justice Statistics,* 1996 (Collingdale, PA: DIANE Publishing, 1998), Table 2.1

his political career. It is widely believed that his use of the Willy Horton episode was influential in his defeat of Michael Dukakis in the 1988 presidential election. Bush was trailing Dukakis in the polls, and his campaign organization searched for crime that could be blamed on Dukakis. As Katherine Beckett put it,

> During the 1988 presidential campaign, the Bush team used the Willie Horton incident as a way of mobilizing outrage about crime and blaming "liberal Democrats" for it. Horton was convicted of murder in Massachusetts, where Michael Dukakis was (later) governor. Subsequently released on furlough, Horton allegedly kidnaped a couple and raped the woman. The Bush campaign used Horton's photograph in its television spots describing the case (and Dukakis's role in it) because, as one of the producers of the advertisement put it, the incident was "a wonderful mix of liberalism and a big black rapist."[62]

President Bush went much further to manipulate the truth with the intent of stirring up fear of black drug dealers when his staff engineered the purchase of crack cocaine in Lafayette Park across from the White House. Craig Reinarman and Harry G. Levine, in their study of the crack cocaine scare, *Crack in America,* described the events:

On September 5, 1989, President Bush, speaking from the presidential desk in the Oval Office, announced his plan for achieving "victory over drugs" in his first major prime-time address to the nation, broadcast on all three national television networks. We want to focus on this incident as an example of the way politicians and the media systematically misinformed and deceived the public in order to promote the War on Drugs. During the address, Bush held up to the cameras a clear plastic bag of crack labeled "Evidence." He announced that it was "seized a few days ago in a park across the street from the White House" (*Washington Post*, September 22, 1989, p. A1). Its contents, Bush said, "were turning our cities into battle zones and murdering our children." The president proclaimed that, because of crack and other drugs, he would "more than double" federal assistance to state and local law enforcement (*New York Times*, September 6, 1989, p. A1). The next morning the picture of the president holding a bag of crack was on the front pages of newspapers across America.

About two weeks later, the *Washington Post*, and then National Public Radio and other newspapers, discovered how the president of the United States had obtained his bag of crack. According to White House and DEA officials, "the idea of the president holding up crack was first included in some drafts" of his speech. Bush enthusiastically approved. A White House aide told the *Post* that the president "liked the prop. . . . It drove the point home." Bush and his advisors also decided that the crack should be seized in Lafayette Park across from the White House so the president could say that crack had become so pervasive that it was being sold "in front of the White House."[63]

The decision set up a complex chain of events. White House Communication Director David Demarst asked Cabinet Affairs Secretary David Bates to instruct the Justice Department "to find some crack that fit the description in the speech." Bates called Richard Weatherbee, special assistant to Attorney General Dick Thornburgh, who then called James Milford, executive assistant to the DEA chief. Finally, Milford phoned William McMullan, special agent in charge of the DEA's Washington office, and told him to arrange an undercover crack buy near the White House because "evidently, the President wants to show it could be bought anywhere."[64]

Despite their best efforts, the top federal drug agents were not able to find anyone selling crack (or any other drug) in Lafayette Park, or anywhere else in the vicinity of the White House. Therefore, in order to carry out their assignment, DEA agents had to entice someone to come to the park to make the sale. Apparently, the only person the DEA could convince was Keith Jackson, an eighteen-year-old African-American high school senior. McMullan reported that it was difficult because Jackson "did not even know where the White House was." The DEA's secret tape recording of the conversation revealed that the teenager seemed baffled by the request: "Where the [expletive deleted] is the White House?" he asked. Therefore, McMullan told the *Post*, "we had to manipulate him to get him down there. It wasn't easy."[65]

Controlling the New Ghetto

The New Ghetto as a Crime Cauldron

As these comments suggest, a great deal (perhaps most) of the increase in post-1967 street crime was committed by 14 to 25-year-old males living in inner-city ghettos. The hoards of young people in these ghettos—who had been teased for years by the opulent lives of characters on television and by commercials with their incessant message of buy, buy, buy—grew up knowing that there was no way that they could live the American "good life" by getting a job, working steadily and hard, and proceeding up the ladder to success. Remember, these youths had been emboldened by the Civil Rights movement, excited by the War on Poverty's promises of economic advancement, and had their hopes dashed by the demise of the radical movements and ensuing conservative reaction. So they did not sit by and passively take it. They did what vigorous young people do. They devised a multitude of ways to get into trouble.

Critical mass further escalated the violence—assaults and homicides—that young ghetto dwellers committed. When violence between the hundreds or thousands of young males who were milling about on the streets of the compacted ghettos reached a certain level, it precipitated a change in the general orientation of everyone living in these locations. The threat of assault or death was seen as a real possibility, and therefore, everyone had to change their behavior to address this perceived threat. William Julius Wilson captured the fears of a 39-year-old divorced schoolteacher and mother of four living on Chicago's South Side:

> I think he was just gettin', buyin' somethin' or whatever—at the restaurant or somethin' and some kid walked up to him on the street and shot him five times. I—I don't know was it gang related or if kids—you know, just a matter of bein' in the wrong place at the wrong time, you know. Those are the kinds of things that you have to be careful about when you live in an environment like this.[66]

Because of the fear of violence, individuals either withdrew and avoided any public place where violence was likely to occur or they got ready to meet violence with counterviolence. Increasingly, young people joined gangs for protection, prepared themselves psychologically to meet violence with violence, and armed themselves. This, in itself, escalated the violence. The ghettos had become true cauldrons of crime, much of it violent crime.

It must be noted that crime is not exclusive to ghetto youth. Americans of all races and throughout the class structure commit a lot of crime. Studies conducted over the last 40 years have revealed that employees regularly steal from employers.[67] White, suburban youths engage in about as much delinquency as inner-city lower-class youths,[68] and businessmen systematically violate the law and government regulations to maximize profits.[69] For example, in 2000–2001, investigators from the California Bureau of Automobile Repair (BAR), responding to years of complaints about the auto repair industry, examined the repairs of 1,315 vehicles owned by people who had requested a check through a toll-free hotline. In 42 percent of the repairs, the BAR uncovered billing fraud, with an average of $811 in overcharges for parts or labor not received.[70] The recent revelations of theft of staggering amounts by some of the top executives of the nation's most prestigious and powerful corporations, such as Enron, have revealed that theft is a way of life even at the very top of the class system.[71]

Moreover, ghetto crime is not the most violent. Business executives arrange to have deadly chemicals illegally disposed of and, moreover, ignore and cover up evidence of harm caused by many of their manufacturing processes and their products. Physicians knowingly perform unnecessary and risky, but profitable, operations that, Dr. Sidney Wolfe estimated, caused 16,000 deaths in 1965.[72] These practices harm and kill many more people each year than all of the violent crimes perpetrated by lower-class ghetto dwellers. What is unique about ghetto crime is that it is more likely to involve face-to-face, hostile interaction—as in a mugging—and it is frequently committed by African Americans or Latinos. These factors, not its uniquely violent nature or the monetary expense of street crime, have caused the intense public reaction. Jeffrey H. Reiman has put it very well:

> Is a person who kills another in a bar brawl a greater threat to society then a business executive who refuses to make his plant a safe place to work? By any measure of death and suffering the latter is by far a greater danger than the former. But because he wishes his workers no harm, because he is only indirectly responsible for death and disability while pursuing legitimate economic goals, his acts are not called *crimes*. Once we free our imagination from the irrational shackle of the one-on-one model of crime can there be any doubt that the criminal justice system does *not* protect us from the gravest threats to life and limb? It seeks to protect us when that threat comes from a young, lower-class male in the inner city. When that threat comes from an upper-class business executive in an office, it looks the other way. And this in the face of growing evidence that for every American citizen murdered by some thug, six American workers are killed by their bosses.[73]

Leo Drutman, writing in the *Los Angeles Times*, made the same points when he commented on what the FBI crime reports do not report:

> Conspicuously absent from the report, however, was an assessment of corporate crime. The report contains no statistics on the accounting and securities frauds that have rocked the economy in the last two years. It does not list details on the litany of food safety violations, product safety violations, workplace safety violations, environmental pollution and countless other crimes that kill, injure and sicken millions of Americans each year.

> The reason is simple but troubling. Under federal law, the FBI must collect data on eight crime indexes: murder and manslaughter; forcible rape; robbery; aggravated assault; burglary; larceny-theft; motor vehicle theft; and arson. It also is required to produce a report on hate crimes. . . .

When the costs of corporate crime have been estimated, however, the numbers are staggering. Most credible estimates confirm that, in the [aggregate], white-collar and corporate crimes cost the U.S. hundreds of billions of dollars annually—far more than conventional categories of crime such as burglary and robbery. . . .

By comparison, the FBI estimated that in 2002, the nation's total loss from robbery, burglary, larceny-theft, motor vehicle theft and arson was almost $18 billion. That is less than a third of the estimated $80 billion Enron alone cost investors, pensioners and employees.

But corporate crime isn't just about the money. It's also about people's lives. The national murder rate has hovered around 16,000 a year in recent years. (In 2002 the FBI reported 16,204 murders.) But a respected group of occupational health and safety investigators, led by J. Paul Leigh, a UC Davis School of Medicine professor, has estimated that in 1992 alone there were 65,971 deaths resulting from job-related injuries and occupational diseases. These numbers do not include the thousands of annual deaths caused by cancers linked to corporate pollution, deaths from defective products, tainted foods and other corporate-related causes.[74]

Social Dynamite

From the mid-1970s through the 1990s, the ghetto was viewed as a menacing evil. To the general public, it was a bivouac from which urban predators terrorized the city. N. R. Kleinfield, in an article in the *New York Times*, wrote about the fears of New Yorkers in 1989 that formed the context for the arrest and conviction of five innocent black youths for raping a white, female jogger in Central Park:

The jogger rape case, infused with socking brutality and the intersections of race and class, was a transformative moment in the city's history. What happened that evening in the park seemed to crystalize all that was wrong with New York and to suggest that it had devolved into a tameless and racially polarized battleground in which even its youths were capable of the most wanton acts. No one was safe, not anywhere. New Yorkers were introduced to an unfamiliar urban horror called wilding: marauding bands of teenagers preying on residents seemingly for little more than sadistic pleasure.[75]

For politicians, who had devised policies or allowed and promoted economic changes that helped create the new ghetto, the ghetto was a threat to the political stability of the nation. They saw it as, using Christian Parenti's characterization, "social dynamite":

> The other segment of surplus population—"social dynamite"—are those who pose an actual or potential political challenge. They are that population which threatens to explode; the impoverished low-wage working class and unemployed youth who have fallen below the statistical radar, but whose spirits are not broken and whose expectations for a decent life and social inclusion are dangerously alive and well. They are the class that suffers from "relative deprivation." Their poverty is made all the more unjust because it is experienced in contrast to the spectacle of opulence and the myths of social mobility and opportunity. This is the class from which the Black Panthers and the Young Lords arose in the sixties and from which sprang the gangs of the 1980s. In the 1930s this same class provided the brawn for the Communist Party—organized Unemployed Councils that forcibly stopped evictions in New York's Lower East Side.

> The social dynamite is a threat to the class and racial hierarchies upon which the private enterprise system depends. This group cannot simply be swept aside. Controlling them requires both a defensive policy of containment and an aggressive policy of direct attack and active destabilization. They are contained and crushed, confined to the ghetto, demoralized and pilloried in warehouse public schools, demonized by a lurid media, sent to prison, and at times dispatched by lethal injection or police bullets. This is the class—or more accurately the caste, because they are increasingly people of color—which must be constantly undermined, divided, intimidated, attacked, discredited, and ultimately kept in check with what Fanon called the "language of naked force."[76]

As Parenti suggested, politicians, government officials, and criminal justice practitioners did militate against the ghetto. They greatly increased the number of police, passed new laws criminalizing more and more of the behavior of ghetto youths (such as joining gangs and possessing or using crack), greatly lengthened sentences for most street crimes, sent a higher percentage of people charged with felonies to prison, increased the prison populations, and devised a new system of imprisonment and parole supervision that managed, controlled, and eventually disposed of a large portion of the young males and a growing percentage of the females in the ghetto. At one point, in 2001, one-third of young black males were either in prison, in jail, or on parole or probation. On any given day in 1999, 41 percent of black male high school dropouts, 22 to 30 years old, were in jail or prison.[77] We have, in effect, established a new form of apartheid. Loïc Wacquant, in his examination of the incarceration of African Americans in recent years, put it well:

> To understand these phenomena [black hyperincarceration], we first need to break out of the narrow "crime and punishment" paradigm and examine the broader role of the penal system as an *instrument for managing dispossessed and dishonored groups*. And second, we need to take a long historical view of the shifting forms of ethno-racial domination in the United States. This double move suggests that the astounding upsurge in black incarceration in the past three decades results from the obsolescence of the ghetto as a device for caste control and correlative need for a substitute apparatus for keeping (unskilled) African Americans in a subordinate and confined position—physically, socially, and symbolically.[78]

Inner-city crime has not stopped, however. New ghetto youth grow up and face the same life circumstances, the same range of options, which do not include paths to the good life through conventional and legitimate efforts. They still clique up, join gangs, deal drugs, "thug," or do whatever they can to avoid the dull, mundane, impecunious, disrespected life that is in store for them if they follow the legal and recommended paths available to them—such as minimum-wage jobs flipping hamburgers at McDonald's. But they too will be managed, controlled, and disposed of. The criminal justice system will grind most of them up and spit them out. Like their predecessors, they will be converted from social dynamite to—using Christian Parenti's other characterization of the surplus population—"social junk":

> "Social junk" are those whose spirits and minds are shattered; they are the deinstitutionalized mentally ill, alcoholics, drug addicts, and cast-off impoverished seniors; the lonely, beaten drifters with no expectations of a future and little will to fight.[79]

Increasingly, ex-convicts can be added to this category. Their descent into dereliction is the final step in their disposal.

Endnotes

1. Even David Garland, a leading scholar of the history of punishment, seems to place most emphasis on the rising crime rates in explaining the punitive swing. See *The Culture of Control,* 153.
2. There is considerable disagreement on the rates of crime increases in these years. This issue is taken up more thoroughly later on in the chapter.
3. See especially James Q. Wilson, *Thinking About Crime,* and John Dilulio, "Crime in America: It's Going to Get Worse."
4. Each time, I was fired after the first week because I decided immediately that I could not work there and did not report to the foreman to whom I was assigned.
5. Tamar Lewin, "Low Pay and Closed Doors Confront Young Job Seekers," *New York Times,* 10 March 1994, p. B12.
6. William Julius Wilson, *When Work Disappears: The World of the New Urban Poor* (New York: Vintage Books, 1996), 58–59.
7. Ibid., 59.
8. Michael Harrington, *The Other America: Poverty in the United States* (New York: Macmillan, 1962).
9. David Halberstam, *The Reckoning* (New York: Avon, 1986), 366–367.
10. Bennett Harrison and Barry Bluestone, *The Great U-Turn* (New York: Basic Books, 1988), 4.
11. Marshall Frady, "The Big Guy," *New York Review of Books,* 7 November 2002, p. 6.
12. Michael Harrington, *The New American Poverty* (New York: Penguin, 1984), 19–22, emphasis added.
13. Barbara Tuchman, in one of her insightful works of history, *The March of Folly* (New York: Ballantine, 1984), pointed to our involvement in the Vietnam War as a example of a folly leaders undertake that ends in disastrous consequences, despite the fact that many informed persons are warning that the undertaking is folly.
14. Harrison and Bluestone, *The Great U-Turn,* 7.
15. Ibid., 8.
16. Ibid., 11.
17. Ibid., 25.
18. Ibid., 28.
19. Ibid., 36.
20. See Harrington, *New American Poverty,* 60.
21. Harrison and Bluestone, *The Great U-Turn,* 39–40.

22. Ibid., 42–43.

23. Ibid., 45.

24. Ibid., 48.

25. David Gordon, *Fat and Mean* (New York: Simon & Schuster, 1996), 64.

26. Harrison and Bluestone, *The Great U-Turn*, 76.

27. Ibid., 77.

28. Harrington, *New American Poverty*, 48.

29. Wacquant, "The New Urban Color Line," 251.

30. Harrington, *New American Poverty*, 125–126.

31. The 1970s' violence of the Charles Manson Family, Venceremos, the Weathermen, and the Symbionese Liberation Army was the final death throe of the 1960s revolutionary movements.

32. Harrington, *New American Poverty*, 24.

33. See Nicholas Lemann, *The Promised Land* (New York: Knopf, 1991) for an excellent dicussion of the failures of many of the Chicago housing projects.

34. Quoted in Wilson, *When Work Disappears*, 5.

35. See William Julius Wilson, *The Truly Disadvantaged* (Chicago: University of Chicago Press, 1980), for a discussion of this migration of the more affluent blacks out of the inner-city neighborhoods.

36. Wilson, *When Work Disappears*, xiii.

37. Pierre Bourdieu, "Le Capital social," *Acts de la Recherche en Sciences Sociales* 31 (January): 2–3, and "The Forms of Capital," in John G. Richardson, ed., *Handbook of Theory and Research for the Sociology of Education* (New York: Greenwood, 1986), 723–744.

38. Loïc Wacquant, "Negative Social Capital: State Breakdown and Social Destitution in America's Urban Core" *Netherlands Journal of the Built Environment* 13, no. 1 (1998): 25, 40.

39. Wacquant, "The New Urban Color Line," 233–234, 238.

40. Wacquant, "Deadly Symbiosis: When Ghetto and Prison Meet and Mesh," 107–108. Quotes within the quote were from Jerome G. Miller, *Search and Destroy: African American Males in the Criminal Justice System* (Cambridge, MA: Cambridge University Press, 1997), 101, and Suhdir Verkatesh, *American Project: The Rise and Fall of a Modern Ghetto* (Cambridge, MA: Harvard University Press, 2000), 123–130.

41. Douglas G. Glasgow, *The Black Underclass* (New York: Vintage, 1981), 9.

42. In the early 1970s, many young ghetto youths aspired to be pimps. Though they didn't have any whores, they carried around a copy of the paperback book *The Pimp,* by Ice Berg Slim (Los Angeles: Holloway House, 1987), practiced the pimping style spelled out in this manual, and talked about being a pimp. See Tom Wolf, *Radical Chic*

and Mau Mauing the Flack Catchers (New York: Pan Macmillan, 2002), Chapter 8.

43. Wilson, *The Truly Disadvantaged*, 25.

44. Quoted in Allen Matusow, *The Unraveling of America* (New York: Harper Torchbooks, 1984), 143.

45. Lyndon B. Johnson, "Remarks on the City Hall Steps, Dayton Ohio," in *Public Papers of the Presidents, 1964, Vol. 2* (Washington, DC: Government Printing Office, 1965), 1371.

46. Katherine Beckett, *Making Crime Pay* (New York: Oxford University Press, 1997), p. 37.

47. Beckett, *Making Crime Pay*, 38. The Nixon quotes are from Nancy E. Marion, *A History of Federal Crime Control Initiatives* (Westport, CT: Praeger, 1994), 401, and Matusow, *Unraveling of America*, 401.

48. Beckett, *Making Crime Pay*, 38.

49. Daniel Patrick Moynihan, *The Politics of Guaranteed Income* (New York: Random House, 1973), 42.

50. Wilson, *Thinking About Crime*, 235.

51. Sarnoff Medenick, W. F. Gabrielli, and B. Hutchings, "Genetic Influences in Criminal Convictions," *Science* 224 (1984): 891–894.

52. Peter Greenwood, *Selective Incapacitation* (Santa Monica, CA: Rand, 1982).

53. See particularly Alfred Blumstein, Jacqueline Cohen, Jeffrey Roth, and Christy Visher, eds., *Criminal Careers and Career Criminals* (Washington, DC: National Academy of Sciences, 1986).

54. James Q. Wilson and Richard Herrnstein, *Crime and Human Nature* (New York: Simon and Schuster, 1985).

55. The quote is from Bertram Gross, "Reagan's Criminal Anti-crime Fix," in Alan Gartner, Colin Greer, and Frank Riessman, eds., *What Reagan Is Doing to Us* (New York: Harper and Row, 1962).

56. Beckett, *Making Crime Pay*, 48.

57. Ronald Reagan, "Remarks at the Conservative Political Action Conference Dinner," in *Public Papers of the Presidents, 1983: Vol. 1* (Washington, DC: Government Printing Office, 1984b), 252.

58. Ronald Reagan, "Remarks at the Annual Conference of the National Sheriff's Association in Hartford, Connecticut," in *Public Papers of the Presidents of the United States, 1984: Vol. 2* (Washington, DC: Government Printing Office, 1985), 886.

59. Ronald Reagan, "Remarks at a White House Ceremony Observing Crime Victims' Week," in *Public Papers of the Presidents, 1983: Vol. 1* (Washington, DC: Government Printing Office, 1984a), 553.

60. Quote in Steven Wisotsky's criticism of the drug war: "Crackdown: The Emerging 'Drug Exception' to the Bill of Rights," *Hastings Law Review Journal* 38 (1987): 890.

61. Beckett, *Making Crime Pay*, takes these percentages from George Gallup, ed., *The Gallup Poll* (Wilmington, DE: Scholarly Resources, 1990).

62. Katherine Beckett, quoted in Kenneth Karst, *Law's Promise, Law's Expression: Visions of Power in the Politics of Race, Gender, and Religion* (New Haven, CT: Yale University Press, 1993), 73–74.

63. Quoted in Michael Isikoff, "Drug Buy Set Up by Bush: DEA Lured Seller to Lafayette Park," *Washington Post*, 30 September 1989, p. A1.

64. Quoted ibid.

65. Craig Reinarman and Harry G. Levine, *Crack in America* (Berkeley: University of California Press, 1997), 22–23. The quote within the quote is from Isikoff, "Drug Buy Set Up," A1.

66. Wilson, *When Work Disappears* (New York: Vintage, 1996), 6–7.

67. See, for instance, R. Hollinger and J. Clark, *Theft by Employees* (Lexington, MA: Lexington).

68. See Travis Hirschi, *Causes of Delinquency* (Berkeley: University of California Press, 1969, 1983).

69. See Edwin H. Sutherland, *White Collar Crime* (New York: Dryden, 1949); Jeffrey H. Reiman, *The Rich Get Richer and the Poor Get Prison* (New York: Wiley, 1979); and James W. Coleman, "Respectable Crime," in James F. Shelley, ed., *Criminology: A Contemporary Handbook* (Belmont, CA: Wadsworth, 1995).

70. Jenifer Warren and Virginia Ellis, "Fraud Rampant in Body Shops," *Los Angeles Times*, 10 September 2003.

71. New York Attorney General Elliot Spitzer, in his sustained investigation of Wall Street fraud, uncovered a new form in the mutual fund industry. Certain traders were allowed by employees of Bank of America to trade stock after closing hours, which, according to a *Los Angeles Times* article (17 September 2003, p. C1), "may have cost small investors billions of dollars." Spizer had earlier "spear headed a probe of Wall Street stock analysts, which resulted in a $1.4 billion settlement with 10 major brokerage firms over conflicts of interest." These later actions did not result in criminal charges, but they could have.

72. See Fleetwood Blake and Arthur Lubow, "America's Most Coddled Criminals," in *New Times*, 19 September 1975, pp. 26–29.

73. Reiman, *The Rich Get Richer*, 72.

74. Leo Drutman, "Corporate Crime Acts Like a Thief in the Night," *Los Angeles Times*, 4 November 2003, B3.

75. N. R. Kleinfield, "New Yorkers Reminded of Fears Left Behind," *New York Times*, 6 December 2002, p. A29.

76. Christian Parenti, *Lockdown America* (New York: Verso, 1999), 46.

77. See Bruce Western, Becky Pettit, and Josh Guetzkow, "Black Economic Progress in the Era of Mass Imprisonment," in Marc Mauer and Meda Chesney-Lind, eds., *Invisible Punishment* (New York: New Press, 2003), 172.

78. Wacquant, "Deadly Symbiosis," *Boston Review,* April/May 2002, p. 23.

79. Ibid., 46. ✦

Chapter 9

Aftermath

The federal and state governments' wars on crime and drugs over the last 25 years have not significantly reduced crime or drug use, because these activities are deeply woven into the fabric of society. There is little chance of doing much about them without undertaking massive economic, social, and cultural changes. Crime is spread throughout the class hierarchy, with most serious crime committed by those at the top. The punitive measures have been aimed, almost exclusively, at the lower classes who, because of severely reduced life options, are less deterrable by threats of punishment. However, the reduction of crime was not the major purpose of the wars on crime and drugs, and our rulers have actually succeeded in their real purposes. These were to divert the general public's attention away from other pressing social and economic problems and onto street crime and drug use *and* to neutralize the new dangerous class—nonwhite, ghetto youths. As pointed out in the preceding chapter, on any given day in 1999, 41 percent of black male high school dropouts, 22 to 30 years old, were in jail or prison. Enough ghetto youths were incarcerated and held long enough under mean and socially crippling conditions to force them to "lay low" and accept impecunious, at most bothersome but not threatening, life adjustments on the edges of society. In this way, they have been contained and converted from potentially dangerous "social dynamite" to "social junk."

In the 1990s, crime rates dropped dramatically. This had little or nothing to do with the escalation of punishment. James Austin and I compared the changes in crime rates across the United States from 1981 to 1990, the period of the greatest increases in incarceration rates, and discovered that crime rates were just as likely to stay the same, go down, or rise whether or not states increased their rates of incarceration.[1] Probably one of the most important causes of the decline in street crime in the 1990s was that during this period, with the general dip in unemployment, the number of people residing in high-poverty neighborhoods decreased by 24 percent.[2] In 1990, almost one-third of the country's black population lived in high-poverty neighborhoods, and in 2000, only 19 percent did. Marc Mauer, who has monitored the shifts in crime rates over the past several decades, and Meda Chesney-Lind, a prominent criminologist, made this observation regarding the 1990s dramatic drop in crime rates: "Most of the responsibility for the crime drop rests with improvements in the economy, changes in the age structure, or other social factors."[3]

It is not clear what lies ahead for both employment and crime. It appears, however, that we have reached the end of the road in the expansion of prison populations. States are groaning under the weight of their prison budgets and desperately thrashing around in search of some way to extricate themselves from financial disaster. It is a good time to take a critical look at the destruction and debris left over from the wars on crime and drugs.

Collateral Damage

In this book, I examine the direct consequences of the wars on crime and drugs: the imprisonment of hundreds of thousands of people, most of whom were guilty of relatively petty crimes; their lengthy and debilitating incarceration; and their ejection back into the society—ill-prepared, handicapped by their stigmatized social status, and hindered by parole agents who police rather than assist them. The direct financial cost of the imprisonment binge has been well publicized—at least $35 billion a year. What has not been recognized enough are the collateral damages the wars have wrought—the harm done to other social programs because so much money has been siphoned off into "corrections," the diminution of civil rights, the erosion of our traditional values of fairness and tolerance, and the creation of new interest groups that will be significant impediments to the reformation of the excessive and punitive criminal justice system.

Diversion of Tax Money to Prisons

While the amount of money spent to build new prisons and to fund state and federal prison enterprises has steadily risen, the money to support other government services has shrunk. It has not been just the high cost of building new prisons and keeping the hundreds of thousands of new prisoners locked up—for about $40,000 a year per prisoner—that has gobbled up the tax dollars.[4] The new prisons have been built by issuing bonds that burden states with high interest costs requiring payment over extended periods, eating up more tax money. In many states, such as California, voters finally rejected issuance of new bonds for prison construction. State governments slyly circumvented this by funding prison construction through other types of bonds that did not require public approval but which incurred much higher interest rates than the regular bonds.

The most obvious reduction in services has been in higher education. California built 22 new prisons during the 1980s and 1990s but not one new state college or university. Expenditures for higher education in most of the other states that experienced significant expansion in prison populations leveled off or declined during this period. Medical and social welfare service funding was similarly affected. In 2002, because of the recession, most states faced huge tax deficits and began to slash social services. A few looked at their excessive prison costs and began searching for ways to cut them. California, the state with the largest prison budget in the country and one of the worst tax deficits ($38 billion at the last count), was not among them. Gray Davis, former California governor, who consistently presented himself as "tough on crime" and received significant financial support and votes from the California Corrections and Peace Officers Association, approved a 39 percent pay raise for prison guards and increased the prison budget while slashing other social services.

Social Costs

In our earlier study, James Austin and I evaluated some of the additional social costs of imprisonment:

> . . . many prisoners sent to prison are married and have children. Moreover, all of them have mothers, fathers, brothers, sisters, uncles, aunts or cousins. Though it is sometimes true that a prisoner was causing family and friends a great deal of difficulty, usually relatives experience some disruption and pain when persons are

sent to prison. The removal of an individual from his social contexts does some harm to his family, friends, and employer, though the amount of harm is hard to calculate.[5]

The impact of the imprisonment binge on the social fabric of poor neighborhoods has not been fully appreciated or adequately studied. A large percentage of young, inner-city, nonwhite males (one-third or more) are in jail, in prison, on parole, or on probation. Since the late 1960s, politicians have fulminated on the problem of fatherless homes in the ghetto. The excessive incarceration of African American and other nonwhite young males in the last three decades has greatly exacerbated this problem. Donald Braman examined the impact of imprisonment on families:

> When most families in a neighborhood lose fathers to prison, the distortion of family structure affects relationship norms between men and women as well as between parents and children, reshaping family and community across generations. And, while families in poor neighborhoods have traditionally been able to employ extended networks of kin and friends to weather hard times, incarceration strains these sustaining relationships, diminishing people's ability to survive material and emotional difficulties. As a result, incarceration is producing deep social transformations in the families and communities of prisoners—families and communities, it should be noted, that are disproportionately, poor, urban, and African American.[6]

Todd R. Clear argued that concentrated incarceration of ghetto members rended their communities' social fabric *and* reduced public safety:

> I argue that very high concentrations of incarceration may well have a negative impact on public safety by leaving communities less capable of sustaining the informal social control that undergirds public safety. This happens not only because incarceration, experienced at high levels, has the inevitable result of removing valuable assets from the community, but also because the concentration of incarceration affects the community capacity of those who are left behind.[7]

High rates of incarceration of ghetto dwellers flowing back and forth between the inner-city neighborhoods and the jails and prisons has resulted in outside values, meanings, and social organizations being affected by prisoner culture and prisoner social organizations. In earlier periods, prison culture and prison slang were somewhat exclusive to the prison. Today, the values, meanings, relationships, and language of the two worlds—the prison and the ghetto—are intertwined. Gangsta rap, to some great extent, reflects this mixture.

With the influence of prison culture, outside relationships have become more violent and rapacious. Though gangs have been part of life in lower-class and working-class urban neighborhoods for decades, even centuries, since the 1960s, gang culture has been cultivated and reshaped in prison, and the new forms have been exported to outside communities. In California, for instance, the two major Chicano gangs—the Mexican Mafia (EME) and La Nuestra Familia—arose in the prisons and then carried their violent and predatory activities to outside neighborhoods.[8] The African American street gangs—the Bloods and the Crips—were likewise influenced by prison gang activities.

Many inner-city communities that traditionally exercised less political clout have been further politically weakened by the imprisonment boom because of the disenfranchisement of convicts and ex-convicts. The District of Columbia and 46 states bar prisoners from voting. Ten states impose lifetime disenfranchisement on convicted felons. The effect of this was starkly evident in the 2000 presidential election when George W. Bush won Florida and the election. In the tight and controversial Florida vote, large numbers of African American voters (who are traditionally Democrats) were denied a vote because of their legal status. This is a dramatic example of a group's loss of national political power. Marc Mauer reported on the findings of two sociologists, Christopher Uggen and Jeff Manza, on the impact of the disenfranchisement of African Americans on U.S. Senate races:

> Even with a projected lower turnout rate, they concluded that disenfranchisement policies have affected the outcome of seven U.S. Senate races from 1970 to 1998, generally in states with close elections and a substantial number of disenfranchised voters. In each 2case the Democratic candidate would have won rather than the Republican victor. Projecting the impact of these races over time leads them to conclude that disenfranchisement prevented Democratic control of the Senate from 1986 to 2000.[9]

This weakening of voting power operates daily at the city and state level, and the political clout of inner-city people is greatly diminished by incarceration and its aftermath.

Vindictiveness

The conservative ideology behind the excessively punitive reaction toward street crime has encouraged vindictiveness, which has profound, negative social consequences. James Austin and I wrote about these consequences:

> In America, according to the dominant ideology, everyone is responsible for his or her acts, and every act is accomplished by a willful actor. Consequently, every undesirable, harmful, "bad" act is the work of a blameful actor. This belief has resulted in our being the most litigious people in the world and has given us the world's largest legal profession. It has also led us to criminalize more and more behavior and to demand more and more legal action against those who break laws. Today many Americans want someone blamed and punished for every transgression and inconvenience they experience.
>
> Social science should have taught us that all human behavior is only partially a matter of free will and that persons are only partially responsible for their deeds. Everyone's actions are always somewhat influenced or dominated by factors not of one's own making and beyond personal control (with economic situation being the most influential and obvious).
>
> Moreover, seeking vengeance is a pursuit that brings more frustration than satisfaction. It has not only been an obstacle in solving many social problems and in developing cooperative, communal attitudes (the lack of which are one of the important causes of the crime problem), but it is in itself a producer of excessive amounts of anxiety and frustration. Ultimately, vindictiveness erects barriers between people, isolates them, and prevents them from constructing the cooperative, communal social organizations that are so necessary for meaningful, satisfying human existence. Ironically, it is just these social structures that contain the true solutions to our crime problem.[10]

Broad Sweep of the Wars on Crime and Drugs

Ghetto crime was the main source of the public's fear, but the punitive criminal justice policies that have resulted from this fear have reached much farther than the ghetto. The enhanced police forces and the new punitive laws swept up hundreds of thousands of nonghetto citizens, though most of them were from the lower rungs of the class ladder. At least one-third of state and federal prisoners are white, and they come from small towns and rural areas as well as the big cities. Moreover, the drug war brought into play a variety of "gung ho" enforcement operations, such as California's Campaign Against Marijuana Production (CAMP) and the federal Drug Enforcement Agency (DEA), that have tramped over the social landscape, arresting and imprisoning more or less respectable middle-class and even upperclass wives, mothers, husbands, fathers, farmers, stockbrokers, teachers, lawyers, politicians, and policemen. Mikki Norris, Chris Conrad, and Virginia Resner collected many examples of this brutal overextension of the law in the drug war:

> Before his arrest in Oakland, California, David Ciglar was being retrained for a promising new career as a MRI technician.
>
> He had been injured on his job as a firefighter/paramedic as he was carrying a woman from a building. He has been credited with saving over 100 lives. Based on a tip to the DEA, he was caught with a plastic tray of 167 small marijuana seedlings growing in his garage.
>
> Under a threat that his wife would also be sent to prison and his children sent to a foster home, David pleaded guilty. His family home was seized. He received the mandatory minimum sentence of ten years.[11]

Kay Tanner, serving 10 years, described her arrest and conviction for cocaine conspiracy:

> The night before Christmas Eve, my front door was rammed in and approximately fifteen fully armed DEA and police invaded my home.
>
> This was all related to my tenants that had moved. I was handcuffed and interrogated for eight hours about people I didn't even

know. I was threatened with arrest and they tore my house apart looking for evidence. I was not arrested as they found nothing they were looking for.

I was later indicted for one count of Conspiracy to Traffic Cocaine. Conspiracy does not require any evidence. All you need is testimony by a government witness, which is bought with plea bargains. There were two witnesses who faced twenty year sentences and got only 12–18 months for their testimony. I was convicted for having knowledge of my tenants actions by hearsay only.

I have lost my home and spent all of my money defending myself, trying to undo this nightmare.

Prison is about loneliness and despair. About mothers and grandmothers without their families, most of which were victims themselves. Victims of their husbands, boyfriends or poorly chosen friends. Now they are victims of the federal government with no hope in sight.[12]

Loss of Civil Rights

The punitive campaign has undermined our civil rights. From the late 1970s through the 1980s and 1990s, legislators not only passed laws that greatly increased the number of people sent to prison and their length of sentences but also passed many laws that significantly encroached on the civil liberties of all American citizens. They passed laws that cut back on the rights of citizens to file habeas corpus petitions to the courts; began restricting the scope of the exclusionary rules that had been introduced by the Warren Court to impede police misconduct; instituted widespread drug testing laws; passed "forfeiture laws" by which police jurisdictions could legally confiscate the property of anyone *charged* with, but not convicted of, drug law violations. Norris, Conrad, and Resner described the operation of this law:

In federal forfeiture cases, law enforcement gets to keep the seized assets. Some states provide that a portion goes into their General Fund. What property can the government take? Any property can be seized if the police suggest that it was:

- Bought from profits of illegal activity.

- Used to facilitate a crime (such as a family car that was driven to buy drugs).

How much evidence does the government need for this? No hard evidence; just probable cause—the same standard required for a search warrant or arrest. Police can use hearsay evidence, such as a tip from an informant whose name is not revealed. In all other type[s] of cases, hearsay is inadmissible.

Can seized property be reclaimed? You must file a "claim" that you are the owner of the seized property and, except for real estate or property worth more than $500,000, post a cash bond equivalent to ten percent of the value of the property in order to have the right to a hearing to contest the seizure.

At trial, the burden of proof is on you, not the government. You are required to prove that your property is innocent by a "preponderance of the evidence"—a higher standard [than that] used by police to seize the property.[13]

Between 1985 and 1995, the U.S. Department of Justice seized property worth more than $4 billion.

The result of these new laws is that citizens have been subjected to more searches of their persons and property; lost their cars, homes, and boats and had to engage in lengthy civil procedures to have them returned when charges were dropped or disproved; have been forced to submit to drug testing at their place of employment or schools; and, if convicted of a crime, have had much less success in having their convictions reviewed by higher courts.

The Prison-Industrial Complex

The wars on crime and drugs introduced private profit into the imprisonment enterprise. The massive prison expansion greatly benefitted existing industries devoted to prison construction or created new ones. An excellent demonstration of the growth of these industries is the expansion of the commercial activities at the annual meeting of the American Correctional Association (ACA), the current extension of the original National Prison Association (NPA). The NPA, which formed in 1870, issued, in that year, a far-sighted statement of principles that eventually (after 1950) dominated "correctional" thinking. These principles emphasized indeterminate sentences appropriate for a rehabilitative ("correctional") imprisonment strategy, education for prisoners, and "moral regeneration." In recent years, the modern organization, ACA, talks mostly about products, profits, and costs. Joseph Hallinan, a journalist who spent four years traveling around the country visiting and writing about prisons, gave his impressions of the 2000 ACA meeting in Cincinnati, Ohio, the site of the formation of the National Prison Association:

> But in the halls of the Cincinnati convention center not much is heard these days about moral regeneration. The NPA's members, many of them ministers, debated questions of the human soul. Their counterparts today talk mostly about money. . . .
>
> The scent of so much money has caught the noses of corporate giants like AT&T and Procter & Gamble, which have rented space here at the convention center in Cincinnati, along with lesser-known groups like the Aleph Institute ("Helping institutions meet the needs of Jewish inmates"). The surprising thing is the number of small and midsize companies here that have prospered with the prison boom. Many of them once made products almost exclusively for the "civilian" world. But today, with so many convicts behind bars, they have retooled themselves.[14]

Though in the last two years its fortunes have greatly declined, the private prison business had flourished, generated large fortunes for some of its founders, and had significant influence in shaping governmental prison policies. In the words of Christian Parenti, who likewise studied America's imprisonment binge,

> Another player in the matrix of interests referred to as the prison industrial complex is the fast growing and powerful private prison industry. Through assiduous cultivation of state officials the private prison industry is increasingly active in shaping criminal justice policy, but their partnership with the state also faces problems: recent events have unveiled private jailers as cheats, liars, and liabilities.[15]

As it has turned out, after promising significant improvements in the cost and quality of the prison enterprise, private prisons have proven to be at least as costly as state facilities and have had serious problems in the treatment and control of prisoners. It has been disclosed that low-paid employees lack sufficient training, turn over frequently, and abuse prisoners. The Government Accounting Agency investigated one facility:

> [Eighty] percent of the CCA [Corrections Corporation of America—the largest private prison organization] had no corrections experience; many of the guards were only eighteen or nineteen years old; prison medical records went unaccounted for while more than 200 chronically ill inmates were left untreated in the general population; and almost no effort was made to separate violent psychotics from peaceful convicts. Later inmate civil rights suits alleged that guards violated regulations by using tear gas inside; that prison tactical teams dragged inmates naked and shackled across floors; and that during cell searches convicts were forced to strip, kneel, and were shocked with stun guns if they moved.[16]

New Interest Groups

The prison expansion has given rise to other powerful interest groups, particularly prison employee unions. The California Correctional Peace Officers Association (CCPOA) is the leading example.

> Originally little more than a moribund social club, the CCPOA has become one of the most fearsome political machines in California history. Since 1983, the number of COs [correctional officers] in California has ballooned from 1,600 to more than 28,000 and their real salaries have more than doubled to an average of $41,000. The CCPOA now commands a budget of $17 million, an assault force of twenty-two in-house lawyers, and a huge political war chest. In just the first half of 1998 the guards doled out over $1 million in political contributions.[17]

In 2001, the power of the CCPOA was demonstrated when California governor Davis, in spite of the state's tremendous tax deficit, approved a 39 percent raise for prison guards.

Reforming Criminal Justice

There is a small but politically influential cadre of "experts," including Charles Murray and James Q. Wilson, who still believe that locking up hundreds of thousands of people and making them serve extremely long sentences was the right thing to do. As Charles Murray argued in the *Times of London* in 1997, "We figured out what to do with criminals. Innovations in policing [helped], but the key insight was an old one: Lock 'em up."[18] In 1998, Wilson reported that "putting people in prison is the single most important thing we've done to decrease crime."[19] These conservative spokespersons have a following that will remain influential as long as we have a conservative government that is served by a punitive ideology and has control over the awards it can distribute to "intellectuals" who serve the government's interest.

However, a growing number of criminologists and informed citizens agree that it is time for a dramatic decrease in the number of prisoners and a much greater emphasis on preparing them for life after prison. To accomplish the first of these, most agree that many fewer people should be sent to prison and those who are imprisoned should serve less time. There is less agreement on who should be sent to prison and how much time they should serve.[20] In regard to the second point, preparing released prisoners for life after prison, most agree that much more effort and money must go toward education, vocational training, and prerelease preparation. All who have studied the success and failure of "rehabilitative programs" recognize the great need for substantial transitional programs—halfway houses, job training and placement services, after-prison support efforts, mentoring programs, and temporary financial assistance.

There are no magic formulas for solving the crime problem through penal practices, such as those that were promised by the conservative politicians and academic theorists in the 1970s and 1980s. Most informed social scientists understand that state penal practices have limited influence on crime. The evidence suggests that there is some general deterrence accomplished in the threat and delivery of punishment, but its extent is more related to certainty of punishment than severity. Also, it is well known that the effectiveness of the threat of punishment varies according to the type of criminal activity and the life circumstances of the potential criminal. People who have many options, and therefore many commitments, are highly deterrable, particularly on property crimes. Those, such as ghetto youths, with fewer options are much less deterrable. Also, the evidence from three decades of evaluating the effectiveness of rehabilitative efforts suggests that most attempts make little if any difference. There is some evidence that we worsen the crime problem if we damage the people we punish so that they have less chance of living a crime-free life after their punishment. From this knowledge we must conclude that we will have some but not a huge impact on crime through variations in our criminal justice policies.

It is clear that the general threat of penal sanctions does deter *some* crime. In several historical instances, when the threat of penal sanctions were withdrawn, crime increased.

> When the Nazis arrested the entire police force of Copenhagen and left that city without official law enforcement for some months, there were marked increases in some kinds of crime, in some instances as much as tenfold.[21]

Several nations' successful reduction of drunk driving through harsher penalties and increased police surveillance reveals that for some types of behavior and against certain populations, deterrence works. Also, we must recognize, when we reflect back on the argument made by Emile Durkheim, that the delivery of punishment serves important integrating social functions. The public's commitment to society increases or is sustained if it witnesses something being done about transgressions of the rules that it believes are important. On the other hand, it loses its commitment when nothing is done.

These understandings lead us to accept that we must deliver penal sanctions but that we cannot expect too much in terms of crime reduction from them. Also, we must recognize that too much punishment does more harm than good. We should accept the principle of restraint and deliver enough punishment to accomplish the deterrence that is possible, but not so much that it backfires and degrades or corrupts our humanity. Accepting this principle of restraint should lead to a greatly reduced use of imprisonment and much more attention paid to prisoner rehabilitation, shorter sentences, minimal harm perpetrated on prisoners during imprisonment, and improving efforts to prepare them for a productive, noncriminal life after prison.

These goals seem very rational, that is, if we accept the premises on which they are based. Reaching them, however, will be extremely difficult, because the current punitive situation has become heavily buttressed by many relationships and features in our society. First, the persistent campaign to arouse Americans' fear of crime has succeeded in deeply instilling distorted or false definitions related to crime, criminals, and what works regarding crime control. It will be very difficult, therefore, for politicians to reverse their positions.[22] Additionally, there are many interest groups in place that are favorably served by the present punitive policies. These include the employee unions (such as California's CCPOA), private prison corporations, state and federal prison bureaucracies, and businesses involved in prison construction or in supplying prisons with services and products—all of which constitute a powerful prison-industrial complex. Finally, the elites of our society and conservative politicians have been well served by the punitive campaign, which they largely mounted themselves. The bloated, superactive criminal justice operation never hurts them (except on the relatively rare occasion when one of their children or close relatives is arrested for something like drug possession). Crime has been a neat diversion away from other much more serious social and political problems, the solutions of which would require sacrifice by them (such as paying their share of taxes to support social programs). Consequently, to achieve significant reform of our penal system, Americans must see through the myths about America that have been generated by the power elite and spread by the mass media, which the elites increasingly control. The public will have to come to understand that economic arrangements are the major (but not total) cause of our high crime rates, both street and suite. They will need to see that we do have a class system that results in unfair distribution of all goods and privileges in the society, and that the important decisions about our present situation and future arrangements are made by people who are mainly serving the interests of a few, not the majority. Neal Gabler, writing in the *Los Angeles Times*, discussed why Americans believe there is no class system in the United States and concluded with what he thinks they do believe:

> After 20 years of inspirational tales of wealth, and as many years of government-bashing, this is where we find ourselves now. Most of us believe fervently in the American Dream. Most of us believe that the rich are deserving and that, with a few breaks, we might get ours, too. Most of us believe that taxes are some kind of confiscatory scheme rather than a tool for correction of an imbalance.

And most of us believe that to think in terms of class under these circumstances is to deny the ideal of individual responsibility. This is the very basis of America. That's why the rich will keep getting richer, the middle class will keep losing ground, the poor will keep getting ignored, and no one will say a single word about it.[23]

I would add that "and the poor, particularly, the nonwhite poor, will continue to get prison."

Endnotes

1. Irwin and Austin, *It's About Time*, 150–152. More recently, Jenni Gainsborough and Marc Mauer examined the rates of change in crime rates and rates of incarceration and came to the same conclusion. They found that the states that had above-average increases in their rates of incarceration had an average reduction in crime rates of 13 percent. The states that had below-average increases in incarceration rates had a 17 percent reduction in crime rates. See Gainsborough and Mauer, *Diminishing Returns: Crime and Incarceration in the 1990s* (Washington, DC: The Sentencing Project, September 2000), 7.

2. Paul Jargowsky, Report for the Brookings Institution, 2003, cited in William Julius Wilson, "There Goes the Neighborhood," *New York Times*, 16 June 2003, p. 19.

3. Marc Mauer and Meda Chesney-Lind, eds., *Invisible Punishment* (New York: New Press, 2003), 8.

4. The actual annual cost per prisoner is difficult to determine because there are so many less visible, indirect costs, such as the loss of taxes paid by those prisoners who would have been employed, the added welfare costs paid to wives, taxes lost by tying up government property with non tax-producing buildings, and so forth. James Austin and I, using the data available to us in 1993, calculated the total cost to be approximately $30 thousand per prisoner. With the general increases in all prices since then, $40 thousand seems like a sound estimate. See Irwin and Austin, *It's About Time*, 138.

5. Irwin and Austin, *It's About Time*, 160.

6. Donald Braman, "Families and Incarceration," in Mauer and Chesney-Lind, eds., *Invisible Punishment*, 118.

7. Todd R. Clear, "The Problem With 'Addition by Subtraction': The Prison-Crime Relationship in Low-Income Communities," in Mauer and Chesney-Lind, eds., *Invisible Punishment*, 181–182.

8. See Moore et al., *Homeboys: Gangs, Drugs, and Prison in the Barrios of Los Angeles*.

9. Marc Mauer, "Mass Imprisonment and Disappearing Voters," in Mauer and Chesney-Lind, eds., *Invisible Punishment*, 55.

10. Irwin and Austin, *It's About Time*, 151–152.

11. Mikki Norris, Chris Conrad, and Virginia Resner, *Shattered Lives: Portraits From America's Drug War* (El Cerrito, CA: Creative Expressions, 1998), 33.

12. Ibid., 11.

13. Ibid., 53–54.

14. Joseph Hallinan, *Going Up the River* (New York: Random House, 2001), 156.

15. Parenti, *Lockdown America*, 217.

16. Ibid., 223.

17. Ibid., 226.

18. Charles Murray, "The Ruthless Truth," *Times of London*, 1997.

19. James Q. Wilson, "The Crime Bust," *U.S. News & World Report*, 25 May 1998.

20. Many "liberal" critics of the overuse of incarceration have suggested that we make a distinction between violent and nonviolent offenses and be more lenient on the nonviolent. I am uncomfortable with this distinction, because many unserious crimes, such as second degree robbery, are included in the violent category. Also, separating out the perceived nonviolent offenders could lead to harsher penalties for the remaining offenders.

21. See Working Party for the American Friends Service Committee, *Struggle for Justice*, 56.

22. As related before, a group of us prison reformers met with Robert Presley, the chair of the Public Safety Committee of the California Senate, in 1978, at a time when he was introducing or supporting bills that would lengthen sentences and send more people to prison. He told us that there was nothing he could do. The public wanted harsher sentences, and no politician could afford to be seen as "soft on crime." He indicated that we (citizens groups) would have to get them (the legislators) out of the corner they had got themselves into.

23. Neal Gabler, "Class Dismissed," *Los Angeles Times*, 2 January 2002, p. M1. ✦

Afterword

The Case of the Women

Gendered Harm in the Contemporary Prison

Barbara Owen

Prisons have typically responded to female criminal behavior with little thought to the unintended consequences for women, their children, and the community. Since prisons for women have been modeled after those designed for their "louder and bigger brothers," they damage women incommensurately with the level of threat most convicted women present to society.[1] Women have long been invisible in conventional studies of the criminal justice system and in the literature of the prison.[2] As the numbers of women imprisoned in contemporary America attain unimagined size, these issues therefore require an investigation through a gendered lens.

Women and the Imprisonment Binge

Women's Pathways to Prison

As Irwin argued in his work on imprisoned men, their previous involvement in outside criminal behavior systems and the acquisition and importation of criminal identities during lockup shape their prison world. This analysis is less applicable to the

261

majority of female prisoners because there is little evidence that women participate routinely in outside criminal behavior systems or develop a commitment to a criminal identity.[3] Like incarcerated men, most women in prison disproportionately belong to a minority, are poor, and possess few educational or vocational skills. They also tend to come from families that are fractured by poverty; as a result, violence, unemployment, and substance abuse predominately shape their life chances. However, women prisoners have been more marginalized from conventional institutions than imprisoned men. For example, they are less likely than male offenders to be employed at the time of arrest or to be looking for work when unemployed, less likely to be married, and more likely to come from single-parent families. Women are also more likely to come from families in which parents used drugs and alcohol.[4] These individual circumstances play out in their pathways to prison, which are much different than men's. Marginalized women, who struggle with what Barbara Bloom called "triple jeopardy" as a result of their class, race, and gender position in society[5], are funneled into the prison for reasons only tangentially related to their criminal behavior. The majority of women who wind up in prison have struggled in a world framed by poverty and have experienced explicit racial and gender discrimination within a patriarchal society.

Intimate violence and its effect on life chances are key differences between female and male prisoners. Many incarcerated women and men report that their early family life was marked by abuse, typically at the hands of their parents or adult caretakers. However, imprisoned women report abuse at over three times the rate of that reported by men. These women have also experienced violence from intimate adult partners, which often continues throughout the life course.[6] For many traumatized women, drug and alcohol use becomes a psychological survival strategy, further reducing their options and life chances. Although women may have always used substances to address untreated trauma, the recent increased criminalization of drug use has fueled the concomitant rise in their imprisonment.

When the consequences of violence, trauma, and subsequent drug use are combined with a lack of opportunity for girls and women, early childbearing, and the inadequate protection of patriarchy and public policy, women's prisons become home to those who have no other place in contemporary life. Women's prisons have become the repository for discounted women, not because they are dangerous to society but because these women violate conventional expectations of gender. The prison has become a tool for managing women who are dispossessed and dishonored through multiple marginalization—much of which is tied to their gender. In addition to these processes of dispossession and dishonor, described by Irwin and others cited in this text, prison harms women in an another way: Women, by virtue of their subordinate place in society, have been further discounted, demeaned, and ultimately, dismissed.

The War on Drugs as a War on Women

Since 1980, the female prison population has risen at a rate much faster than that of males. In absolute terms, the number of women incarcerated in state and federal prisons has risen nearly eightfold, from 12,000 in 1980 to more than 96,000 in mid-2003. While the total number of male prisoners between 1990 and 2000 grew 77 percent, the number of female prisoners increased 108 percent during the same period.[7] Although Bureau of Justice Statistics (BJS) data indicate that violent offenses are the major factor in the growth of the male prison population, this is not the case for women prisoners.[8] For them, drug offenses represent the largest source of growth. Almost 50 percent of male prisoners are locked up for crimes of violence, with 18 percent doing time for property offenses, 19 percent for drug crimes, and 11 percent for public order offenses. Women, in marked contrast, have a much more even distribution across the three major offense categories: 32 percent of incarcerated females are serving time for violent offenses, 26 percent for property offenses, 30 percent for drug crimes, and 11 percent for public order crimes.[9] Chesney-Lind pointed out that even in the violent crime category, female violence tends to occur in family and friendship contexts.[10] BJS data also show that female violent offenders are more likely to know their victims and less likely to cause them serious physical harm.[11]

Several sources demonstrate that the increase in female prison populations cannot be explained solely by increasing crime rates. According to BJS statistics, the rate for women has risen only about 32 percent in the last two decades, while the imprisonment rate has increased 159 percent.[12] Steffensmeier and Allan confirmed that an increase in crime and arrest rates cannot alone account for the explosion in the female prison population.[13] In their analysis of Uniform Crime Reports (UCR) data collected between 1960 and 1995 and offender information from the National Crime Victimization surveys, they found that gender and crime seriousness are indirectly related. The root of female crime, they argued, is found in the criminalization of drug use and "female inequality and economic vulnerability that shape most female offending patterns."[14] Scholars also point to the differential effect of drug war policy on the lives of women, particularly women of color. Bloom, Chesney-Lind, and Owen,[15] Mauer, Potler, and Wolf[16] and Bush-Baskette[17] are among those who argue that women have been disproportionately penalized by the war on drugs.

In addition to gender differences between male and female crime, women's arrest and incarceration rates vary by race.[18] Minority women are overrepresented in the U.S. prison population, with the percentage of African-American women who are incarcerated growing at increasing rates. In 1991, African-American women made up about 40 percent of the female prison population; by 1995, this population had grown to 48 percent. The percentage of Hispanic and Latina women is also growing at a somewhat slower rate. As Harrison and Beck stated,

> [F]emale incarceration rates, though substantially lower than male incarceration rates at every age, reveal similar racial and ethnic disparities. Black females (with an incarceration rate of 191 per 100,000) were more than twice as likely as Hispanic females (80 per 100,000) and 5 times more likely than white females (35 per 100,000) to be in prison on December 31, 2002. These differences among white, black, and Hispanic females were consistent across all age groups.[19]

Punishment in Society: Making Law

With a focus on perceived dangerousness, the power of the propertied class, and the role of the state, Irwin described the general process through which social control is legitimated in law and differentially applied to those in less propertied and less powerful classes. A gendered analysis adds that, under conditions of patriarchy, women are the least powerful actors across all class lines.

Social control regarding women typically involves the application of patriarchal rules that control women's positions in society by controlling their bodies and their sex role behaviors and limiting their life chances. For men, "dangerousness" is defined as their threat to social order through physical violence or property damage. For women, "dangerousness" has been seen as the threat their behavior poses to conventional morality and oppressive patriarchal order. When women violate sex role and sexual expectations, they must be controlled and punished. While the purest examples of this process are historical, recent research points to more contemporary attempts to control the sexual and reproductive aspects of women's lives. For example, Bagley and Merlo argued that law, science, and the state have colluded in regulating women's bodies and women's lives. They reported that "[c]riminal sanctions that focus on women's reproductive roles and capacities not only define and treat women as 'bodies' rather than persons, but they also ignore or trivialize the social problems that bring these women to the attention of agents of formal and informal social control."[20]

History of the Imprisonment of Women

In Western societies, the prison for men evolved as the primary mechanism for controlling the threats they represent to the social and economic order. In contrast, women's prisons evolved to control behavior that challenged the gender order rather than social or economic institutions. Throughout history, the female criminal has been cast as "double-deviant"—first, because she violates the criminal or moral law, and second, and perhaps more important, because she has violated the narrow strictures of the female role within society.[21] As a precursor to the contemporary prison, the workhouse, in its various forms, was used to confine a range of less serious offenders, including penniless women and prostitutes. Women could also be sent to bridewells, poorhouses, or nunneries by fathers or husbands who wanted to punish an unruly, disobedient, or unchaste woman. In England, one of the first models for the modern prison was intended to provide a place of penitence for prostitutes. Up until the late 1800s, women, men, and children were confined together in these attempts at correction, often with no provision for food, clothing, or bedding. Women who did not have families to provide for them resorted to prostitution with more propertied inmates or prison officials to survive.

In the late 1700s and early 1800s, England transported over 60 percent of convicted offenders to work as indentured servants in the colonies of America and Australia. The small percentage of women who were transported had typically been convicted of crimes relating to poverty or sexual behavior. Ironically, women transported to the colonies were often used as prostitutes or mistresses—willing or not—to meet the demand for sexual partners in these rough new worlds. Those escaping forced prostitution became indentured servants to the managerial class.

Women were excluded from imprisonment in the first penitentiaries, which were oriented toward redeeming prisoners, because "the common conception was that a criminal woman was beyond redemption."[22] Johnson reported that women and minorities were "barely considered human," and thus they were not fit candidates for the penitentiary's regime.[23] The harsh treatment of women was justified by the argument that "women convicts were more depraved than men, since having been born pure, they had fallen further than their male counterparts in crime."[24]

Women were held in facilities intended for males—usually local jails rather than centralized prisons—and were often locked away in crowded and dirty rooms above the guardhouse or mess hall.[25] Without consistent supervision, women were vulnerable to attacks by one another and the male guards, and had few opportunities to work and exercise.[26] Freedman stated that women were subjected to the "worst debasement at the hands of the prison officials and guards" and that sadistic beatings, rape, and illegitimate births combined to make the prison experience even more terrifying.[27] Matrons were eventually hired to supervise women prisoners and protect them from the sexual advances of the male staff and other prisoners. Pollock stated that matrons in these female units were paid less than their male coworkers, and those working in institutions for white women were paid more than matrons employed in facilities housing African-American women.[28]

The Reformatory and the Correctional Institution

By the mid-nineteenth century, prisons for women had diverged in two directions, custodial institutions and the reformatory.[29] The custodial model was the traditional male prison, adopting the retributive purpose, high-security architecture, and male-dominated authority and harsh discipline.[30] While some women—typically young, white, and often middle-class—were sent to the new reformatory, lower-class women and women of color remained confined to the male prison.

In the 1870s, the reformatory movement led to the development of separate women's prisons. The reformatory was a new form of punishment creating institutions designed to house only women with female matrons and programs planned to reform women by promoting appropriate gender roles. Training in cooking, sewing, laundry, and other domestic arts was designed to return the female prisoner to free society as either a well-trained wife or a domestic servant.

After the 1930s, Rafter wrote, the custodial and reform institutions merged, combining elements of their two styles with differing results throughout the United States.[31]

By the 1940s and '50s, a new philosophy of punishment, based on a medical model of treatment, had emerged in the United States. Called "correctional institutions," U.S. prisons moved away from the harsh discipline and work orientation of the custodial prison by attempting to introduce treatment to a newly defined inmate population. It appears that most women's prisons of this era melded the reformatory model with the new approach to "corrections" and yet changed little.

The Contemporary Prison

Beginning in the late 1970s, the majority of prison systems returned to a custodial or "warehouse" model, with few prisons offering rehabilitative programs, although many of the reformatory prisons remained in use. By the 1980s, the numbers of women in prison began to increase exponentially, due primarily to enhanced sanctions against drug offenders. Most states have a relatively small number of prisons for women and thus house women prisoners at only one or two geographically isolated institutions. A few states with small female prison populations even ship their women prisoners to other states for a price; Hawaii is the most extreme example with a policy of shipping women from island institutions to Oklahoma. Some states have built new prisons for women. California is typical of the states that built new, larger institutions, using designs based on male prisons. California has the largest female prison population in the United States (at over 11,000 in 2003) with five prisons for women.

Due to the relative rarity of violence in the women's prison, female prisoners' housing arrangements are not as problematic as they usually are in male institutions. Unlike male prisons, the majority of women's facilities in the United States encompass all classification and security levels. These institutions are often rated at an "administrative security level" and either mix women of all security levels or attempt some internal housing categories by housing women of differing security levels in separate housing units. With the exception of newly arrived prisoners and the small numbers held in the more restrictive special housing units (SHUs) (also known as administrative segregation, security housing units, or segregated housing units), most women prisoners remain in what is referred to as the general population. Regardless of security level classification, these prisoners work, attend school, and participate in programs in close contact with all inmates, whose classification may range from minimum to maximum custody. Lifers and short-termers mingle in housing units, in work and education assignments, and in recreational areas.

This commingling of all custody levels within a few general-purpose facilities often results in the "overclassification" of women prisoners. Few jurisdictions in the United States have developed classification instruments that adequately assess the custody and security needs of women. As a result, the majority are subjected to the more severe custody conditions required by the small number of high-risk women. Additionally, women who represent a minimal risk to the community are often "overconfined" due to the lack of lower-custody facilities, such as camps, community placements, and work furlough facilities.

The small number of women housed in SHUs are usually confined to their cells and experience the most restrictive custody. In their cells for an average of 23 hours a day, they are allowed very limited recreation and visiting privileges. Only a small percentage of the total female prison population is held in SHUs, but conditions there are often severe.

The prison that I studied, Central California Women's Facility (CCWF), was the first prison in the state designed to hold women in the new generation of prison buildings.[32] Here I found that women organize their time and create a social world that is markedly different than the world of the contemporary male prisoner. Just as offense patterns are tied to differences between men and women, so is prison social organization. Like male prisoners, women in prison develop a range of strategies and tactics as they accommodate to a life in prison.

In 1994, over half of the women in California prisons were first-timers.[33] For first-time prisoners, coming to prison can be frightening and filled with apprehension. To manage this uncertainty, the women begin to negotiate routines and strategies that allow them to make a life in this new world. Learning to live in the prison comes primarily through interaction with other prisoners, and relationships are a critical aspect of this new socialization process. As one woman whom I interviewed explained, "Some women are way out of their territory here; they need help from someone who knows what is happening."[34]

As women adjust to their imprisonment, they develop friendships and other forms of relationships with other prisoners. One common type is the "prison family" or the "play-family." A woman often learns how to do her time through interaction with these social units, becoming prisonized in certain ways of behaving, feeling, and thinking. At CCWF, these families developed out of complicated emotional relationships, sometimes based on practical or sexual ties. Families had social and material responsibilities, such as providing friendship and support; celebrating birthdays and holidays; providing food, cigarettes, and clothing; and taking care of a member's possessions when she was transferred out of the unit.

The Mix

A key element in surviving prison is negotiating an aspect of prison life known as "the mix." In its shortest definition, this term refers to one aspect of prisoner informal social activities that can bring trouble and conflict with staff and other prisoners. The mix is the "fast life" or "la vida loca" (that is, the crazy life), lived while "running the yard" in prison. Becoming involved with the mix can lead to violating the prison rules, developing destructive relationships with other prisoners that lead to fights, and generally getting into trouble. A variety of behaviors can put one in the mix—same-sex relationships (known as "homo-secting"), involvement in drugs, fights, and "being messy" (which means making trouble for yourself and others). As one prisoner told me, "The mix is continuing the behavior that got you here in the first place."[35]

For the vast majority of the women at CCWF, however, "the mix" is generally something to be avoided. Most women want to stay out of trouble and do their time on their own terms. The majority of women at CCWF serve their sentences, survive the mix, and return to society, resuming their lives in the free community. For many women, prison life becomes a time for reflection on the trajectory of their lives. One woman said, "Coming to prison was the best thing that ever happened to me. I know I would be dead if I hadn't been sent here. It has made me stop and think about what I was doing to myself and my kids."[36] But these women's feelings notwithstanding, it is important to emphasize the damage of imprisonment and the ways in which this harm is gendered. Next, I review salient elements of women's prisons strictly in terms of how the structure of the contemporary prison introduces and reinforces harm to incarcerated women.

Gendered Harm and the Contemporary Prison

Imprisoning Women

Coming to prison affects women differently than men. Many men who are embedded in some form of a criminal identity system have a definition of self based on an image of "criminal," "thug," or gang member. Membership in these identity systems usually includes some expectation of arrest and incarceration. Many of the men I have interviewed indicated that going to prison is the cost of doing illegitimate business and that given the way their lives were unfolding, prison seemed inevitable. As Irwin has shown (see Chapter 8), a majority of the men in prison come from neighborhoods and families in which going to prison is commonplace. While women come from these same families and neighborhoods, their gender position does not lend itself to the same expectation of going to prison. And because women are typically less involved in serious criminal activity, there is also a lower expectation that they will go to prison.

Moreover, women have fewer cultural maps about this introduction to prison life. Men often enter prison with bravado and may seek out existing social networks, such as homeboy relationships, gang affiliations, tips, or cliques. They may also draw on a set of emotional, social, and physical strategies, developed in their street lives, to confront and solve problems encountered in prison entry. With the exception of ties among a few women who share in these meaning systems or have membership in community homegirl networks, few pre-existing social networks are present in the female prison. The life experiences of most women have not prepared them for prison in the ways that most men's experiences (particularly minority men) have exposed them to this expectation. Most women face the introduction to prison life alone. Therefore, a sense of loneliness and isolation commonly shapes their initial experience.

Harm and the Pains of Imprisonment

Irwin described the ways in which imprisonment harms human beings (see especially Chapter 6). I suggest here that incarcerated women face further gender-based harm through their imprisonment and their reintegration back into the free community. Following Irwin, I, too, see that prison is harmful in both obvious and subtle ways.

Privacy

In prison, as well as the free world, women have a larger expectation of privacy than men. Perhaps relating to biological needs (such as sitting down to urinate) but more likely tied to social proscriptions about modesty and the need to hide from the male gaze, recent court decisions have held that women have a greater expectation of privacy in the prison.[37] While older prisons may continue to use group showers or unprotected toilets, the modern prison for women typically has more private shower and toilet areas. "Modesty panels," covering the "average" woman[38] from shoulder to knee, provide somewhat more privacy. Women can be afforded such shielding because, unlike men, their lower level of reported inmate-on-inmate violence lessens security concerns. The potential for violence among male prison populations precludes such privilege.

But, with these few exceptions, prison design works against expectations of privacy. In the contemporary prison, privacy is an ever-decreasing, and greatly desired, resource. For women, more so than for men, the lack of physical and psychological privacy becomes one of the pains of imprisonment due to one central fact: Women in prison rarely escape the male gaze. Irwin discussed the opposite process in his description of "reckless eyeballing," whereby male inmates were sanctioned for staring at female officers. In most women's prisons, males make up the majority of correctional staff. While privacy is already eroded by crowded conditions, shared housing units, and the need for surveillance, the presence of male staff further undermines one's ability to attend to personal hygiene and grooming without the scrutiny of men. Male staff supervise housing units, observing showers, toilets, and rooms or cells where women dress. However, most prison systems prohibit male staff from performing strip searches, and several recent court cases (Canada and Michigan) have established restrictions on male involvement in this area of operational practice.

Separation From Children

Women prisoners also react differently than men to the separation from children and significant others. Most research describes the importance of family, particularly children, in the lives of imprisoned women.[39] National surveys of women prisoners found that three-fourths were mothers, with two-thirds having children who were under the age of 18.[40] For mothers, separation from their children is the most painful aspect of incarceration. Bloom and Chesney-Lind stated that distance between the prison and the children's homes, lack of transportation, and very limited economic resources compromise a woman prisoner's ability to maintain these relationships.[41] Slightly over half of the women responding to Bloom and Steinhart's 1993 survey of imprisoned mothers reported never receiving visits from their children.[42] Lord, a prison warden in New York, has stated that while men in prison "do their own time," women "remain interwoven in the lives of significant others, primarily their children and their own mothers . . . ."[43] Connections to the free world can make it much harder to "do time," particularly for those with a long time to serve. As Divine said,

You cannot do your time in here and out on the streets at the same time. That makes you do hard time. You just have to block that out of your mind. You can't think about what is going on out there and try to do your five, ten [years] or whatever in here. You will just drive yourself crazy.[44]

Pregnant Women

Although their numbers are small, pregnant women who are in the CCWF population remind others of the separation from their own children. For the majority who are mothers, the presence of a pregnant woman is a reminder of loss and reinforces feelings of separation and guilt because of leaving their children. Most women in special medical housing units do not participate in prison programs; instead, they are "medically unassigned" and may not earn the "good time credits" that reduce time in prison. At the time of delivery, women are taken to a community hospital under escort by the correctional staff. After the baby is born, the inmate stays in the hospital only one or two days. Some women make arrangements for a relative, usually a mother or sister, to pick up the baby. If there are no prior arrangements, the county social service agency provides foster care for the child. The pain of a prison pregnancy takes several forms. First, most women reported that being pregnant in prison was an "ugly feeling." Second, not having a place to send one's child was very painful. Third, many women said that returning to prison after giving birth was extremely difficult.[45]

Acoca also argued that pregnancy during incarceration must be understood as a high-risk situation, both medically and psychologically, for inmate mothers and their children.[46] She noted that deficiencies in the correctional response to the needs of pregnant inmates include lack of prenatal and postnatal care, little education regarding childbirth and parenting, and inadequate preparation for separation from the infant after delivery.

Legal Services for Prisoners With Children (LSPC) has reviewed the treatment of pregnant women in prison.[47] Their investigation has uncovered cases in which obvious danger signs, such as high blood pressure, no fetal heartbeat, and vaginal bleeding, have been ignored. This has led directly to late-term miscarriages, premature deliveries, stillbirths, and sick infants. One of the most troubling aspects of in-prison pregnancies involves the shackling of all pregnant women. This appears to be the policy in almost all state and federal prisons, leading to many negative effects on the delivery, including hemorrhage and decrease in fetal heart rate.

Clothing and 'Hygiene'

Generally, clothes and styles of dress have more meaning for women than men. However, all California prisoners—female and male—wear a "uniform of the day," usually blue denim pants, "baseball" style caps, long-sleeved cotton tee shirts, and state-issued shoes. At the time of my study, few of these clothing items had been specifically designed for women: Women at CCWF were issued shirts and shoes made for men. Women were also issued muumuus, underwear, and a bra. Until recently, female prisoners in California were allowed to wear "street clothes," usually sent by their families or others on the outside, during nonprogramming times. As the clothing and grooming rules for women become more similar to those for men, such arrangements that allow more personal expression seem to be decreasing.

Irwin provided details of current CDC grooming standards for female and male inmates (see Chapter 6). While clothing and grooming standards do not, at first glance, appear to be an onerous aspect of imprisonment, such regulations are a subtle but corrosive aspect of the demeaning nature of the prison. Women are accused by prison staff of not being "feminine," but they are required to wear male clothing. Another charge against women prisoners is that they often do not act like responsible adults. The female state-issued clothing is anything but empowering, however. Although muusmuus look like they are to be used only as housedresses, women are required to wear them in public places. Walking around in a housedress does little to promote feelings of adulthood and, in my view, further serves to demean women. Another demeaning aspect of the **muumuu** as a garment is found at postrelease. If any prisoner does not receive a "going-home package" with street clothes to wear at release or does not have personal clothing, the inmate is required to purchase his or her "state-issue" clothing. Women with few resources often choose to purchase the muumuu because it is the least expensive item. Wearing a muumuu home, like appearing in a housedress in public, is a very discouraging experience. I have been told that drug dealers hang out at the bus station, targeting recently released women wearing these muumuus as potential customers.[48]

A small but significant indignity suffered by women relates to material needs created by menses. Some women have resources that allow them to purchase sanitary supplies in the prison canteen, or to have them sent from home in quarterly packages. Those without such resources must ask staff (who are frequently male) for these products, standing in line in the housing unit to make this request. In one instance, I observed male staff responding to such a request by saying, "I just gave you a pad an hour ago. Why do you need another one?"

Dignity

For both women and men, imprisonment can be an undignified environment. For women, however, much of this indignity occurs though assaults on their definitions of self, specifically as women. There is much discussion in the literature about low self-esteem among female prisoners. Others have written about the ways in which prison infantilizes women. Imprisonment does little to raise one's sense of self-worth. Even among some of the most progressive prison managers, the habit of calling adult women "girls" remains. Calling these women girls conveys the patriarchal subtext of women's imprisonment, but even more demeaning names occur. I have heard, and others have reported, that women are infrequently called "bitches" and "whores."

Programming

The contemporary prison offers a range of programming theoretically designed to address the problems that bring both women and men into prison, although there is significant disagreement about the efficacy of these programs in all prisons. Further, there are problems in providing effective programs for women without gendered elements. Prison systems have been sued by women prisoners and legal advocates over their failure to provide equal programming in female institutions. Since the 1980s, litigation has established that female prisoners have equal rights when it comes to programming, although many jurisdictions have been unable to provide comparable programming for both women and men.[49] *Glover v. Johnson,* one of the most famous cases, was adjudicated in

Michigan, where women sued under the equal protection clause of the Fourteenth Amendment. In the Michigan litigation, the comparison between female and male programs showed a dramatic difference across several areas. Male prisoners had access to 22 vocational programs, but women had access to only 3. Jobs in the women's facilities were fewer in number, lower-paying, and sex-stereotyped. In the same job classification, women were paid less than their male counterparts. Men had access to college classes at the bachelor level; women could take only high school courses. Male prisons had fully equipped libraries, but female institutions did not. Perhaps most unfair was the fact that women did not have similar opportunity to earn earlier release through good time as the men did. The state court found in favor of the women prisoners, ordered Michigan to improve and increase its programming for women, and instituted heavy fines over a 20-year monitoring period.[50] In addition, many prison systems provide fewer visits and work release and recreational programs in women's facilities[51.]

Another gendered element in programming involves the provision of gender-responsive, or women-centered, services. Our 2003 National Institute of Corrections identified the ways in which programs and policies designed for male offenders are often inappropriate and many times damaging for female prisoners.[52] One specific example lies in the current research on in-prison drug programming for women. Although women offenders are likely to have an extensive history of drug and alcohol use, a relatively small percentage of women receive any treatment specifically intended for women within the justice system. A large body of empirical research agrees that treatment within criminal justice systems is less intense, having been modeled after programs for men and therefore unable to meet the gendered needs of women.[53] In my current ethnography, I found that many prison drug programs often use curricula designed for men (with pictures of men and the use of male examples); do not provide treatment staff trained with women-specific information; and continue to use confrontational approaches that do not work well with women.

Mental and Physical Health

The majority of imprisoned women have significant health care problems. LSPC described in compelling detail the health problems of women prisoners in California.[54] They argued that adequate medical care is one of the most pressing problems facing women prisoners and presented data to demonstrate that women in custody have an increased incidence of chronic health problems, including asthma, gynecological disease, inadequate nutrition, and convulsive seizure disorders, often a result of their exposure to violence. Moreover, care is provided with an eye toward reducing costs and is based on the military model, which assumes a healthy male. LSPC concluded that medical care for women in California prisons is woefully inadequate. These problems and conditions occur across the nation.

LSPC reviewed problems common to both women and men in detailing the minimal training of medical technical assistants (MTAs), who are the gatekeepers to the system. More important, MTAs are considered custodial staff and are members of the correctional officers union. LSPC also agreed with Irwin that MTAs demonstrate a custodial approach to medical care rather than a health-professional approach. Other common problems include cancellation of a sick call, the $5.00 copayment now required of all prisoners, and delays in receiving regular medication.

While men also suffer from irregular preventive care, women suffer in terms of their gendered diseases.[55] LSPC stated that many reproductive cancers, such as breast and uterine cancers, go undiagnosed and untreated because there is no systematic plan in place to provide for regular Pap smears and mammograms. They also document that women prisoners seeking medical assistance for tumors or chronic pain are likely to experience delays at every step in the process: access to a doctor, tests, and follow-up care or surgery. In California—and elsewhere—there is little preventive health care education that would allow women to learn how to manage their own medical problems.

Psychological Damage

Mental health disorders appear to be more prevalent for women prisoners. While few studies assess the prevalence and incidence of these conditions, estimates suggest that 25 percent to over 60 percent of the female prison population require mental health services.[56] Evidence in our National Institute of Corrections (NIC) report demonstrates that the violent and traumatic experiences of women prisoners contribute to increased levels of mental health disorder. Prison policies and everyday operational practice have also been shown to aggravate post-traumatic stress disorders (PTSD) in female prisoners.[57] Heavy medication is often used by administrators to control the behavior of women rather than treat mental health problems without such corresponding psychological therapy.[58]

More so than males, female inmates are often dually diagnosed, experiencing both substance abuse and mental health problems.[59] Singer et al. reported that incarcerated women have had experience with both the criminal justice and mental health systems.[60] Teplin, Abraham, and McClelland found that over 60 percent of female jail inmates had symptoms of drug abuse, over 30 percent had signs of alcohol dependence, and 33 percent had PTSD.[61] Few women's prisons are prepared to deal with these complex mental health needs.

Rule Enforcement

Although male prisons typically hold a much greater percentage of violent offenders and have a higher rate of in-prison violence, women tend to receive disciplinary infractions at a greater rate than men. In her comparative study of Texas prisons, Dorothy McClellan found that women prisoners were cited more frequently and punished more severely than males. The infractions committed by the women in McClellan's Texas sample were overwhelmingly petty and, she suggested, perhaps a result of a philosophy of rigid and formalistic rule compliance expected of the women but not of the men.[62] The most common infractions among the women were "violation of a written or posted rule" and "refusing to obey an order." She also found that women were more strictly supervised than men and cited for behavior that would be overlooked in an institution for men.[63] Pollock also suggested that reasons for this disparate practice can be found in staff expectations and differential responses to the behavior of women and men.[64] The patriarchal patterns of social control that propel women into the prison may also be responsible for the differential rule enforcement patterns between male and female institutions.

Physical and Psychological Safety

Compared with prisons for men, almost all women's prisons are physically safer. Physical violence between female prisoners is infrequent, with serious assaults involving weapons even less likely. Verbal threats and loud arguments are more typical expressions of conflict. Physical fights do occur but usually in the context of a personal relationship or, less often, as a result of a drug deal or other material conflict. Organized conflicts related to gangs and ethnic strife have not been reported in the research literature. Women prisoners strike or scratch each other, but they usually do not inflict serious injury. Occasionally, women will resort to a "lock in a sock" as an improvised weapon. The extremely rare stabbing may occur with a pair of scissors or a tool in a spontaneous fight. Riots and other collective disturbances are also atypical. Isolated reports of sexual assaults between female prisoners have been made, but prison sexual assaults are many times more likely in a male facility. In 2003, Congress passed the Prison Rape Elimination Act, designed to address the problem of prison sexual assault, but few separate provisions for women are described in this legislation. In fact, the concept of gender is largely absent.

Women prisoners, like women in the free community, are at a much greater risk of violence and sexual assault from males than females. Multiple reports of staff sexual misconduct have been released from Human Rights Watch, Amnesty International, and other women's rights advocates.[65] In *All Too Familiar: Sexual Abuse of Women in U.S. State Prisons,* Human Rights Watch examined this serious problem.[66] In their careful review of sexual abuse in selected prisons, the Human Rights Watch investigators identified four specific issues: (1) the inability to escape one's abuser; (2) ineffectual or nonexistent investigative and grievance procedures; (3) lack of employee accountability (either criminally or administratively); and (4) little or no public concern. They bluntly stated that their "findings indicate that being a women in U.S. state prisons can be a terrifying experience."[67] As Bloom and Chesney-Lind noted, the sexual victimization of women prisoners is difficult to uncover due to inadequate protection of women who file complaints and an occupational subculture that discourages complete investigation of these allegations. Additionally, they suggested, the public stereotype of women as "bad girls" compromises the legitimacy of their claims.[68]

Reentry and the Gendered Problems of Parole

Both women and men face almost insurmountable odds in re-integrating into the free community. Like men, women who are re-turning to their communities from correctional facilities must comply with conditions of supervised release, achieve financial stability, access health care, locate housing, and reunite with their families or create new social networks. These tasks are compli-cated by gender. A major consideration is reunification with chil-dren. Most incarcerated mothers expect to take responsibility for their children upon release and rarely receive any financial or emo-tional support from the fathers. Families who have taken care of the children often expect the paroled woman to take custody im-mediately following release. For those without formal custody of their children, reunification with children is an important but of-ten elusive goal of released mothers. If a child has been placed in foster or state care during the mother's incarceration, it is espe-cially difficult for the released mother to demonstrate to state agencies that she is capable of caring for her child adequately. Many states now require a paroled offender (female or male) to re-pay the state for any child-related welfare or foster care expenses incurred during incarceration.

Two current studies examine the experience of parole for women. Marilyn Brown investigated the role of motherhood in the parole process in her sensitive description of parole in Hawaii.[69] Patricia O'Brien examined the transition from prison into the free world through case studies of 18 women returning to the commu-nity.[70] While finding a place to live is a central problem for both fe-male and male offenders, O'Brien suggested that, for women, establishing a home, "with all its concrete and metaphorical possi-bilities, is the foundation for other experiences of 'making it' after being released from prison."[71] O'Brien described the way women create a web of social relationships as an "enabling environmental niche"[72] that provides both material and psychological support for women transitioning from prison. She reported

> that in addition to establishing a physical shelter and meeting ba-
> sic needs, they [the women] had to address a multitude of internal
> issues related to how they chose to present themselves in the
> world. Implicit in many women's narratives were their relations

about the impact of incarceration on their relationships, their everyday behavioral choices and how they thought and felt about themselves as a consequence.[73]

Brown placed her discussion of parole within the context of Hawaii's history with rehabilitation. She argued that

[u]nder the guise of rehabilitation, the state attempts to alter the consciousness of women in the hopes that these new selves will leave prison as rational, choice-making and responsible individuals. Penal authorities imagine that their reforms will make a difference in the lives women lead after prison and present further troubles with the law. However, I found that women's post-prison experiences look very much like their lives prior to prison in terms of their economic, social, and family troubles. Little attention is paid to the pathways women travel to prison, journeys that are shaped by abuse, poverty and the dynamics of gender inequality. I found the central role that relationship and family play in the formation of women's subjectivity makes them more vulnerable to criminalization in some contexts—their relations with drug-abusing men being but one example. But relationship can also be a domain in which the state can exercise its power over women. There is no gendered domain of which this is more true than that of motherhood. For, despite their unconventional life-styles, I found that women parolees remain powerfully committed to their children's welfare. Regardless of women's parenting concerns and despite these new notions of selfhood they are exposed to in prison, the structural features of their experience (poor education, alienation from institutions, under employment, and little support for child welfare) remain stubbornly in place. My main claim is that the ideology of the modern schemes of rehabilitation promises autonomy and the capacity to make better choices—but does little or nothing to alter the array of choices that poor women . . . actually face after prison.[74]

For the women in Brown's study of parole, economic dependency and a lack of other material options often forced them into living situations not of their choosing. Living with a violent man and living in drug-involved or dangerous communities, most frequently with dependent children, limit a woman's "choices" while on parole. As Brown stated, "Financial instability precludes attaining secure housing and women's economic dependence increases the potential for living in an unstable familial environment. Economic dependency is a common reason that women remain in violent households. Or households plagued with family troubles and conflict."[75] She further stated that "[t]he fates of women on parole and their children are shaped extensively by such links to social and economic capital, links that often rest on the few tenuous social ties women are able to build with friends, families and lovers."[76]

Developing new relationships was one way these women met the struggles of parole. Brown showed us that "[b]ecause women had previously attempted to sustain relationships by meeting the unrealistic and sometimes harmful expectations of family members and significant, though often abusive or exploitative, partners, a major part of new relational strategies involved focusing oneself and to building a new web of support with professionals, others in recovery, ex-inmates and peers."[77] O'Brien noted, too, that one element of frustration for women transitioning from prison "lay in their struggle to remake these relationships, particularly with their mothers, or to connect with significant others in the hope of moving toward empowering development and ongoing support."[78]

These studies and my current work on drug treatment for imprisoned women underscore the role that drug use and subsequent addiction play in the parole experience.[79] While on parole, treatment options for women are limited and are frequently derived from effective male-based models. Kassebaum suggested that once released from custody, women have greater difficulty in reintegrating into the community. This may be due to the more advanced and severe nature of their addiction, the broader range of problems intertwined with their drug use, and the complexity of their family and community relations. Families, she argued, are often not supportive of treatment and may discourage women from seeking treatment after release.[80]

Relationships With Parole Officers

Women on parole have different relationships with their parole agents than do men. There are three aspects of these relations: expectations of help and assistance, resisting surveillance, and the potential for sexual demands. O'Brien noted that the ways "women negotiated meeting their conditions of parole and their relationships with their parole or probation officer were instrumental to the women's transitions."[81] Elena, a women in O'Brien's sample, reported that she was primed for difficulties with her parole officer:

> Yeah, I thought she was out to send me back. I did not trust her. I didn't like her. . . . And, I just heard stories from the other girls at the halfway house, but later on I found out that they just ended up usin' and they sent their ownselves back. She didn't send them back. . . . That is one thing she doesn't tolerate is using. She even told me that if I ever had a dirty UA or anything she was sending me back. But, like, if I have any problems or any questions, I call her up and I talk to her and she is very understanding.[82]

Not all of the women in O'Brien's study had such mutual relationships: Negative characteristics mentioned by the women included arbitrary interpretation of the rules, excessive intrusion in their lives, and a lack of understanding of the obstacles they had to address when coming out of prison.[83]

Brown noted that women "share a surprising amount of information about their lives and problems with their parole officers. Some paroled women clearly see their parole officer as a social worker type if not a friend."[84] In focus group interviews around the country for the NIC report, many parole officers reported that some of the women on their caseloads said that their parole agent was their best friend.[85] For women who have been victimized by the partners in their lives, an interested and helpful parole agent may well be the only friend a paroled woman has, even if she has been assigned by the criminal justice system.

Excessive intrusion in their lives typically revolved around definitions of sexual behaviors and privacy. O'Brien wrote that one woman felt her parole agent was projecting his moral standards on her sexual behavior by enforcing rules related to not sleeping away from home.

In my current study of prison drug treatment programs for women, I have followed a small group of 20 women ex-prisoners into the community.[86] The story of these women parallels that described by O'Brien and Brown. Difficulties in making a living, reunifying with children, accommodating the demands of families and significant others, finding nonabusing (and sober) sexual partners, and struggling with alcohol and drug problems are marked gender-based differences during the parole period. I have also had some women report to me that their parole agent demanded sexual favors in return for allowing them to remain free on parole.[87] One woman, Maureen, actively resisted these advances and had her home ransacked several times. The agent told her that "This could stop" if she acceded to his sexual demands. She refused and was returned to custody for a series of technical violations. She has since been discharged from parole and has left the state.

Conclusion

One of my respondents in *In the Mix* offered this observation about the damage of imprisonment:

> Prison makes you very bitter . . . and you become dehumanized. I've been in prison since I was 17. I have been abandoned by my family members, and anyone else who knew me out there. Being in prison forces you to use everything that you have just to survive. From day to day, whatever, you know it's very difficult. It's difficult to show compassion, or to have it when you haven't been extended it.[88]

The problems that lead women to prison—abuse and battering, economic disadvantage, substance abuse, and unsupported parenting responsibilities—have become increasingly criminalized as contemporary society continues to dismiss marginalized women. As I have argued previously, society expects the women's prison to address problems that result from the devaluation and marginalization of women under patriarchy. While prison is the wrong place to address the complex issues that shape women's pathways to prison, in pursuing a policy of increasing imprisonment, U.S. society incarcerates women who would be better served in community settings. But for huge numbers of women, prison has become the uniform response to problems created by inequality and gender discrimination. Women in prison have been damaged by the oppression of patriarchy, economic marginalization, and the far-reaching effects of such short-sighted and detrimental policies as the war on drugs and the over-reliance on incarceration.

The upward spiral in the number of women in prison represents a serious failure of conventional society and public policy. Under current policy, these complex problems are laid at the feet of the prison by a society unable—or unwilling—to confront the problems of women on the margin. Women confined in U.S. prisons are enmeshed in a criminal justice system that is ill-equipped and confused about handling their problems—the problems that brought them to prison and the problems they confront during and after incarceration.

I am convinced that the vast majority of modern prisons for women are not organized or operated with the intention of harming women. In many of the female prisons I have observed over the past 10 years, enlightened administrations have sought the opposite: to operate a prison that is safe for women and to create a staff culture that recognizes the gendered nature of the prison experience. But despite the best efforts of prison managers (both women and men) around this country who seek to develop a gender-responsive environment,[89] prisons are increasingly harmful to women, both in terms of their immediate reality while incarcerated and the effect on their lives and their families over time. I am forced to conclude that the fundamental inhumanity of penal confinement and the corresponding processes of "otherizing" diminishes all human beings—whether they are female or male.

Endnotes

1. Thanks to my student, Daniel Grigg, for this image.
2. Joanne Belknap, *The Invisible Woman: Gender, Crime, and Justice* (Belmont, CA: Wadsworth, 2001).
3. Joycelyn Pollock, *Criminal Women* (Cincinnati, OH: Anderson, 1999); Meda Chesney-Lind and Lisa Palmore, *The Female Offender: Girls, Women, and Crime* (Thousand Oaks, CA: Sage, 2004).
4. William Collins and Andrew Collins, *Women in Jail: Legal Issues* (Washington, DC: National Institute of Corrections, 1996); Barbara Bloom, Barbara Owen, and Stephanie Covington, *Gender-Responsive Strategies: Research, Practice, and Guiding Principles for Women Offenders* (Washington, DC: National Institute of Corrections, 2002); Barbara Owen and Barbara Bloom, "Profiling Women Prisoners: Findings From National Survey and California Sample," *Prison Journal* 75, no. 2 (1995): 165–185; Joycelyn Pollock, *Women, Prison, and Crime* (Pacific Grove, CA: Brooks/Cole, 2003); Belknap, *The Invisible Woman;* Angela Browne, Brenda Miller, and Eugene Maguin, "Preva-

lence and Severity of Lifetime Physical and Sexual Victimization Among Incarcerated Women," *International Journal of Law and Psychiatry* 22, nos. 3–4 (1999): 301–322.

5. Barbara Bloom, "Triple Jeopardy: Race, Class, and Gender as Factors in Women's Imprisonment" (Ph.D. diss., University of California Riverside, 1996).

6. Carolyn Wolf Harlow, *Prior Abuse Reported by Inmates and Probationers* (Washington, DC: U.S. Department of Justice, 1999); Bloom, Owen, and Covington, *Gender-Responsive Strategies;* Pollock, *Women, Prison, and Crime;* Belknap, *The Invisible Woman.*

7. Allen Beck and Paige Harrison, *Prisoners in 2000.* (Washington, DC: U.S. Department of Justice, 2001).

8. Paige Harrison, and Allen Beck, *Prisoners in 2002* (Washington, DC: U.S. Department of Justice, 2003).

9. Ibid.

10. Chesney-Lind and Palmore, *The Female Offender.*

11. Lawrence Greenfeld and Tracy Snell, *Special Report: Women Offenders* (Washington, DC: U.S. Department of Justice).

12. Ibid.

13. Darrell Steffensmeir and Emilie Allan, "The Nature of Female Offending: Patterns and Explanations," in R., Zupan ed., *Female Offenders: Critical Perspectives and Interventions,* (Gaithersburg, MD: Aspen, 1998), 5–30.

14. Ibid., 11.

15. Barbara Bloom, Meda Chesney-Lind, and Barbara Owen, *Women in California Prisons: Hidden Victims of the War on Drugs* (San Francisco: Center on Juvenile and Criminal Justice, 1994).

16. Marc Mauer, Cathy Potler, and Richard Wolf, *Gender and Justice: Women, Drugs, and Sentencing Policy* (Washington, DC: The Sentencing Project).

17. Stephanie Bush-Baskette, "The War on Drugs: A War Against Women?" in S. Cook and S. Davies, eds., *Harsh Punishment: International Experiences of Women's Imprisonment* (Boston: Northeastern University Press, 1999), 211–229.

18. Chesney-Lind and Palmore, *The Female Offender.*

19. Harrison and Beck, *Prisoners in 2002,* 9.

20. Kate Bagley and Alida Merlo, "Controlling Women's Bodies" in A. Merlo and J. Pollock, (eds.), *Women, Law and Social Control* (Nedham Heights, MA: Allyn & Bacon, 1995), 147.

21. See Belknap, *The Invisible Women,* and Pollock, *Women, Prison, and Crime,* for a more detailed discussion of these histories.

22. Pollock, *Women, Prison, and Crime,* 9.

23. Robert Johnson, "Race, Gender and the American Prisons: Historical Observations, in J. Pollock, ed., *Prisons: Today and Tomorrow* (Gaithersburg, MD: Aspen, 1997), 32.

24. Estelle Freedman, *Their Sisters' Keepers.* (Ann Arbor: University of Michigan Press, 1987), 78.

25. Pollock, *Women, Crime, and Prison.*

26. I recently visited a midwest, state with a very small prison population. Women and men were confined to a multistory building, previously used as a hospital. The 50 or so women locked up on one floor were confined indoors the majority of the time, but the several hundred men had open movement. The women were allowed to go outside only when the males were locked down.

27. Freedman, *Their Sister's Keepers,* 60.

28. Pollock, *Women, Prisons, and Crime.*

29. Nicole Rafter, *Partial Justice: State Prisons and Their Inmates, 1800–1935* (Boston: Northeastern University Press, 1985).

30. Ibid.

31. Ibid., 182.

32. Owen, *In the Mix.*

33. Owen and Bloom, "Profiling Women Prisoners."

34. Owen, *In the Mix,* 109.

35. Ibid., 179.

36. Ibid., 189.

37. Bloom, Owen, and Covington, *Gender-Responsive Strategies.*

38. Although short and tall women have told me that these panels do not provide privacy to them.

39. Owen, *In the Mix,* 119–120.

40. Greenfeld and Snell, *Special Report,* 341.

41. Barbara Bloom and Meda Chesney-Lind, "Women in Prison: Vengeful Equity," in R. Muraskin, ed., *It's a Crime: Women and Justice* (Upper Saddle River, NJ: Prentice Hall, 2000), 183–204.

42. Barbara Bloom and David Steinhart, *Why Punish the Children? A Reappraisal of the Children of Incarcerated Parents* (San Francisco: National Council on Crime and Delinquency, 1993).

43. Elaine Lord, "A Prison Superintendent's Perspective on Women in Prison" *Prison Journal* 75, no. 2 (1995): 266.

44. Owen, *In the Mix* 129.

45. Owen, *In the Mix.*

46. Leslie Acoca, "Defusing the Time Bomb: Understanding and Meeting the Growing Health Care Needs of Incarcerated Women in America," *Crime and Delinquency* 44, no. 1 (1998): 49–70.

47. Derived from the Legal Services for Prisoners With Children website: *http://prisonerswithchildren.org/issues/health.htm*. Retrieved March 3, 2004.

48. Interviews at CCWF, 2001.

49. Pollock, *Women, Prison, and Crime,* 156.

50. Ibid., 158–159.

51. Ibid., p. ??

52. Bloom, Owen, and Covington, *Gender-Responsive Strategies.*

53. Jean Wellisch, M. Douglas Anglin, and Michael Prendergast, "Treatment Strategies for Drug-Abusing Women Offenders," in James A. Inciardi, ed., *Drug Treatment and Criminal Justice* (Newbury Park, CA: Sage, 1993), 5–25; National Institute on Drug Abuse, "Gender Differences in Drug Abuse Risks and Treatment" *NIDA Notes* 15, no. 4 (2000): 15; Patricia Kassebaum, *Substance Abuse Treatment for Women Offenders: Guide to Promising Practices* (Rockville, MD: U.S. Department of Health and Human Services, 1999).

54. Retrieved January 18 2004 from *http://www.prisonerswithchildren.org*.

55. Bloom, Owen, and Covington, *Gender-Responsive Strategies.*

56. Acoca, "Defusing the Time Bomb."

57. Bloom, Owen, and Covington, 45–47.

58. Elizabeth Leonard, *Convicted Survivors: The Imprisonment of Battered Women Who Kill* (Albany: State University of New York Press, 2002).

59. Acoca, "Defusing the Time Bomb."

60. Mark Singer, Janet Bussey, Li-Yu Song and Lisa Lunghofer, "The Psychosocial Issues of Women Serving Time in Jail," *Social Work* 40, no. 1 (1995): 103–114.

61. Linda Teplin, Karen Abraham, and Gary McClelland, "Prevalence of Psychiatric Disorders Among Incarcerated Women," *Archives of General Psychiatry* 53 (1996): 505–512.

62. Dorothy McClellan, "Disparity in the Discipline of Male and Female Inmates in Texas Prisons," *Women and Criminal Justice* 5, no. 2 (1994): 71–97.

63. Joycelyn Pollock, *Counseling Women in Prison* (Thousand Oaks, CA: Sage, 1998), 35.

64. Pollock, *Women, Prison, and Crime,* 83.

65. Amnesty International USA, *Not Part of My Sentence: Violations of the Human Rights Watch in Custody* (New York: Publisher, 1999); Human Rights Watch Women's Rights Project, *All Too Familiar: Sexual Abuse of Women in U.S. State Prisons* (New York: Ford Foundation, 1996); B.V. Smith, "Sexual Abuse Against Women in Prison" *Criminal Justice* 16, no. 1 (2001): 30–38; A. Moss, "Sexual Misconduct Among Staff and In-

mates," in P. Carlson and J. Garrett, eds., *Prison and Jail Administration: Practice and Theory* (New York: Aspen, 1999), 185–195.

66. Human Rights Watch Women's Rights Project, *All Too Familiar.*
67. Ibid., 1.
68. Bloom and Chesney-Lind, *Women in Prison,* 24.
69. Marilyn Brown, "Motherhood on the Margin: Rehabilitation and Subjectivity Among Female Parolees in Hawaii" (Ph.D. diss., University of Hawaii, Manoa, 2003).
70. Patricia O'Brien, *Making It in the "Free World": Women's Transition From Prison* (Albany: State University of New York Press, 2001).
71. Ibid., 25.
72. Ibid., 64.
73. Ibid., 67.
74. Brown, *Motherhood on the Margin,* 6–7.
75. Ibid., 150.
76. Ibid.
77. O'Brien, *Making It in the "Free World,"* 119.
78. Ibid.
79. Owen, "Changing Lives, A Pathways Perspective on Prison Drug Treatment for Women Offenders." (Ms. in preparation).
80. Kassebaum, *Substance Abuse Treatment* (Rockville, MD: U.S. Department of Health and Human Services, 1999), 113.
81. O'Brien, *Making It in the "Free World,"* 75.
82. Ibid., 80.
83. Ibid.
84. Brown, *Motherhood on the Margin,* 239.
85. Bloom, Owen, and Covington, *Gender-Responsive Strategies.*
86. Owen, "Changing Lives."
87. Ibid.
88. Owen, *In the Mix,* 198.
89. Here I must acknowledge the work of the National Institute of Corrections, which has long supported gender-based research, policy, and practice. ✦

Table of Cases

References

Acoca, L. (1998). "Defusing the Time Bomb: Understanding and Meeting the Growing Health Care Needs of Incarcerated Women in America." *Crime and Delinquency* 44 (1), 49–70.

Amnesty International USA. (1999). *Not Part of My Sentence: Violations of the Human Rights Watch in Custody.* New York:[?].

Arax, M. (1996, August 21). "Tales of Brutality Behind Bars." *Los Angeles Times*, p. A1.

Bagley, K., and Merlo, A. (2001). "Controlling Women's Bodies." In A. Merlo and J. Pollock (Eds.), *Women, Law, and Social Control* (pp. 135–147). Nedham Heights, MA: Allyn & Bacon.

Bartlett, G. L. (1915). *Thru the Mill by '4342.'* St. Paul, MN: McGill-Warner.

Beaumont, G., and Tocqueville, A. (1964). *On the Penitentiary System in the United States and Its Application in France.* Carbondale and Edwardsville: Southern Illinois University Press.

Beck, A., and Harrison, P. (2001). *Prisoners in 2000.* Washington, DC: U.S. Department of Justice.

Beckett, K. (1997). *Making Crime Pay.* New York: Oxford University Press.

Belknap, J. (2001). *The Invisible Woman: Gender, Crime, and Justice.* Belmont, CA: Wadsworth.

Bentham, J. ([1789] 1996). *An Introduction to the Principles of Morals and Legislation.* Oxford: Clarendon Books.

Berkman, A. (1912). *Prison Memoirs of an Anarchist.* New York: Mother Earth Publishing.

Blake, F., and Lubow, A. (1975, September 19). "America's Most Coddled Criminals." *New Times*, pp. 26–29.

Blankstein, A., and Winton, R. (2002, November 21). "130 Arrested in Sweep of Skid Row." *Los Angeles Times*, p. B12.

Bloch, H. A., and Niederhoffer, A. (1958). *The Gang: A Study of Adolescent Behavior.* New York: Philosophical Library.

Bloom, B. (1996). "Triple Jeopardy: Race, Class, and Gender as Factors in Women's Imprisonment." PhD diss., University of California, Riverside.

Bloom, B., and Chesney-Lind, M. (2000). "Women in Prison: Vengeful Equity." In R. Muraskin (Ed.), *It's a Crime: Women and Justice* (pp. 183–204). Upper Saddle River, NJ: Prentice Hall.

Bloom, B., Chesney-Lind, M., and Owen, B. (1994). *Women in California Prisons: Hidden Victims of the War on Drugs.* San Francisco: Center on Juvenile and Criminal Justice.

Bloom, B., Owen, B., and Covington S. (2002). *Gender-Responsive Strategies: Research, Practice, and Guiding Principles for Women Offenders.* Washington, DC: National Institute of Corrections.

Bloom, B., and Steinhart, D. (1993). *Why Punish the Children? A Reappraisal of the Children of Incarcerated Parents.* San Francisco: National Council on Crime and Delinquency.

Blumstein, A., Cohen, J., Roth, J., and Visher, C. (Eds.). (1986). *Criminal Careers and Career Criminals.* Washington, DC: National Academy of Sciences.

Bourdieu, P. (1986). "The Forms of Capital." In J. G. Richardson (Ed.), *Handbook of Theory and Research for the Sociology of Education.* New York: Greenwood.

———. (1980, January). "Le Capital social." *Acts de la Recherche en Sciences Sociales,* 31, (pp. 2–3).

Braman, D. (2003). "Families and Incarceration." In M. Mauer and M. Chessney-Lind (Eds.), *Invisible Punishment,* (pp. 117–135). New York: New Press.

Bromber, W., et al. (1973). "The Relation of Psychosis, Mental Defect, and Personality Types to Crime." *Journal of Criminal Law and Criminology,* 28, 70–89.

Brown, M. (2003). "Motherhood on the Margin: Rehabilitation and Subjectivity Among Female Parolees in Hawaii." University of Hawaii, PhD diss., Manoa.

Browne, A., Miller, B., and Maguin, E. (1999). "Prevalence and Severity of Lifetime Physical and Sexual Victimization Among Incarcerated Women." *International Journal of Law and Psychiatry* 22 (3–4), 301–322.

Bunker, E. (1977). *Animal Factory.* New York: Viking.

———. (2000). *The Education of a Felon.* New York: St. Martin's.

Bureau of Justice Statistics. (2001, September 9). *National Victimization Survey.* Retrieved 2003, *http://www.ojp.usdoj.gov/bjs.*

Burns, R. E. (1932). *I Am a Fugitive From a Georgia Chain Gang!* New York: Vanguard.

Burr, L. S. (1833). "Voice From Sing Sing, Giving a General Description of the State Prison," Letter addressed to the Honorable, the Senate, and Assembly of the State of New York. Albany, NY, 17.

Burt, M. (1992). *Over the Edge.* New York: Urban Institute and Russell Sage.

Bush-Baskette, S. (1999). "The War on Drugs: A War Against Women?" In S. Cook and S. Davies (Eds.), *Harsh Punishment: International Experiences of Women's Imprisonment* (pp. 211–229). Boston: Northeastern University Press.

Butler, P. (1977). "Tap Codes: Ascribed Meaning in Prisoner Communication." *Urban Life* 5 (4), 399–416.

Cahn, E. (1975). *The Sense of Injustice.* Bloomington: Indiana University Press.

California Department of Corrections (CDC). (1965). *Parole-Agent Manual.* Sacramento: California Department of Corrections.

———. (1986, November). *Violence in California Prisons: Report of the Task Force on Violence, Special Housing, and Gang Management.*

———. (1999). *California State Prison, Solano, Mission Summary.* Sacramento: California Department of Corrections.

———. (2000). *California Code of Regulations: Title 15; Crime Prevention and Corrections* (pp. 36–37). Sacramento: California Department of Corrections.

———. (2000). *Operations Manual,* updated through May 1, 2000, p. 581. Sacramento: California Department of Corrections.

Callahan, J. (1928). *Man's Grim Justice: My Life Outside the Law.* New York: J. Sears.

Carroll, L. (1974). *Hacks, Blacks, and Cons: Race Relations in Maximum Security Prison.* Lexington, MA: Lexington.

———. (1998). *Lawful Order.* New York: Garland.

Chesney-Lind, M., and Palmore, L. (2004). *The Female Offender: Girls, Women, and Crime.* Thousand Oaks, CA: Sage.

Clark, C. L. (1927). *Lockstep and Corridor.* Cincinnati: University of Ohio Press.

Clear, T. R. (1994). *Harm in American Penology: Offenders, Victims, and Their Communities.* Albany: State University of New York Press.

———. (2003). "The Problem With 'Addition by Subtraction': The Prison-Crime Relationship in Low-Income Communities." In M. Mauer and M. Chesney-Lind (Eds.), *Invisible Punishment,* (pp. 181–193). New York: New Press.

Clemmer, D. (1965). *The Prison Community*. New York: Holt, Rinehart, and Winston.

Cloward, R., and Ohlin, L. (1960). *Delinquency and Opportunity*. New York: Free Press.

Cohen, A. (1955). *Delinquent Boys*. Glencoe, IL: Free Press.

Coleman, J. W. (1995). "Respectable Crime." In J. F. Shelley (Ed.), *Criminology: A Contemporary Handbook*. Belmont, CA: Wadsworth.

Collins, W., and Collins, A. (1996). *Women in Jail: Legal Issues*. Washington, DC: National Institute of Corrections.

Crane, A. (2001). "Prison Story." Manuscript, written at Solano State Prison.

Criminal Justice Institute. (1995). *The Corrections Yearbook, 1995, Adult Corrections*. South Salem, NY: Criminal Justice Institute.

Crouch, B. M., and Marquart, J. W. (1989). *An Appeal to Justice*. Austin: University of Texas Press.

Dalton, M. (1959). *Men Who Manage*. New York: Wiley.

De Fornaro, C. (1917). *A Modern Purgatory*. New York: Mitchell Kennerley.

Delvecchio, R. (2003, February 1). "Gang of Killers Stopped, Oakland Police Say." *San Francisco Chronicle*, p. A17.

Dickens, C. (1972). *American Notes for General Circulation*. London: Penguin.

Dilulio, J. (1995, August). "Crime in America: It's Going to Get Worse." *Reader's Digest*.

Drutman, L. (2003, November 4). "Corporate Crime Acts Like a Thief in the Night." *Los Angeles Times*, pp. B3.

Durkheim, E. (1933). *The Division of Labor*. New York: Macmillan.

Earley, P. (1992). *The Hot House*. New York: Bantam.

Finnis, J. (1990). *Natural Law and Natural Rights*. New York: Oxford University Press.

Fogel, D. (1975). *The Living Proof: The Justice Model of Corrections*. Cincinnati, OH: Anderson.

Foucault, M. (1977). *The Birth of the Prison*. London: Allen & Unwin.

———. (1977). *Discipline and Punish*. London: Allen & Unwin.

Frady, M. (7 November, 2002) "The Big Guy." *New York Review of Books*, p. 6.

Freedman, E. (1987). *Their Sisters' Keepers*. Ann Arbor: University of Michigan Press.

Fuller, R. (1964). *The Morality of Law*. New Haven, CT: Yale University Press.

Gabler, N. (2002, January 2). "Class Dismissed." *Los Angeles Times*, p. M1.

Gainsborough, J., and Mauer, M. (2000, September). *Diminishing Returns: Crime and Incarceration in the 1990s*. Washington, DC: The Sentencing Project.

Gallup, G. (Ed.). (1990). *The Gallup Poll*. Wilmington, DE: Scholarly Resources.

Garland, D. (1985). *Punishment and Welfare: A History of Penal Strategies*. Aldershot, England: Gower.

——. (1990). *Punishment in Modern Society*. Chicago: University of Chicago Press.

——. (2001). *The Culture of Control*. Chicago: University of Chicago Press.

Giallombardo, R. (1966). *Society of Women: A Study of a Women's Prison*. New York: Wiley.

Glaser, D. (1964). *The Effectiveness of a Prison and Parole System*. Indianapolis: Bobbs-Merrill.

Glasgow, D. G. (1981). *The Black Underclass*. New York: Vintage.

Glasser, J. (2000, May 1). "Ex-cons on the Street." *U.S. News and World Report*, p. 18.

Gordon, D. (1996). *Fat and Mean*. New York: Simon & Schuster.

Greenfeld, L., and Snell, T. (1999). *Special Report: Women Offenders*. Washington, DC: U.S. Department of Justice.

Greenwood, P. (1982). *Selective Incapacitation*. Santa Monica, CA: Rand.

Gross, B. (1962). "Reagan's Criminal Anti-crime Fix." In A. G. Gartner, C. Greer, and F. Riessman (Eds.), *What Reagan Is Doing to Us*. New York: Harper & Row.

Gunnison, R. B., and Lucas, G. (1998, March 18). "Guard Union's Clout Impeding Prison Investigation, Critics Say." *San Francisco Chronicle*, pp. A1, A13.

Gusfield, J. (1981). *The Culture of Public Reform: Drinking and the Symbolic Order*. Chicago: University of Chicago Press.

Guze, S. B. et al. (1969). "Criminality and Psychiatric Disorders." *Archives of General Psychiatry*, 20, 583–591.

Hairgrove, D. D. (2000). "A Single Unheard Voice." In R. Johnson and H. Toch (Eds.), *Crime and Punishment: Inside Views* (pp. 147–149). Los Angeles: Roxbury.

Halberstam, D. (1986). *The Reckoning*. New York: Avon.

Hallinan, J. (2001). *Going up the River*. New York: Random House.

Harlow, C. W. (1999). *Prior Abuse Reported by Inmates and Probationers*. Washington, DC: U.S. Department of Justice.

Harrington, M. (1962). *The Other America: Poverty in the United States*. New York: Macmillan.

——. (1984). *The New American Poverty.* New York: Penguin.

Harrison, B., and Bluestone, B. (1988). *The Great U-Turn.* New York: Basic Books.

Harrison, P., and Beck, A. (2003). *Prisoners in 2002.* Washington, DC: U.S. Department of Justice.

Hay, D. (1975). "Property, Authority, and the Criminal Law." In D. Hay, P. Linebaugh, J. G. Rule, E. P. Thompson, and C. Winslow (Eds.), *Albion's Fatal Tree* (pp. 17–63). New York: Pantheon.

Heffernan, E. (1972). *Making It in Prison: The Square, the Cool, and the Life.* New York: Wiley.

Herre, R. S. (1950). "A History of Auburn Prison From the Beginning to About 1867." D.Ed. diss., Pennsylvania State University.

Hirschi, T. (1969). *Causes of Delinquency.* Berkeley: University of California Press.

Hollinger, R., and Clark, J. (1983). *Theft by Employees.* Lexington, MA: Lexington.

Holtzer, H. (1996). *What Employers Want: Job Prospects for Less-Educated Workers.* New York: Russell Sage.

Hopkins, E. D. (1997, February 24 and March 3). "Lockdown: Life Inside Is Getting Harder." *New Yorker,* pp. 61–71.

Hughes, R. (1988). *The Fatal Shore: The Epic of Australia's Founding.* New York: Vintage.

Human Rights Watch Women's Rights Project. (1996). *All Too Familiar: Sexual Abuse of Women in U.S. State Prisons.* New York: Ford Foundation.

"Inmates Go to Court to Earn Interest on Prison Accounts." (1999, November 17). *Wall Street Journal: California,* p. 1.

Irwin, J. (1970). *The Felon.* Englewood Cliffs, NJ: Prentice Hall.

——. (1974 June). "The Trouble With Rehabilitation." *Criminal Justice and Behavior* 1 (2), 141–142.

——. (1980). *Prisons in Turmoil.* Boston: Little, Brown.

——. (1985). *The Jail.* Berkeley: University of California Press.

——. (2000). "Rogue." Manuscript.

Irwin, J., and Austin, J. (1994). *It's About Time: America's Imprisonment Binge.* Belmont, CA: Wadsworth.

Irwin, J., and Cressey, D. (1963, Fall). "Thieves, Convicts, and the Inmate Culture." *Social Problems,* pp. 144–155.

Isikoff, M. (1989, September 30). "Drug Buy Set Up by Bush: DEA Lured Seller to Lafayette Park." *Washington Post,* p. A1.

Jackson, G. (1970). *Soledad Brother.* New York: Bantam.

Jacobs, J. (1977). *Stateville: The Penitentiary in Mass Society.* Chicago: University of Chicago Press.

Johnson, J. A. (2000). "A Career Statement." In R. Johnson and H. Toch (Eds.), *Crime and Punishment: Inside Views* (pp. 164–167). Los Angeles: Roxbury.

Johnson, L. B. (1965). "Remarks on the City Hall Steps, Dayton Ohio." In *Public Papers of the Presidents, 1964: Vol. 2* (p. 1371). Washington, DC: Government Printing Office.

Johnson, R. (1997). "Race, Gender, and the American Prisons: Historical Observations." In J. Pollock (Ed.), *Prisons: Today and Tomorrow* (pp. 26–32). Gaithersburg, MD: Aspen.

———. (2002). *Hard Time.* Belmont, CA: Wadsworth.

Johnson, R., and Toch, H. (2000). *Crime and Punishment: Inside Views.* Los Angeles: Roxbury.

Karr, R. E. (2002). "In My World." Poem.

Karst, K. (1993). *Law's Promise, Law's Expression: Visions of Power in the Politics of Race, Gender, and Religion.* New Haven, CT: Yale University Press.

Kassebaum, P. (1999). *Substance Abuse Treatment for Women Offenders: Guide to Promising Practices.* Rockville, MD: U.S. Department of Health and Human Services.

Kleinfield, N. R. (2002, December 6). "New Yorkers Reminded of Fears Left Behind." *New York Times*, p. A29.

Kloech, J. (1968). "Schizophrenia and Delinquency." *The Mentally Abnormal Offender*, p. 1928.

Kupers, T. A. (1961). "Authoritarianism and the Belief System of Incorrigibles." In Donald R. Cressy (Ed.), *The Prison.* New York: Holt, Rinehart, & Winston.

"Legal Services for Prisoners With Children." Retrieved March 3, 2004, from *http://prisonerswithchildren.org/issues/health.htm.*

Lemann, N. (1991). *The Promised Land.* New York: Knopf.

Leonard, E. (2002). *Convicted Survivors: The Imprisonment of Battered Women Who Kill.* Albany: State University of New York Press.

Leonhardt, D. (2002, September 29). "Out of a Job and No Longer Looking." *New York Times*, p. D4.

Lewin, T. (1994, March 10). "Low Pay and Closed Doors Confront Young Job Seekers." *New York Times*, p. B12.

Lewis, W. D. (1965). *From Newgate to Dannemora: The Rise of the Penitentiary in New York, 1796–1848.* Ithaca, NY: Cornell University Press.

Lord, E. (1995). "A Prison Superintendent's Perspective on Women in Prison." *Prison Journal* 75 (2), 257–269.

Lusky, J. (2002, Summer/Fall). "The Plagues of Prison." *New Letter of the Western Prison Project*, p. 8.

Lynch, M. (1999). "Waste Managers? New Penology, Crime Fighting, and the Parole Agent Identity." *Law and Society* 32 (4), 839–869.

Macallair, D. (2003, April 21). "Reforming California's Failed Parole System." *San Francisco Chronicle*, p. B7.

MacLean, P. A. (2000, January 26). "Inmate Denounces Guard Who Shot Him." *Daily Journal*, p. 1.

Marion, N. E. (1994). *A History of Federal Crime Control Initiatives*. Westport, CT: Preager.

Martin, D. (1989, June 19). "The Gulag Mentality." *San Francisco Chronicle*, Sunday Punch section, p. 5.

———. (1992, August 9). "Home—but Not Free: Prison Is Tough but Getting Out Is Tougher." *San Francisco Chronicle*, Sunday Punch section, p. 3.

Martinson, R. (1974). "What Works?—Questions and Answers About Prison Reform." *The Public Interest* 35, 22–54.

Matusow, A. (1984). *The Unraveling of America*. New York: Harper Torchbooks.

Mauer, M. (2003). "Mass Imprisonment and Disappearing Voters." In M. Mauer and M. Chesney-Lind (Eds.), *Invisible Punishment* (pp. 50–58). New York: New Press.

Mauer, M., and Chesney-Lind, M. (Eds.). (2003). *Invisible Punishment*. New York: New Press.

Mauer, M., Potler, C., and Wolf, R. (1999). *Gender and Justice: Women, Drugs, and Sentencing Policy*. Washington, DC: Sentencing Project.

McClellan, D. (1994). "Disparity in the Discipline of Male and Female Inmates in Texas Prisons." *Women and Criminal Justice*, 5 (2), 71–97.

McKelvey, B. (1977). *American Prisons: A History of Good Intentions*. Montclair, NJ: Patterson Smith.

Medenick, S., Gabrielli, W. F., and Hutchings, B. (1984). "Genetic Influences in Criminal Convictions." *Science* 224, 891–894.

Melossi, D. (1980). *The Prison and the Factory: The Origins of the Penitentiary System*. Berkeley: University of California Press.

Menninger, K. (1968). *The Crime of Punishment*. New York: Viking.

Miller, J. G. (1997). *Search and Destroy: African American Males in the Criminal Justice System*. Cambridge, UK: Cambridge University Press.

Miller, M. B. (1980). "Dread and Terror: The Creation of State Penitentiaries in New York and Pennsylvania, 1788 to 1833." D. Crim. diss., University of California, Berkeley.

Mobley, A. (2001 November). "Guess Who's Coming to Dinner? A Prisoner Perspective on the Possibilities of Reentry." Manuscript.

Moore, J. W. (1991). *Going Down to the Barrio: Homeboys and Homegirls in Change.* Philadelphia: Temple University Press.

Moore, J. W., Garcia, C., Garcia, L., and Valencia, F. (1978). *Homeboys: Gangs, Drugs, and Prison in the Barrios of Los Angeles.* Philadelphia: Temple University Press.

Morris, N. (1974). *The Future of Imprisonment.* Chicago: University of Chicago Press.

Moss, A. (1999). "Sexual Misconduct Among Staff and Inmates." In P. Carlson and J. Garrett (Eds.), *Prison and Jail Administration: Practice and Theory* (pp. 185–195). New York: Aspen.

Moynihan, D. P. (1973). *The Politics of Guaranteed Income.* New York: Random House.

Murray, C. (1997). "The Ruthless Truth." *Times of London.*

Murton, T., and Hyams, J. (1979). *Accomplices to the Crime.* New York: Grove.

National Institute on Drug Abuse. (2000). "Gender Differences in Drug Abuse Risks and Treatment." *NIDA Notes* 15 (4), 15.

Nelson, V. (1933). *Prison Days and Nights.* New York: Grove.

Nieves, E. (2001, May 22). "Rash of Violence Disrupts San Quentin's Death Row." *New York Times*, p. A10.

Norris, M., Conrad, C., and Resner, V. (1998). *Shattered Lives: Portraits From America's Drug War.* El Cerrito, CA: Creative Expressions.

O'Brien, P. (2001). *Making It in the "Free World": Women's Transition From Prison.* Albany: State University of New York Press.

Owen, B. (1988). *The Reproduction of Social Control.* New York: Praeger.

———. (1998). *In the Mix.* New York: State University of New York Press.

———. (in preparation). "Changing Lives: A Pathways Perspective on Prison Drug Treatment." Manuscript.

Owen, B., and Bloom, B. (1995). "Profiling Women Prisoners: Findings From a National Survey and California Sample." *Prison Journal* 75 (2), 165–185.

Parenti, C. (1999). *Lockdown America.* New York: Verso.

Pashukanis, E. B. (1978). *Law and Marxism: A General Theory.* London: Ink Links.

Patrick, E. (2000). "Meaning of 'Life' in Prison." In R. Johnson and H. Toch (Eds.), *Crime and Punishment: Inside Views* (pp. 141–143). Los Angeles: Roxbury.

Petersilia, J. (2003). *When Prisoners Come Home*. New York: Oxford University Press.

Pollock, J. (1998). *Counseling Women in Prison*. Thousand Oaks, CA: Sage.

———. (1999). *Criminal Women*. Cincinnati, OH: Anderson.

———. (2003). *Women, Prison, and Crime*. Pacific Grove, CA: Brooks/Cole.

Powelson, H., and Bendix, R. (1951). "Psychiatry in Prison." *Psychiatry* 14.

Powers, G. (1826). *A Brief Account of the Construction, Management, and Discipline of the New York State Prison at Auburn*. Auburn, New York.

Preggar, J. (2003). "Memo—Parole," memos for a master class. University of California, Los Angeles, Department of Sociology.

The President's Commission on Law Enforcement and Administration of Justice. (1967). *Task Force Report: Corrections*. Washington, DC: Government Printing Office.

Rafter, N. (1985). *Partial Justice: Women in State Prisons, 1800–1935*. Boston: Northeastern University Press.

Rawls, J. (1971). *A Theory of Justice*. Cambridge, MA: Harvard University Press.

Reagan, R. (1984a). "Remarks at a White House Ceremony Observing Crime Victims Week." In *Public Papers of the Presidents, 1983: Vol. 1* (p. 553). Washington, DC: Government Printing Office.

———. (1984b). "Remarks at the Conservative Political Action Conference Dinner." In *Public Papers of the Presidents, 1983: Vol. 1* (p. 252). Washington, DC: Government Printing Office.

———. (1985). "Remarks at the Annual Conference of the National Sheriff's Association in Hartford, Connecticut." In *Public Papers of the Presidents of the United States, 1984: Vol. 2* (p. 886). Washington, DC: Government Printing Office.

Reiman, J. H. (1979). *The Rich Get Richer and the Poor Get Prison*. New York: Wiley.

Reinarman, C., and Levine, H. G. (1997). *Crack in America*. Berkeley: University of California Press.

Riemer, H. (1937). "Socialization in the Prison Community." In *Proceedings of the American Prison Association* (pp. 151–155). American Prison Association.

Ripley, A. (2002, January 21). "Outside the Gates." *Time*, pp. 58–62.

Rivera, C. (2002, November 30). "Homeless Often Take a One-Way Street to Skid Row." *Los Angeles Times*, p. A1.

Robinson, B. (1971, September). "Love: A Hard-Legged Triangle." *Black Scholar*, p. 39.

Rothman, D. (1980). *The Discovery of the Asylum: Social Order and Disorder in the New Republic*. Boston: Little, Brown.

Rusche, G., and Kirchheimer, O. (1939). *Punishment and Penal Discipline*. New York: Columbia University Press.

——. (1939). *Punishment and Social Structure*. New York: Columbia University Press.

Schrag, C. (1944). "Social Types in a Prison Community." Master's thesis, University of Washington.

Schultz, R. (1991). "Life in SHU: An Ethnographic Study of Pelican Bay State Prison." Master's thesis, Humboldt State University.

Sheldon, R. G., and Brown, W. B. (2000). "The Crime Control Industry and the Management of the Surplus Population." *Critical Criminology* 9, 39–40.

Silverman, I. J., and Vega, M. (1996). *Corrections: A Comprehensive View*. New York: West.

Simon, J. (1993). *Poor Discipline: Parole and the Social Control of the Underclass*. Chicago: University of Chicago Press.

Singer, M., Bussey, J., Song, L., and Lunghofer, L. (1995). "The Psychosocial Issues of Women Serving Time in Jail." *Social Work* 40 (1), 103–114.

Slater, A. (1994, May). "The Same, Only Worse." *Pelican Bay Prison Express* 2 (4), 1–2.

Slater, R. (1986). "Psychiatric Intervention in an Atmosphere of Terror." *American Journal of Forensic Psychiatry* 7 (1), 8–9.

Slim, Ice Berg [Robert Beck]. (1969). *The Pimp: The Story of My Life*. New York: Holloway House.

Smith, B. V. (2001). "Sexual Abuse Against Women in Prison." *Criminal Justice* 16 (1), 30–38.

Steffensmeir, D., and Allan, E. (1998). "The Nature of Female Offending: Patterns and Explanations." In R. Zupan (Ed.), *Female Offenders: Critical Perspectives and Interventions* (pp. 5–30). Gaithersburg, MD: Aspen.

Sutherland, E. H. (1949). *White Collar Crime*. New York: Dryden Press.

Sutherland, E. H., Cressey, D. R., and Luckenbill, D. F. (1992). *Principles of Criminology*, 11th ed. New York: General Hall.

Sykes, G. (1958). *The Society of Captives*. Princeton, NJ: Princeton University Press.

Teplin, L., Abraham, K., and McClelland, G. (1996). "Prevalence of Psychiatric Disorders Among Incarcerated Women." *Archives of General Psychiatry*, 53, 505–512.

Terry, C. M. (2003). *The Fellas: Rocky Roads Toward Addiction, Prisonization, and Reintegration*. Belmont, CA: Wadsworth.

Thrasher, F. (1963). *The Gang*. Chicago: University of Chicago Press.

Toch, H. (1977). *Living in Prison: The Ecology of Survival*. New York: Free Press.

Toch, H., Adams, K., and Grant, J. D. (1989). *Coping: Maladaptation in Prisons*. New Brunswick, NJ: Transaction Publishers.

Travis, J. (2001, June). *From Prison to Home*. Washingtion, DC: Urban Institute.

Travis, J., and Lawrence, S. (2002). *Beyond the Prison Gates: The State of Parole in America*. Washington, DC: Urban Institute.

Tuchman, B. (1984). *The March of Folly*. New York: Ballantine.

Updike, J. (1994). *Brazil*. New York: Facett Columbine.

Vasconcellos, J. (1998, October 22). "Closing Statement," Corcoran State Prison Hearings, California State Senate.

Verkatesh, S. (2000). *American Project: The Rise and Fall of a Modern Ghetto*. Cambridge, MA: Harvard University Press.

Vigil, J. D. (1988). *Barrio Gangs*. Austin: University of Texas Press.

Von Hirsch, A. (1976). *Doing Justice*. New York: Hill and Wang.

Wacquant, L. (1994). "The New Urban Color Line: The State and Fate of the Ghetto in Post-Fordist America." In C. J. Calhoun (Ed.), *Social Theory and the Politics of Identity* (pp. 231–276). Oxford and Cambridge: Blackwell.

——. (1998). "Negative Social Capital: State Breakdown and Social Destitution in America's Urban Core." *Netherlands Journal of the Built Environment*, 13 (1), 95–133.

——. (2001). "Deadly Symbiosis: When Ghetto and Prison Meet and Mesh." *Punishment and Society* 3 (1), 95–133.

——. (2002, April/May). "Deadly Symbiosis." *Boston Review*, pp. 23–24.

Ward, D. A., and Breed, A. F. (1984). *The United States Penitentiary, Marion, Illinois: A Report to the Judiciary Committee, United States House of Representatives, October 1984*.

Ward, D., and Kassebaum, G. (1958). *Women's Prison: Sex and Social Structure*. Chicago: Aldine-Atherton.

Warren, J., and Ellis, V. (2003, September 10). "Fraud Rampant in Body Shops." *Los Angeles Times*, p. A3.

Webster's Third New International Dictionary. (1971). Springfield, MA: G & C Merriam.

Wellisch, J., Anglin, M., and Prendergast, M. (1993). "Treatment Strategies for Drug-Abusing Women Offenders." In J. A. Inciardi (Ed.), *Drug Treatment and Criminal Justice* (pp. 5–25). Newbury Park, CA: Sage.

Western, B., Pettit, B., and Guetzkow, J. (2003). "Black Economic Progress in the Era of Mass Imprisonment." In M. Mauer and M. Chesney-Lind (Eds.), *Invisible Punishment* (pp. 165–182). New York: New Press.

Wiersnian, D. (1966). "Crime and Schizophrenics." *Excerpta Criminologica,* Vol. I, 169–181.

Williams, V., and Fish, M. (1974). *Convicts, Codes, and Contraband.* Cambridge, MA: Ballinger.

Wilson, J. Q. (1975). *Thinking About Crime.* New York: Random House.

——. (1998, May 25). "The Crime Bust." *U. S. News & World Report.*

Wilson, J. Q., and Herrnstein, R. (1985). *Crime and Human Nature.* New York: Simon & Schuster.

Wilson, W. J. (1980). *The Truly Disadvantaged.* Chicago: University of Chicago Press.

——. (1996). *When Work Disappears: The World of the New Urban Poor.* New York: Vintage.

——. (2003, June 16). "There Goes the Neighborhood." *New York Times,* p. 19.

Wines, E. C., and Dwight, T. (1867). *Report on the Prisons and Reformatories of the United States and Canada.* New York.

Wisotsky, S. (1987). "Crackdown: The Emerging 'Drug Exception' to the Bill of Rights." *Hastings Law Review Journal,* 38, 890.

Wolf, T. (2002). *Radical Chic and Mau Mauing the Flack Catchers.* New York: Pan Macmillan.

Working Party for the American Friends Service Committee. (1971). *The Struggle for Justice.* New York: Hill and Wang.

Yablonsky, L. (1962). *The Violent Gang.* London: Macmillan.

Yee, M. S. (1973). *The Melancholy History of Soledad Prison.* New York: Harper & Row.

Zimmer, L. (1986). *Women Guarding Men.* Chicago: University of Chicago Press. ✦

Author Index

Subject Index